'An extraordinary and unsettling journey into the way modern Britons work. It is *Down and Out In Paris and London* for the gig economy age.'
Matthew d'Ancona, *Guardian* columnist and bestselling author of *Post-Truth*

'A tautly written exposé of the swindle of the gig economy and a call to arms.'
Nick Cohen, journalist and author of *What's Left?*

'I emerged from James Bloodworth's quietly devastating and deeply disturbing book convinced that the "gig economy" is simply another way in which the powerful are enabled to oppress the disadvantaged.'
D. J. Taylor, author of *Orwell: The Life*

'A truly devastating examination of the vulnerable human underbelly of Britain's labour market, shining a bright light on the unjust and exploitative practices that erode the morale and living standards of working-class communities.'
Frank Field, MP

'James Bloodworth pulls back the carpet and exposes the rotten floorboards of Britain's low-wage, insecure and exploitative economy, describing living and working conditions that Dickens would recognise. It must surely act as a wake-up call to our political elites to genuinely tackle the gross inequality at the heart of our society.'
Wes Streeting, MP

'Whatever you think of the political assertions in this book – and I disagree with many of them – this is an important investigation into the reality of low-wage Britain. Whether you are on the Right, Left or Centre, anybody who believes in solidarity and social justice should read this book.'
Nick Timothy, former Chief of Staff to Theresa May, now columnist for the *Daily Telegraph* and *The Sun*

———

ABOUT THE AUTHOR

James Bloodworth is a journalist, broadcaster and author. He writes a weekly column for the *International Business Times* and his work has appeared in the *Guardian*, *New York Review of Books*, *New Statesman* and *Wall Street Journal*. He is the former editor of *Left Foot Forward*, an influential political blog in the UK.

🐦 @J_Bloodworth

HIRED

SIX MONTHS UNDERCOVER IN LOW-WAGE BRITAIN

JAMES BLOODWORTH

Atlantic Books
London

Published in trade paperback in Great Britain in 2018 by Atlantic Books, an imprint of Atlantic Books Ltd.

10 9 8 7 6 5 4 3 2 1

A CIP catalogue record for this book is available from the British Library.

Trade paperback ISBN: 978 1 78649 014 8

E-book ISBN: 978 1 78649 015 5

Printed in Great Britain by Bell & Bain Ltd, Glasgow

Atlantic Books
An imprint of Atlantic Books Ltd
Ormond House
26–27 Boswell Street
London
WC1N 3JZ

www.atlantic-books.co.uk

CONTENTS

Preface   1

Part I: RUGELEY

Chapter 1   11

Chapter 2   28

Chapter 3   42

Chapter 4   54

Chapter 5   64

Part II: BLACKPOOL

Chapter 6   79

Chapter 7   91

Chapter 8   106

Chapter 9   121

Chapter 10   132

Part III: SOUTH WALES VALLEYS

Chapter 11   143

Chapter 12   153

Chapter 13   165

Chapter 14   180

Chapter 15   187

Part IV: LONDON

Chapter 16   203

Chapter 17   211

Chapter 18   219

Chapter 19   228

Chapter 20   243

Epilogue   258

Notes   266

Index   272

Life is good, and joy runs high
Between English earth and sky

William Ernest Henley,
'England, My England'

PREFACE

Early in 2016, as the sun crept out from behind the clouds and the bitter winter frosts began to subside, I left London in a beaten-up old car to explore a side of life that is usually hidden from view.

Around one in twenty people in Britain today live on the minimum wage. Many of these people live in towns and cities that were once thriving centres of industry and manufacturing. Many were born there and an increasing number were born abroad.

I decided that the best way to find out about low-paid work in Britain today would be to become a part of that world myself: to sink down and become another cog in the vast, amorphous and impersonal machine on which much of Britain's prosperity is built. I would penetrate the agencies that failed to pay their staff a living wage. I would live among the men and women who scratched a living on the margins of a prosperous society that had supposedly gone back to work after a long, drawn-out recession. And I would join the growing army of people for whom the idea of a stable, fulfilling job was about as attainable as lifting an Oscar or the *Ballon d'Or*.

In the aftermath of the financial crisis of 2008, 'austerity' became the *raison d'être* of the British government. There was 'no money left' – so it was confidently proclaimed – and public services had to be cut back drastically or else contracted out to private companies who supposedly knew better how to run them than the state.

Since then the mood music has grown more optimistic: Britain is enjoying record levels of employment. Yet sunny optimism about the labour market masks the changing nature of the contemporary economy. More people are in work, but an increasing proportion of this work is poorly paid, precarious and without regular hours. Wages have been failing to keep pace with inflation. A million more people have become self-employed since the financial crisis, many of them working in the so-called 'gig' economy with few basic workers' rights. Toiling away for five hours a week may keep you off the government's unemployment figures, but it is not necessarily sufficient to pay the rent. Even for those in full-time work the picture is hardly rosy: Britain has recently experienced the longest period of wage stagnation for 150 years.

I set out to write about the changing nature of work, but this is also a book about the changing nature of Britain. Half a century ago Arthur Seaton, the anti-hero of Alan Sillitoe's cult novel *Saturday Night and Sunday Morning*, may have hated his dull job as a lathe worker in a Nottingham factory, but he could at least take a day off now and then when he was ill. There was a union rep on hand to listen to his grievances if the boss was in his ear. If he did get the sack he could usually walk into another job without too much fuss. There were local pubs and clubs at which to drink and socialise after work. All in all, there was a definite sense that, while the struggle between bosses and workers was not at an end, there had been a fundamental change in its terms.

The social democratic era probably ended in 1984, when the police batons came crashing down onto the heads of working men whom the former Conservative Prime Minister Harold Macmillan had once described as 'the best men in the world, who beat the Kaiser's and Hitler's armies and never gave in'. The stunned faces of the miners, knocked for six by the police and plastered luridly across the tabloids, seemed to capture the realisation of the time that, after a brief interregnum, to be a working man or woman was once again to be, if not despised, then only just tolerated.

Life in Britain has improved a great deal for many over the past forty years. Unthinking nostalgia is a dead end, the equivalent of an attempt to reside in the ruins of a crumbling old house that is full of cobwebs and on the verge of collapse. A sepia-tinged yearning for the mid-twentieth century is especially insulting to those for whom the century of the 'common man' was just that: the century of the white, heterosexual *man*. We live in a time that is both richer and more free than the era of hanging and the Notting Hill race riots.

But as our world of liberal progress was being built, another world was being dismantled. The mines are gone but so, almost, are the trade unions, reduced to rump organisations largely confined to the public sector. Were Arthur Seaton alive today, he would conceivably be trapped on a zero-hours contract in a dingy warehouse, cowed, fearful and forever trying to slip off for a two-minute toilet break out of sight of a haughty middle manager. Or maybe he would have gone on to university – a prospect quite unthinkable for most working-class young men and women when the novel that made him famous was first published in 1958.

A book about work is inevitably a book about class. Each generation we tell ourselves that class is dead, yet with every generation we fail to dispose of the cadaver. Those who lose their footing and slip down the social order very often sink into poverty; but even today a relegation to the lower depths of the social hierarchy can invite onto one's head a class hatred that burns every bit as painfully as economic dislocation.

I would not claim that what follows is an original or pioneering way of reporting on working-class life. Nor did I set out with the intention of confirming my already-existing prejudices. I did not know what to expect on my travels. It would be more truthful to say that I went into the project with an open mind and was to some extent radicalised by the process. Many of the things I found were worse than anything I had expected to see in one of the richest countries in the world.

But then, pick up almost any newspaper in Britain today and the message leaps off the page at you: poor people are the way they are because of their moral laxity or their irresponsible life choices. The old Victorian attitude still prevails. As Henry Mayhew subtitled the fourth volume of his epic nineteenth-century documentary on London, there are: *Those that will work, those that cannot work, and those that will not work.*

Neat divisions of this sort are as illusory today as they were when Queen Victoria was on the throne: an era when pseudo-scientific theories of class put people in the workhouse at home and threatened them with a bayonet in the guts abroad. The gap between comfortable prosperity and miserable squalor is not always as vast as many would like to believe. It is easy enough to sink down into poverty in modern Britain, and it can happen regardless of the choices you make along the way.

I do not claim that my going undercover was the same as experiencing these things out of necessity. Ultimately, I was a tourist. If things got too bad I could always draw on money in the bank or beat a hasty retreat back to a more comfortable existence. But my aim was never to get drawn into an ego-driven squabble over the 'authenticity' of my approach. I simply decided that going undercover would be the most effective way of learning about low-paid work, and I still believe that to be true.

I will, of course, be denounced by some for writing this book at all. A healthy fear of paternalism can occasionally be replaced among well-meaning people with a blanket lionisation of 'authenticity'. Many would undoubtedly have preferred that I deferred the task of writing this book to an 'authentic working-class voice'. This desire to hand working people the pen or the microphone is an admirable impulse in its own right; yet it can lead to quietism if treated as an absolute. Few of the people I would meet on my journey had the time to pontificate in the *Guardian* about their lifestyle. One of the reasons there are so few working-class authors today is precisely because a working-class job is typically incompatible with the sort of existence required to dash off books and articles. At a very basic level, a prerequisite to sitting down to quietly turn out 80,000 words is not having to worry about the electric being turned off or the discomfort of an empty stomach. There are many factors that can obstruct the paths of working-class authors. The existence of this book is probably not one of them. Any movement that seeks to change those circumstances will also have to bring a significant section of the middle classes along with it if it is to succeed. I believe that books like this one are a more effective way of doing that than yet another hair-splitting pamphlet preaching to the already converted.

And besides, if it matters, I was doing precisely the sorts of jobs that appear in this book well into my early twenties. I was born to a single mother in Bridgwater, Somerset. I left school with few qualifications; after various arduous retakes I was the only one of four children to study at university. This book is less an exercise in 'slumming it', and more a return visit to a world I narrowly escaped.

As for what I have sought to avoid, I did not want to write another dry and turgid tome about 'austerity' or 'the poor'. There are enough books of that sort already. I wanted instead to experience at least some of the hardship myself, and to write a book that contained real human beings rather than unusually saintly or malevolent caricatures. The media landscape is already soaked with the opinions of company directors, managers, bureaucrats and the orthodoxies of one political hue or another. Thus I have approached the worker and the man or woman who sleeps in the street with my questions, rather than the boss or the academic with a theory purporting to explain why they sleep there. Ultimately, I wanted to see things for myself rather than read about them second-hand in books and newspaper articles written by those who had never really looked.

In terms of the practicalities, when I set out on my journey I had in my hand a scrap of paper with a rough plan scrawled upon it: I would spend six months taking whatever minimum-wage jobs I was offered. The aim was not to travel to every part of the country, but nor did I want to stay too firmly rooted in one spot. Outside of London I would look for work in the sort of towns that rarely interest governments or the media unless there is an election in the offing. I did not begin with a plan to go to anywhere in particular; I simply went where I was offered a job and when I got there I lived, where possible, on the salary I was paid. The only people who knew what I was up to were those I sat down with and interviewed along the way. In those instances, I stepped temporarily out of my adopted persona and became once again a writer. Had any of my employers ever got wind of what I was up to they would undoubtedly have fobbed me off with some PR dogsbody, which is what happened whenever I tried to speak to an organisation openly. I was tired of people telling me things they knew to be untrue simply because they had been paid to say them.

Politically speaking, a lot has happened since I first set out to write the book. One government has fallen and another has taken its place. The present Conservative regime clings on but only just. The Labour Party has moved to the left and, for the first time in a generation, there is a whiff of socialism in the air. All of this – together with the ascendancy of a mercurial American President – has ignited a renewed interest in the plight of the so-called 'left behind' and others thought to be feeling disenfranchised by globalisation. This sympathetic mood may pass soon enough. But when it does, the resentments will linger on: there is much to be in disgust about, and it takes a certain type of comfort and affluence not to see it.

Ultimately this is a book about working-class life in the twenty-first century. It is an attempt at a documentary about how work for many people has gone from being a source of pride to a relentless and dehumanising assault on their dignity. This is a series of snapshots rather than a comprehensive study. I could not go everywhere and work for everyone, but I do not feel that anything in these pages is particularly exceptional. I am certain that someone reading this book could go out and find similar things for themselves, which in a way makes what follows even more disconcerting.

James Bloodworth, November 2017

PART I

RUGELEY

1

It was quarter past six in the evening and the siren had just sounded for lunch: a loud noise pumped through loudspeakers into every corner of the cold and drab warehouse. It sounded like a cheap musical doorbell, or a grotesque parody of the tune a plastic ballerina plays as she slowly spins on top of a jewellery box.

While I stood in the queue, hands in pockets, waiting to get out, a well-built security guard darted forward and made a signal for me to put my arms in the air. 'Move forward, mate, I haven't got all afternoon,' he said firmly in a broad West Midlands accent. I moved along and received a brisk pat-down from the guard. I was followed by a long undulating line of around thirty exhausted-looking men and women of mostly Eastern European nationalities who were shuffling through the security scanners as fast as the three guards could process them. We were in too much of a hurry to talk. We were also emptying pockets and tearing off various items of clothing that were liable to set off the temperamental metal detectors – a belt, a watch or even a sticky cough sweet clinging limply to the inside of a trouser pocket.

There was some sort of commotion at the front of the line: a quarrel had suddenly erupted between a security guard and a haggard-looking young Romanian man over the presence of a mobile phone. We all looked on in befuddled silence.

Security guard: You know you're not supposed to bring those in here. You were told that on your first day.

Romanian: I have to wait for important call. My landlord want to speak with me.

Security guard: Why can't you make personal calls in your own time like everybody else? For the umpteenth time, I'll tell you again. No ... mobile ... phones ...in ... here! Do you understand me? Now, I'll have to tell your manager.[1]

The place had the atmosphere of what I imagined a prison would feel like. Most of the rules were concerned with petty theft. You had to pass in and out of gigantic airport-style security gates at the end of every shift and each time you went on a break or needed to use the toilet. It could take ten or fifteen minutes to pass through these huge metal scanners. You were never paid for the time you spent waiting to have your pockets checked. Hooded tops were banned in the warehouse and so were sunglasses. 'We might need to see your eyes in case you've had too much to drink the night before,' a large, red- and waxy-faced woman named Vicky had warned us ominously on the first day. 'Your eyes give you away.'[2]

For hour after sweating hour we had traipsed up and down this enormous warehouse – the size of ten football pitches – tucked away in the Staffordshire countryside. Each day this short break came as temporary relief.

Lunch – we still called it lunch despite it being dished out at six o'clock in the evening – marked the halfway point in a ten-

and-a-half-hour shift. After going through the usual rigmarole of security, the men and women would spill into the large dining hall and fan out in every direction like an army of ants in flight from the nest. Most of us rushed headlong into the hall to grab a tray and establish a respectable position in the lunch queue. The whole panicked dash was punctuated by a chorus of yells and fiery laments. The best of the hot food had usually gone by the time the first twenty or so men and women had hurriedly passed through the canteen. It was therefore of great importance to secure a spot in the queue as quickly as possible, even if it meant shoving one of your co-workers out of the way in order to do so. Solidarity and the brotherhood of man did not exist in this world. You trampled on the other guy before he walked over you. If you were that sorry unkempt Romanian who had fallen foul of security – yelled at incoherently in a language you barely understood – you might be waiting six or seven hours before you got to see another inviting plate of mincemeat soaked in gravy and stodgy carbohydrates.

Eastern European languages filled the air of the shiny-floored dining hall, which was brightly lit like an operating theatre and always smelt strongly of disinfectant. There were around fifty men and women perched at the canteen tables, hunched over little black lunch trays furtively shovelling huge dollops of meat and fistfuls of chips into their mouths. The Romanians would always unfailingly clean up after themselves. They were, in fact, the most fastidious workers I had ever come across. Along with those of us who sat at the tables, another ten or so men stood milling around next to the coffee machines – head to toe in sportswear, hands in pockets and surreptitiously following every woman who shimmied past with leering eyes. On the opposite side of the dining hall was a huge window which looked out onto the big grey cooling towers of the local power station. 'Proper work,' you would think as you gazed up at the vast chimneys that puked white clouds of steam into the sky as jackdaws glided round and round like burnt pieces of paper.

One of the perks of the job was the relatively cheap food and the free teas and coffees available from the many vending machines. Mincemeat, potatoes or greasy chips plus a can of drink and a Mars bar for £4.10 – not a great deal more than the cost of preparing food beforehand, and most of it piping hot, unlike sandwiches made at home. The challenge was finding sufficient time to eat and drink during the short window allocated for break. I could count on one hand the number of times I managed to finish a full cup of tea.

We were allocated half an hour for lunch, but in practice spent only around half of that in a state of anything resembling relaxation. By the time you made it to the canteen and elbowed your way through a throng of ravenous workers, you had around fifteen minutes to bolt down the food before you started the long walk back to the warehouse. Two or three English managers would invariably be waiting for you back at the work station, pointing at imaginary watches and bellowing peremptorily at anyone who returned even thirty seconds late: 'Extended lunch break today, is it?' 'We don't pay you to sit around jabbering.'[3]

This was life at Amazon, the world's largest retailer. I was an order picker in one of its huge distribution centres in the small Staffordshire town of Rugeley. The warehouse employed around

1,200 people. The majority of my co-workers were from Eastern Europe and most of those were from Romania. The Romanians were often dumbfounded as to why any English person would want to degrade themselves doing such lowly work. 'Excuse me if this sounds offensive, but are you English? Born here?' *Yes, I am English*. 'Then why are you picking? No offence,' asked a chubby young red-haired girl on my second day.[4] A week later the same girl grabbed me by the arm, shook me violently and told me she wanted to pack her bags and return home as soon as possible. 'I hate it, I hate it here,' she hissed through chipped teeth. She said that she had only planned to stay at Amazon for a month, and that she had come here with her boyfriend to save money to take back to her small village just outside Transylvania. But neither the work nor the city she had ended up in – Birmingham – had matched her expectations of what Britain was supposed to be. 'I hate the people, I hate the dirt and I hate the work ... I don't like this country ... Too many Indian people. Indian people everywhere!'

Amazon's vast warehouse sat on waste ground between the local canal and the power station. Down the road was a company that bought and sold dead cattle. The massive shoebox-like structure of the building in which we worked was the pale blue colour of a swimming pool, and looked incongruous amid the industrial landscape of belching chimneys and sodden green fields. It contained four floors, and Amazon's workforce was similarly split up into four main groups. There were those who checked and unpacked the incoming orders; those who stowed the items on shelves; another group – which I was part of – that picked the orders; and finally the workers who packed the products up ready for delivery. It was the picker's job to march up and down the long narrow aisles selecting items from the two-metre-high shelves before putting them in big yellow plastic boxes – or 'totes', as they were called. These totes were wheeled around on blue metal trolleys before being sent down huge, seemingly never-ending conveyor belts that followed the length of the building the way a stream makes its way towards the sea. On an average day you would expect to send around forty totes down the conveyors, each one filled with books, DVDs and assorted miscellanea.

We lacked a manager in the usual sense of the word; or a flesh and blood manager, at any rate. Instead, each of us carried around with us a hand-held device that tracked our every move as if we were convicts out on house arrest. For every dozen or so workers, somewhere in the warehouse a line manager would be huddled over a desk tapping orders into a computer screen. These instructions, usually an admonishment to speed up, would filter through to our devices in an instant: 'Please report to the pick desk immediately' or 'Your rates are down this hour, please speed up.' We were ranked from highest to lowest in terms of the speed at which we collected our items from the shelves and filled our totes. For example, I was informed during my first week that I was in the bottom 10 per cent in terms of my picking rate. 'You'll have to speed up!' I was told by one of the agency reps. When you allowed your mind to wander, it was easy to imagine a future in which human beings were wired up to devices like this twenty-four hours a day.

As well as a potential forewarning of things to come, this algorithmic system of management was a throwback to the 'scientific management' theories of Frederick W. Taylor. In seeking to root out idleness and inefficient toil, in 1911 the wealthy mechanical engineer from Philadelphia published a monograph on what he saw as the potential for the scientific perfectibility of labour activity. Scientific management held that every workplace task ought to be meticulously monitored: watched, timed and recorded. Workers were units of production whose output ought to be measured in the same way as the machines on which they worked, and were to be directed down to the finest detail. Along with other prominent intellectuals of his day, Taylor did not consider the working class to be fully human: they were more usefully viewed as a resource to be exploited for profit. 'The writer firmly believes that it would be possible to train an intelligent gorilla so as to become a more efficient pig-iron handler than any man can be,' Taylor wrote disparagingly of the men whom he believed 'incapable' through 'lack of mental capacity' of understanding the theories they were to be subjected to.[5] The 'boss-class' has enthusiastically embraced Taylor's theories. In 2001, the Fellows of the Academies of Management voted *The Principles of Scientific Management* the most influential management book of the twentieth century.[6]

Twentieth-century communism also finds its echo in the modern workplace, both in modern *corporatese* and in the admonishments to feel joyful at the prospect of struggle. Socialist realism has mutated into rosy corporate uplift. Feel-good slogans were plastered across the interior walls of Amazon's warehouse next to photographs of beaming workers whose radiant countenances proclaimed that everyone at work was having a wonderful time. *We love coming to work and miss it when we're not here!* declared a life-sized cardboard cut-out of a woman named 'Bez'. Similarly, almost everything that had a name was given a euphemism. Even calling the place a warehouse was a minor transgression. Instead, you were informed on the first day that the building would henceforth be known as a 'Fulfilment Centre' – or FC for short. You were not fired or sacked; instead you were 'released'. Significantly, the potentially antagonistic categories of Boss and Worker had also been abolished. You were all 'Associates' – both high and lowly alike.

Over the course of a single morning the average picker could earn around £29 carting totes back and forth along the dimly lit aisles of the warehouse. Meanwhile Jeff Bezos, Amazon's CEO, who at the time of writing is worth around $60.7 billion, once increased his wealth by a cool £1.4 billion over the course of a similar amount of time. Calling everyone 'associates' was, it seemed, a ruse designed to foster the illusion that you were all one big happy family. 'Jeff Bezos is an associate and so are all of you,' an Amazon supervisor cheerily informed us on the very first day.[7] Which is fine as far as it goes; though the vernacular seemed purposely designed to blur the distinction between the life of a seven-pound-an-hour picker and the sort of life you can lead with £1.4 billion in the bank. The 'associates' who walked home at midnight, heavy legs supporting suppurating feet which over the course of the day had puffed up half a size bigger, were treated at every juncture as lesser human beings than men like Jeff Bezos. This was all the more reason, perhaps, for those who do so well out of such a state of affairs to create a rhetorical universe distinct from the flesh and blood reality.

Amazon's recruitment process ran strictly through two agencies – PMP Recruitment and Transline Group. I landed the job at Amazon through Transline. This agency shot to notoriety in 2013 after one of the company's employees was suspended for cruelly boasting about her apparent ability to 'stop' Jobseeker's Allowance: 'If people from the JC [job centre] don't turn up to an appointment, I stop their benefits for thirteen weeks ... suckers ... I get so much pleasure knowing what I can do if [they] mess me round. I'm going to be shot for it one day I bet!' The employee would later be suspended and never returned.[8]

I encountered a similar relish for lording it over subordinates from several people in minor positions of authority at Transline. Petty führers were ubiquitous, and if you had the temerity to ask why you had not been paid your full wages for that week they would talk to you as if you were something they had scraped off the bottom of their shoe.

Every contract that we pickers were on at Transline was zero-hours and temporary. Despite requesting it several times, I was never given a copy of my actual employment contract, and was eventually told by a Transline rep that a contract did not exist because I was on a zero-hours contract. The documents I *did* see on the day I was invited in for the interview were quickly whisked away as soon as I had filled out the requisite details. After nine months, Amazon would either take you on permanently or cast you aside with no more compunction than if you had been a sack of rotten potatoes. In practice, you were extremely lucky even to make it to nine months. We were informed on our first day that if we were 'outstanding' then Amazon might conceivably retain us. However, we were also told that we should be 'under no illusions that this is a temporary job'.⁹ This was drummed into us *ad nauseam* over the course of the first afternoon. A reward was dangled in front of us – 'we do keep on the best performing staff' – and quickly snatched away like a juicy steak pulled from the jaws of a salivating dog. 'About seventy people are waiting for these jobs, so don't get your hopes up,' a Transline rep said with supercilious relish during the induction. The stream of eager-looking men and women who flooded into the brightly lit office seemed to lend force to the rep's gloomy message.

To be kept on by Amazon as a permanent employee was to find oneself in possession of a coveted 'blue badge'. I was told by several Amazon employees that the prospect of attaining a badge was often used to coax workers into doing things they would not have otherwise entertained.

'Basically, they lie to everybody to get them to do things,' said my housemate Chris, a balding thirty-three-year-old Romanian with soft eyes and the husky voice of a heavy smoker. 'There were some blue badges [available], and [the Amazon managers] said to me, "Hey, you have to change your shift to get a blue badge. Not for a long time, but for a few weeks" ... It turned out to be for three months. Oh, and they gave the blue badges to everyone else anyway.'¹⁰

We were stood about in the kitchen of the small house we were renting along with three others. It was a blackened red-brick shoebox at the end of a gap-toothed terrace which half a century ago would have housed local miners: the 'barracks of an industry', as such settlements were once called. There were clusters of these cramped and huddled houses spread right across the Cannock Chase district. Rugeley was situated in the north, and down the A460 were the towns of Cannock and Hednesford.

It was early spring, and due to the dilapidated state of the house you could never fully escape the dank and filthy weather outside. Everything on the side of the kitchen nearest the window had the same silver film of dew that glazed the small lawn and the black and wet pavement outside. At the bottom of the front garden was a tall hedge where little black bags left by dog-walkers would hang until the sacks broke and spilled their foul contents onto the pavement below.

Chris was frying some potatoes in a pan on the hob to go with the luminous pink sausage he had just pulled out of the fridge. You can usually discern the nationalities of the residents of a house like this by the contents of the kitchen. Cured meat and beer and they are from Eastern Europe. Bacon, eggs and a few ready meals and they are English. Yellow-stained potato and rice dishes and the South Asians have arrived. Rather than traipsing around an old English town all day looking furtively for the signs of multiculturalism, you might save yourself the time by simply opening the door of a fridge.

As is common in rented dwellings, the lounge had been summarily ripped out and turned into an extra bedroom. The house functioned as a cash cow rather than a comfortable place to live. The landlord was one of the better sorts, yet every appliance and article of furniture had been purchased on the cheap – and was thus liable to break down or fall apart at the first opportunity. I slept in a room that permanently reeked of cheap, nauseating paint. The electrics shorted several times over the course of the month, and as a consequence there was often no hot water with which to take a shower before work. There was a stinking toilet with a malfunctioning flush and a grimy washbasin. On one occasion all the lights in the kitchen stopped working because someone had over-run the bath and water had poured down through the light fittings and into the kitchen below. Cockroaches would occasionally scurry out from under the skirting and roam around the overflowing bin, which was permanently stuffed with the filthy wrappers from several days' worth of food. The heating was controlled centrally by a single switch, meaning it was either swelteringly hot or bitterly cold.

Living in the house alongside Chris and myself were three others: another Romanian named Claudiu and an Englishman named Joe who lived in his poky room together with his wife. I rarely saw Claudiu, whereas Joe would often linger outside the side door of the house smoking and spitting large splashes of catarrh onto the pavement. He was bald, heavily tattooed and his face was wrinkled and yellow. He had a nervous disposition and the rapid movements of a bird. The first thing he did when I moved in was to ceremonially shake my hand and greet me as a 'fellow English'. 'We English, we've gotta stick together,' he said, before telling me what an improvement I was on the previous tenant. 'Blinking heck, the last bloke here before you was a right mardy bum.'

Everyone living in the house worked at Amazon, which was about forty minutes away on foot. Chris had worked as a process guide at Amazon for eleven months. A process guide is essentially an assistant manager, and it was Chris's job to monitor fellow workers and to pick up any production quality issues that might occur during the course of a shift. Chris told me that he was a 'respectable guy' back in Romania; yet over here he was a tiny cog in Amazon's giant global distribution machine, a behemoth that employed almost 8,000 people in the UK alone.[11] Like many of the Romanians I met, Chris had been sold an idea of Britain which only vaguely corresponded with the reality he encountered when he arrived.

'There are some agencies that are getting [workers] from Romania, and they're getting a commission for them. It's an English guy who's doing this ... John I think is his name. I came to the UK through this company ... They're lying to you, so they're gonna say, "Hey, you go to John Lewis or somewhere else," but they're sending people to Amazon. OK, maybe their first intention was to send people to John Lewis and they don't have places available, but they're saying this to everyone – even to guys with a better resumé like me.'

The employment agencies constantly drum it into workers like Chris that if they kick up a fuss about the conditions at work there is a vast reserve army of their fellow countrymen ready to take their place. Hearing stories like this brought to mind the words of the working-class writer B. L. Coombes, who in his 1939 novel on Welsh colliery life *These Poor Hands* wrote:

> It is a rotten feeling for a man who is working to come
> outside and see that a crowd of men are waiting for work.
> It warns him that the masters can treat him as they wish,
> for he dare not insist on his rights when there are so many
> waiting for a chance to start.

The house I shared with Chris was one of the better places he had lived since coming to England, at least in the sense that the landlord wasn't constantly scheming to dip his hand into Chris's shallow pockets. The buy-to-let market in the UK has boomed in recent years. There are good landlords, and then there are those for whom acquiring a property 'portfolio' is mostly about ripping off tenants and making a fast buck. Home ownership in Britain is at a thirty-year low.[12] More than a third of former council homes are now owned by private landlords. Meanwhile, between 2007 and 2016 total mortgage lending for buy-to-let properties doubled from 8.5 per cent to 17 per cent.[13] It has become harder to own a house but far easier to find a landlord. Buying-to-let can also be a lucrative occupation in itself. In 2015, 38 per cent of workers earned less than the amount the average homeowner made from the increase in the value of their house.[14]

Men like Chris, who, when they first come to Britain are unaware of their rights as tenants, are walking wedges of currency for this rising class of rapacious rentiers. Unscrupulous landlords – sometimes first- or second-generation migrants themselves – reel in the Eastern Europeans with conviviality and a thin veneer of respectability before their hand darts swiftly towards their new tenant's wallet. They earn your trust before swooping like a ravenous hawk whose eye has locked on to a corpulent vole. Everything sounds reasonable and above board until your feet are comfortably placed under the table and moving out becomes an oppressive chore. Then the landlord ups the ante, demanding ever-more money for rent and deposits – £300, £400, sometimes as much as £1,000. This had been the experience of Chris and many of his friends.

'For many Romanian tenants you're gonna have rats in your house, really small rooms; a single room is gonna be just a bed, and that's it for £65 a week – everything included. And they try to scam you for money – for more money. A lot of these [property] agencies, they're not quite legal, so when they suddenly told me I had to pay £360–£370 more, even if I paid in advance for one more week, I left in a couple of days. I was really disgusted. They suddenly said, "Hey, you have to pay us more." Basically, working for Amazon you don't have time for many other things, and I didn't have time to go and argue with them ... so I just left.'

As we talked, Chris upended the frying pan and poured the crispy discs of potato he was frying onto the plate. Some of them jumped out of the pan and onto the floor, a meal for the various creatures that would dart out from under the skirting boards as soon as it got dark.

'They're just trying to make more money for their pockets. Forcing people to pay more. All of my friends had this problem. Even now, after I left the house, there's one guy there, still living there, and he's having the same issue right now. He's having exactly the same issue. He's having to pay £340 in advance. [They're] suddenly demanding three or four weeks' rent in advance.'

When the agency had unsavoury tenants, they dumped those on the Romanians too.

'They put some drug addicts with us in the house, and another guy was on trial, or waiting for his sentence. If someone is going to pay them money for two weeks, three weeks in advance, they just don't care, they just want money and that's it. There was an addict who was really filthy, and the garbage in his room was like twenty centimetres high. And I was shocked because that smell was really bad, and it was impossible to live there. And then they're stealing the food from the freezer, the drug addicts. And when I told the agency about it, they didn't reply; they just ignored it.'

Unlike Chris, I had walked into the job at Amazon freely, with a viable route out. But more importantly, I knew where to find my next meal if things became unbearable. The alternative for many of the Eastern Europeans was much starker. The average net monthly salary in Romania as of April 2016 was £413. In rural areas it was even less.[15]

'We need the money to survive ... right now I'm helping my family. From time to time I'm helping them to survive. I mean, we can stay in the forest and live but we need more money, that's the problem.'

Chris and the other Romanians realised that what they were doing was wretched work – hence their incredulity when I, an English national, chose willingly to put myself through it. 'Why you do this fucking shit?' 'Why don't you get another job?' 'You English!' I had questions like this fired at me nearly every day. For many of my workmates, however, the alternative was £143 a month and a fairly spartan existence supported by a threadbare social safety net. The cracks in the pavement in Eastern Europe were deeper and the squalor that poverty brought there was more wretched than anything you would have found in our grimy kitchen with its foul-smelling bin. But to say that men like Chris were infinitely glad of the work they were doing at Amazon, as it has become so fashionable to do – *These immigrants want to get on and I say good luck to them* – would not be quite truthful. As another young Romanian put it to me in the pub a few days later: 'You can work here like an animal; you work four days, you know, and you have £240. I am a nobody here, yes; but back in Romania I am a nobody without enough money to eat.'

2

Rugeley is a small Staffordshire town with a population of around 24,000, sandwiched between Stafford and Cannock Chase. Depending on whom you speak to, its name is pronounced either Rudge-ley (rhyming with sludge) or Rouge-ley (as in the make-up). It is one of those down-at-heel market towns that exist as a sort of perpetually ill-treated younger sibling to the bigger local towns and cities like Birmingham or Shrewsbury. Nothing ever seems to happen in places like this. An atomic bomb could go off over London and things would probably carry on much as before. The same pale and slatternly people would still be found floating languidly in and out of the charity shops and takeaway restaurants that pepper the high street. The scrawled-on bedsheets calling attention to 'Sue's 40th' would still be found draped from the local landmarks. And the anonymous wretches who flit in and out of precarious and poorly paid employment would be as invisible to the politicians of the apocalyptic future as they are to the politicians of today. Rugeley is never likely to receive the attention bestowed on a really destitute part of the country like Jaywick, say, or Glasgow. But in a sense it is more instructive. There are towns like it dotted across the Midlands and the North of England. On my days off I would sometimes stop for a cup of tea at a small local cafe on the high street. The shop was brightly lit and welcoming, with the morning sun flooding in through the large front windows onto the red and white checked tablecloths, giving off a dull pink glare. The menu was rudimentary as far as it goes – full English breakfast, bacon and sausage cobs finished off with apple crumble and custard for dessert – and the antiquated feeling of the little shop was augmented by two plastic towers of penny chews and rhubarb and custards which snaked up the back wall. The homely atmosphere would have been complete with the addition of a fly-blown sign perched in the front window advertising 'Tuck Shop Favourites'. The sleepy tea shop existed in restful contrast to the swanky Costa further down the high street, which teemed with people.

The high street in Rugeley is a narrow and winding street of little red-brick shops that leans ever-so-slightly inward, as if trying to squeeze the life out of the cobbled walkway that runs reluctantly down the middle. A little further down the sleepy high street is the pub where the notorious physician William Palmer, aka the Rugeley Poisoner, once did away with several people using strychnine. Charles Dickens described Palmer as 'the greatest villain that ever stood in the Old Bailey'. Thirty-five thousand spectators travelled to Stafford Gaol in 1856 to watch Palmer hang. Above the door of the pub, a dilapidated sign hangs as it would have during the nineteenth century, only today it carries the name of *The Shrew* rather than *The Talbot Arms*. In 1856, one local journalist wrote that the old sign's 'creaking at night must have wearied William Palmer's wife when she lay dying'.

The little tea shop never had more than three or four people in it at any one time. Those who did pass through were almost always on familiar terms with the owner. A radio hummed faintly in the background, but such was the hushed atmosphere of the place that any conversation was invariably started with the entire shop.

'There's a rollover on the National Lottery tonight. Thirty-three million,' announced a fair-haired young woman one afternoon as she wheeled a pushchair through the front door, her overcoat flapping mournfully behind her in the breeze. 'How many have you had in?' she asked the owner, a plump woman of around fifty who always wore a fearful expression.

'It's been quiet around town,' the owner replied. 'Morrisons ain't half as packed as it normally is.'

I asked the women about work in the town, and the lady with the pushchair insisted firmly (and truthfully, from what I had gathered) that it was 'mostly Eastern Europeans' who worked at Amazon.

'They get on the train from Birmingham, and when they get off you'd think you were in a foreign country. They say there's people sleeping under the canal bridge and all sorts.'

Listening keenly, another of the tea shop's patrons, a stooping lady of around seventy with rimless glasses and a sandy-coloured perm, piped in, and tried to explain in a sympathetic tone of voice what was behind the apparent influx of migrants to Rugeley.

'I don't think it's their culture ... I mean, they've just got no money. They're skint ... like us in a way, but they hop on a bus and come over here and go up to Amazon. You feel for them a bit, really.'

She then straightened her shoulders a little, removed her glasses, narrowed her eyes and began to shake her head very slowly. 'You do feel for them, especially when you see them young girls, eighteen or nineteen, traipsing up and down the road to go and do them long hours.'

The woman with the pushchair informed me that when Amazon first arrived in Rugeley in 2011, it had been a 'massive thing for the community'.

'There was gonna be all these jobs, but no one ended up getting one, did they? There's a hell of a lot of anger round here about it now. It's the breaks and things, I've heard. They say it's stopping people wanting to work there ... People are putting those things on their arms checking how many steps they've done.'

But the woman's anger was not directed at the migrants themselves, so much as at the thought that Amazon might be favouring foreigners over the locals. She went on again to tell me stories of migrants sleeping under the bridge that runs over the Trent and Mersey Canal; though I never found any evidence of this on the several occasions I went down to have a look.

'They don't employ local people, do they?' she said accusingly before I left.

'*Can't* or *won't*?' I asked.

'Well, they never seem to take any locals on, that's all I'm saying.'

I asked what year the local Lea Hall Colliery closed.

'Blimey, that's been gone a while now, ain't it? The power station's going altogether.'

'In June,' the owner interposed.

'How many jobs will that be going, then?' I asked finally.

Lady with pushchair: 'About a hundred and fifty, didn't they say? [Or] two hundred at the power station?'

The owner: 'Yeah, two hundred.'

A couple of unemployed twenty-something men would sometimes congregate in the cafe, sipping mugs of tea and furtively poring over copies of the *Sun* and the *Rugeley Chronicle*. Lunchtime arguments occasionally moved next door to the pub, where a frequent topic of conversation would be the 'scroungers' who preferred 'sitting on the sofa snacking to working', and also, inevitably, the migrants. One beer-soaked man whom I regularly bumped into – an out-of-work carpenter with spindly limbs and a rasping voice – grabbed me by the arm several times to recite a story about how his son was unable to find somewhere to live because of – he would lower his voice at this point – 'all them Eastern Europeans'.

According to the 2011 census, Rugeley has fewer foreign-born residents than the national average.[16] Yet peeping out through the frosted glass of the little pub on the high street, the threat of 'the Romanians' loomed ominously over the town like a fearsome raincloud. The handful of migrants the man knew personally were another matter entirely. They were 'not like the rest of them', he told me. Some were even 'decent blokes' who you could have a drink and a laugh with. But given the chance the carpenter would 'shut the door' on the others. 'The lot of them coming in, down the train station and that. Where's the working man supposed to live?' he would ask emphatically, jabbing a tobacco-stained finger into my chest. 'Where's he supposed to work?'

The spread of precarious work, propped up by an army of exploited labourers speaking in incomprehensible tongues, inevitably fuels these sorts of concerns. But there is a feeling of English culture being overwhelmed by capitalism, too. The forces that have ruthlessly turned almost every British high street into a cultural wasteland of dull and identikit chain stores offering the same sensory experience are now so vast and incomprehensible that it is the single *Polski sklep* that is singled out. If English culture is being trampled on then Ronald McDonald should take more of the blame than Eastern European fruit pickers.

One of the first things to catch your eye on arriving in Rugeley is the obtrusively large red shopfront advertising private detectives. *Is your partner cheating? Ask about our tracking service*, reads the huge white lettering in the window. The shop also advertises lie-detector tests for hire. This is the paranoid world of *The Jeremy Kyle Show* writ large. Fidelity and faithfulness have been slowly chipped away by more ephemeral, market-driven principles promising instant gratification. You ditch one lover and take another, just as you might throw away an iPhone and buy a newer model in an emotional flight of fancy. For working-class communities this adds yet another layer of impermanence to an already insecure existence, especially for those men whose sense of masculine inadequacy is reinforced by the lack of any purposeful employment.

On several occasions I saw the same forlorn-looking young man hanging around outside the red-fronted shop. He was thin and gaunt, with protruding cheek bones and nervous-looking soft eyes that would dart about rapidly while he spoke. He was twenty-eight but looked much older. His face was clammy and grey, and he had lost one of his front teeth. He worked in a local shop and had been offered a job at Amazon but had turned it down.

'It was the first job I ever turned down,' he said proudly between short and rapid drags on a cigarette. 'It's foreigners' work, you know? You get in on a job in a place like that and there ain't no one to talk to. They [the Eastern Europeans] keep themselves to themselves, don't they? You try to be friendly and that, but they ain't that interested; they just don't wanna know. It's sort of like they look down on us, because we're English, you know? I don't know why it is, but it always feels like they look down on us.'

I learned soon enough why the young man was always loitering around the Jeremy Kyle shop.

'Women, they end up leaving me for no reason and then going off with another lad. Always happens to me, like. I don't know how I can change that. I'm a man of truth ... I think I'm a nice guy, but they automatically treat me like I'm a pushover, you know.'

He relayed to me the story of how he had met a twenty-three-year-old woman on Facebook. She lived in Blackburn. For the first few weeks, at least, things went well. But it was clear from what the man said that he soon became possessive and domineering. At the first sign of disinterest on the part of the object of his affections he started bombarding her with text messages – around 100 a day.

'She used me. She used me for my money for two months and a half. I accused her of cheating before that. And they [her and her friends] told me, "You better stop texting or you'll be in deep shit." But I ain't scared of anyone. I've got a sword and axes in my house [grinning]. If they come to my house, I'll just take it outside, scare the shit out of them, and then take it back in the house.'

The man expelled the last breath of smoke through the gap in his front teeth and slipped into a lament about the state of the town.

'There's fucking nothing about here. There's like betting shops, Ladbrokes and that, a few pubs, hardly any clothes shops whatsoever – we've got JD Sports and then a few others – and that's it. I wouldn't work at fucking Amazon.'

He crushed the cigarette under his foot and lurched back into the private detective store. In the recent past a man often found a sense of identity through his work. But for those besieged by hostile economic forces today it can be hard to find a sense of belonging in the world. With the decline of trade unionism, discontent is expressed through ephemeral and individual modes of expression or it is driven inward. From the outside, an illusion is fostered that the working classes are the architects of their own destinies. You might be stacking shelves in Tesco or flogging useless junk to pensioners from a cow-shed converted into a call centre, but when you get a tattoo or a celebrity haircut, you feel a temporary affinity with the pop stars, rock stars and footballers who strut across the pages of the tabloids like peacocks. But the conceit at the bottom of this is that, unlike the icons of popular culture you wish to imitate, you invariably have to drag yourself back to the grim drudgery of it all the very next morning.

As for Amazon, I got a sense from the people I spoke to in the town that locals did initially get jobs there. Indeed, the ease with which I got in proved that there was no conspiracy to lock English workers out. Nor, strictly speaking, were there a limited number of jobs on offer. The sheer rapidity at which people dropped out after starting resulted in a constant stream of fresh openings. But few English locals I spoke to were willing to put up with the conditions for any significant period of time. The more I looked into it, the more this did not appear to be a problem confined to Rugeley. According to a recent survey of Amazon's staff by the GMB union:[17]

- 91 per cent would not recommend working for Amazon to a friend.
- 70 per cent of staff felt that they were given disciplinary points unfairly.
- 89 per cent felt exploited.
- 78 per cent felt that their breaks were too short.
- 71 per cent reported that they walked more than 10 miles a day at work.

'Everyone I started with, they're all gone now. I'm the only one left out of eight,' said Claire, a chubby nineteen-year-old with red streaks in her hair, who combined packing at Amazon with a job in a local pub.[18]

I sat with Claire at a table on the upstairs floor of Wetherspoons in Cannock. The pub was dimly lit and the air was heavy with the smell of sugar and hop residue. It was early afternoon on a weekday, and the pub teemed with pensioners, young mothers and the unemployed. Behind the table where we were sat, the luminous plastic spoon a young woman was using to feed her baby stood out against the chestnut-coloured Mock-Tudor interior. Further back, next to the fruit machine, were two slovenly-looking men, one clasping a pint tight to his chest while the other searched anxiously for coins in every pocket of his baggy denim jeans.

Over an orange juice, Claire told me that many of her friends had started working at Amazon with high hopes, but that these were soon dashed when the reality of the job smacked them in the face.

'A few of them left because they got better jobs, but the rest of them, they hated it.'

Claire could have been the poster girl for a younger generation for whom the concept of a job for life feels as antiquated as floppy disks and VHS tapes. She had been forced out of a job at another pub because her hours had suddenly been reduced. She heard that Amazon were recruiting so she applied for one of the packing positions through the Transline agency. There were regular headlines in the paper about Amazon creating hundreds of new jobs in Rugeley, and for a nineteen-year-old the money – £7 an hour – did not seem particularly bad. She turned up at the agency's office in Cannock, filled out the pile of papers and underwent the obligatory drug and alcohol test.

And so Claire started working at Amazon. It was the end of October and Claire had previously been worried about how to pay for Christmas. She lived at home with her mum but still had to pay rent as well as monthly direct debits for a mobile phone. A job at Amazon held out the prospect of at least some seasonal cheer: drinks with friends and presents for the family. Claire had 'got on her bike' (or on a coach laid on by Amazon in this case) and had gone looking for work. She did everything that was asked of her. She had even refused to sign on while she was looking for a job. Yet, as with many others I would go on to meet, her hopes were soon dashed.

'They [Transline] underpaid me multiple times over Christmas, and then it took eight weeks to get [the money] back. All in all, I think it worked out at like twenty-seven hours over three weeks that they'd underpaid me. My mum ... she contacted ACAS a few times to try and resolve it. And when I mentioned it to Amazon that ACAS had been contacted, I got my money back the next week ... After three months, anything that you're owed they [the agency] won't pay it.'

But soon after Claire had wrestled back the first lot of money, the underpayments from Transline started again.

'I got paid eighteen pounds two weeks ago for forty hours. I got paid for two-and-a-half hours.'

During the week in question Claire had effectively been paid 45p an hour. Again, though, it took several weeks to get the money back.

'I should've got £262, I think ... They said, "Sorry, but everyone's pay has been messed up." I was told when I got my wage slip, "Don't worry, it's just the wage slips that are wrong." ... I've been there six months and I've been underpaid about seven times.'

Taking Transline to an employment tribunal might have been an option for Claire, were it not so prohibitively expensive. Employment tribunal fees were introduced in July 2013, meaning that a disgruntled employee must now fork out up to £1,200 to bring a case to a tribunal. The result has been a precipitous fall in the number of claimants coming forward, from 5,847 before fees were introduced to 1,740 in the year afterwards (2014–15) – a drop of 70 per cent.[19]

When you get a professional job you invariably graduate from weekly to monthly pay packets. It is cheaper for companies to do it this way. To do payroll fifty-two times a year is costlier and more time consuming than doing it twelve times. But if you are living hand to mouth, you cannot afford to wait a month before you get your first pay cheque. You need it right away. The idea of falling back on savings is as otherworldly to those at the bottom end of the labour market as taking a loan out from Wonga is to the middle classes. Thus, agencies like Transline pay their workers each week. Or at least that's how it is supposed to work.

'I've had to [borrow] money off my mum quite a few times to pay the rent because of them. If I lived with a landlord I'd be fucked, basically. But yeah, when they paid in that £18 I had a direct debit going out of £40 … I think they also gave me £140 instead of £260. I had to pay £80 out, and I had to pay a £40 direct debit, so I only had £20 for the week. Luckily, I've got another job, so I had £100 coming in that week on the Sunday, but Amazon and Transline didn't know that. I said to them, "Look, when am I getting the rest of my money?" "Oh, next week," they said. This was because they couldn't do same-day transfers, apparently.'

The limited employment rights conferred on Amazon's workforce by the agencies was one thing; however, even these insubstantial safeguards were regularly flouted. Management could also be needlessly capricious, especially with its points-based disciplinary system whereby workers accrued points for things like days off with illness, not hitting pick rates or being late.

'You're allowed six points before release [before you're sacked]. One of my friends had four, and they pointed her for clocking out early when she hadn't. They pointed her [again] because the Amazon bus broke down and she was late for work; [and then again] because her child was in hospital so she had to leave work. When I first started, I was in a car accident ... I managed to get into work but they sent me home and pointed me for it. And I was like, "I've just been in a car accident; you're the ones who sent me home. Why am I being pointed?"'

Claire did not expect to be at Amazon for much longer. She had already clocked up five points, and so was just one point away from being 'released'. The first point was for the car accident; then she received a point for not hitting her productivity rates ('On pack it's ridiculous'); she picked up another when the bus laid on by Amazon was late again; she picked up a point when Amazon tried to force her to do overtime ('they said it was compulsory and I was like, "I've done my five weeks of compulsory overtime, I'm not doing any more"'); and she picked up another point when she was off with a migraine. ('I suffer with really bad migraines, and I said to them, "Can I bring a doctor's note in?" And they were like, "No, you'll still get pointed."')

Claire also told me a story about a friend of hers who was transgender. Before he stopped working for Transline he was on the receiving end of jibes about this.

'To me that's just as bad as being racist,' Claire said firmly, refuting in one breath the lazy stereotype that working-class people are hopelessly unreconstructed on every social issue under the sun.

'He was transgender, and his real name was Elise but he asked to be called Elliot, and Transline point blank refused. They called him Elise, so he just wouldn't answer them. I was like, "He's transgender, he's on testosterone, so he technically is a male. And what does it matter if you call him Elliot or Elise?"'

'Did they say why?'

'Because *she* was a girl, they said. Because *she* "didn't have the bits".'

'Who said that?'

'One of the Transline managers.'

To get one of Amazon's coveted blue badges was fiendishly difficult. You had to be exceptional and even minor infractions seemed to disqualify you.

'You can't have any time off,' Claire told me, 'and you have to have perfect rates all the time ... like 100 per cent all the time on anything.'

Another friend of Claire's was all set to get a blue badge as the end of his nine months approached. He had worn himself out, Claire said, pulling what must have amounted to hundreds of thousands of items off the shelves for Amazon's customers, from books to kitchen appliances. He had hit all his pick rates, had always turned up to work on time and, crucially, had somehow managed not to flout the innumerable petty rules which governed nearly every aspect of the job. Yet this brave new economy – the Darwinian world in which illness was an unpardonable sin – spat him out like a betel nut. His crime was having the temerity to get sick. He even phoned the office an hour before work, in accordance with Transline's rules, to let his manager know. Not that this stopped the agency from getting rid of him.

3

I was back at work and had started to get sick. It was my second week. Because being ill was a punishable offence, I was about to earn myself a 'point'. Never mind that working an obscenely long ten-and-a-half-hour day on a diet of stodge and grease was liable to leave even the healthiest worker ailing. If you were sick you lost a day's pay, which tended to make you even sicker, due to the penurious lifestyle it encouraged. Not that Amazon seemed to worry. They had, after all, developed this cruel system, which saw workers punished for any kind of ailment that kept you at home.

As with so many of the rules at Amazon, the automatic assumption from higher up was that in every aspect of the job you were trying to pull a fast one. All illness was synonymous with a layabout whose sickness is the result of a drunken night on the town. You were not *really ill*; it was obvious that you just didn't want to be at work. Thus, if you informed the agency in good time that you were going to be absent you were still punished for it. *Thanks for letting us know, now here is your point.* If you failed to phone in and give forewarning you were (albeit with rather more justification) sanctioned with three points. A week of notified illness accrued five points, which was a whisker away from getting the sack. Similarly, if you were one minute late for work, as well as being given a point, you risked losing pay equivalent to fifteen minutes. On the whole, sympathy was in short supply. 'You'll just have to self-medicate because we need you here,' an Amazon supervisor had told us on the first day.[20] The canteen was heavily stocked with cough lozenges and it was soon obvious why.

On my return to work an awkward man in gold-rimmed spectacles came looking for me on behalf of Transline. I caught sight of him wending his way in and out of the aisles, clipboard tucked under one arm, looking down each of the long walkways for – as it turned out – me. For the agency's apparent enforcer (it was this man's job to go around informing people of their mistakes and misdemeanours) the man was a surprisingly yielding character. He looked on you with submissive hang-dog eyes as he reeled off your charge sheet. Unlike some of the other managers, he evidently did the job reluctantly. He stuttered and prevaricated, and every attempt at admonishment was rendered feeble by his mousy apprehension. He ought to have been a librarian rather than a person wielding any sort of authority over others.

Nevertheless, he did eventually manage to expostulate that I was to be given a point for the previous day's absence. He did not say it was a punishment but that was effectively what it was. The anger welled up in me as the man was droning on and I was forced to bite my tongue. I did, however, ask if it was legal to discipline me like this merely for being ill – especially when I had gone through the correct procedure of phoning the office an hour before my shift began. He gave me the sort of answer a school teacher would give you when you were five years old. 'It is what Amazon have always done,' he replied, looking at me more in sorrow than in anger, which made the whole thing worse. He might just as well have said, 'Because I said so.' [21]

According to the pedometer I wore on my wrist, I was walking around ten miles a day. The greatest distance I travelled was fourteen miles and the shortest distance was seven. To give some concrete sense of what that entailed, setting off on my first day from the heart of London and heading east, by the evening I would have arrived in Sidcup. By the end of day two I would be approaching Rochester. By the end of the week the coast of Dover would be in sight, and at the end of the month I would have walked to Antwerp in Belgium. The cumulative effect of the monstrous amounts of walking you are expected to undertake is felt most keenly on your feet, which in my case began to resemble two ragged clods of wax gone over with a cheese grater. Traipsing around for ten miles when your feet are soft and you've eaten well and slept soundly is one thing. Doing it for four consecutive days (and that's before any overtime is factored in) with very little let-up and on a diet of ready meals is another thing altogether.

Over the course of a week the tiredness crept up on me to the point where it felt as if someone had fastened manacles around my ankles. Any vitality new employees might possess falls away from them like an old coat within a couple of days. When they start, cordial, bright-eyed young Romanian men and women are so busy running around that they don't even have time to wipe the sweat from their faces. Just a few days later they'll be curled over their trolleys, covertly trying to snatch a morsel of sleep out of sight of the roving supervisors.

This was how I first met Nirmal, a forty-year-old British Indian man from Wolverhampton who had once owned his own business. One evening I had gone charging round a corner in the darkness of the warehouse to retrieve a box of grass seed to complete a customer's order. As I dashed around the bend my trolley went careering into Nirmal's. There was a loud crash and the big man in front of me jerked up like a spring that had been uncoiled. He had evidently been asleep, though for how long it was impossible to tell. Nirmal had a physique like Obelix in the *Asterix* comic strips. His corpulence reminded you of a walrus, but his manner always conveyed an air of amiable good humour that meant you instantly warmed to him. Nirmal had run a corner shop in a previous life, yet it had gone to the wall when the recession of 2008 hit. Since then, he had worked as a van driver for a couple of years, and after tiring of that – 'It was really hard work and mind-numbingly boring after a bit' – had decided to give Amazon a go.

I had first noticed Nirmal when, on the very first day, I saw him scanning the room during the induction, looking around at the assembled young Eastern Europeans with a mixture of disdain and jocularity. A smirk was constantly curving up one side of his face, the way a crease adorns a crumpled shirt. Once you had registered it you could hardly imagine Nirmal with any other expression. His approach to work was characterised by what Richard Hoggart described in *The Uses of Literacy* as a 'go slow – don't put the other man out of a job' attitude. 'It's like a bank,' Nirmal told me cryptically, 'when one person speeds up it ruins it for everyone.'

I immediately liked Nirmal. You could tell, however, that he was not going to last long in the job. By the end of the first week

I was picking around 180 items a session and averaging about ninety items per hour. My score wasn't particularly impressive, either – the red-haired Romanian girl who claimed to 'hate' the job was hitting 230 items per session. Nirmal approached me at lunch on the second day with a wider grin than usual to boast about how he was hitting forty items an hour. I didn't have the heart to tell him just how bad that was, so instead I lied, telling him that I had 'just about managed fifty but that was walking fast'.

The problem, of course, was Nirmal's weight. If you were out of shape at all the work was torturous. The same was true if you were over a certain age. On one occasion[22] I witnessed a particularly disgusting scene. Wheeling a trolley down a deserted corner of the warehouse one dull afternoon, I saw a supervisor – a dead-eyed young middle manager who was puffed up from the gym and pungent with aftershave – set upon an older man.

Shaking his finger at him, the young man called the older worker every name he could think of. The words came out of his mouth like sour milk poured from a jug. He might as well have knocked the old man over with scorn. The man on the receiving end, who must have been at least sixty, grew pale and tense as he cowered under the wave of cruel invective. The wrath of the manager – whose face had turned from red to purple and back to red again – was only abated when he was summoned downstairs by a muffled voice on his walkie-talkie. The old man he left behind had by that time shrivelled up like a melted crisp packet. Nirmal, who had been watching the spectacle unfold from further back, sidled up to me, shaking his head. 'Fucking hell,' he chuckled softly. 'He ain't gonna last long.'

And he didn't. While I was stood outside smoking a cigarette at lunch that day, I watched the old man stagger out of the building and through the second set of tall metal security gates. These sat between hulking black metal fences at the end of the car park. This ungainly man with bloodshot eyes moved as if all the life had been drained out of him. He teetered into the car park and towards a little red Nissan Micra which was sat with its lights on, engine purring away quietly. As he approached the car a dishevelled old lady climbed out of the driver's door as quickly as she could move. Looking fixedly at the man's grief-stricken face, she pulled out a handkerchief from the pocket of her duffel coat and scampered towards him. She dabbed the man's face with her brown mottled hand as she pleaded with him to disclose what had happened. The entire scene, which could not have lasted more than a minute or two, made you want to cry. Off they trundled in the car, heads bobbing like plastic ducks in a bath as they disappeared out through the gate. I never saw either of them again.

The top floor on which I worked was a gloomy place, with the only natural light coming in through small rectangular windows located far above on the high ceiling. Most of the light was provided by grey steel lamps the shape of rugby balls and about the same size. These were dotted about the ceilings on every floor and cast a peculiar yellow glow about the place. During the course of the night – because as soon as we clocked off at 11:30 p.m. another group of workers were bussed in to start their shifts – many of the motion-sensitive lights would malfunction, meaning that a dozen or so workers would be left scuttling around in the dark on the top floor of a warehouse at three o'clock in the morning. Who, when they purchase an iPhone charger or an Adele album with a click on Amazon's website, imagines anything like this?

You discover almost as soon as you begin the job that the admonishment to 'never run' was not meant literally. Rather, it was an illusory prohibition of something which was a necessary requirement if you were to avoid the sack. Like a totalitarian state, rules were laid down that it was impossible not to flout. Dashing around was obligatory if you were to meet the exacting targets set for every worker. Similarly, water breaks were permitted, but to go off in search of a water dispenser was to run the risk of 'idling', another transgression you were often warned about. There were around twelve water machines on each floor, yet in a labyrinth of aisles spread over 700,000 square feet it was nearly always impossible to locate one nearby when you needed it.

I would begin work each day at one o'clock in the afternoon along with the rest of my shift cohort. We would swipe through the outer security gates, walk to our lockers and dispose of our belongings – mobile phones, keys and anything else liable to delay your exit through security later on – and head towards the pick desk. It was impossible to take a recording device into the warehouse (or to be more precise, it would have been impossible to get it back out through the security gates at the end of a shift), and so I carried an innocuous-looking notepad and pen around with me in my back pocket. The security guards at Amazon were endowed with a great deal of power, which included the right to search your car if they suspected you of stealing something. Such was the weight of suspicion falling on you from day one that even carrying the little pen and paper in my pocket felt like I was committing some disgraceful crime.

There is something unusually oppressive about an environment like that. I suspect it makes a person more rather than less likely to misbehave. The entire time I was working at Amazon I felt as though I was under a dark cloud of suspicion. I would find myself cringing under the accusatory questions of a supervisor or security guard when I had done nothing wrong. The sheer oppressiveness of the place built up over time to become a self-fulfilling prophecy: you soon began to fantasise about scheming against the company and its petty rules. The first time you were accused of idling you felt a burning sense of injustice. The second or third time it happened you would be annoyed only because you had been caught. You would soon find yourself carrying out small rebellions against authority: a misplaced item you would once have picked up, you now left on the floor. You would snack in the warehouse and defile the floor with the empty wrapper, or deliver a satisfying boot to the spines of a row of tightly packed books or DVDs.

Arriving at the pick desk to start a shift, you would typically receive something between a briefing and a telling-off from one of the Amazon line managers. Prizes would be offered for the best-performing pickers – though I never did see anyone win anything – and a manager would run through all the mistakes your shift had made on the previous day. These would include things like not stowing boxes properly after picking an item and taking too much idle time. Most of what was disparagingly called 'idle time' involved things like going to the toilet, yet the wickedness of 'idling' was brought up unfailingly at every briefing, as if the need to perform bodily functions would eventually melt away in the name of productivity. 'You need to get your productivity up, guys,' intoned various managers in the corporate jargonese that seeks to sugar-coat admonishments. 'You're clocking up too much idle time.'[23] Rather than complaining when people had the temerity to go to the toilet, productivity-obsessed Amazon might instead have installed more toilets. For those of us who worked on the top floor of this huge building, the closest toilets were down four flights of stairs. So far, in fact, that on one occasion I came across a bottle of straw-coloured liquid perched inauspiciously on a shelf next to a box of Christmas decorations.

'They put me on pick the other day and asked me why I had fifteen minutes' idle time,' Claire had told me in the pub. 'I was like ... I needed to go to the toilet. I had to walk all the way down the stairs – like four floors – to go to the toilet. It's like, what do you expect?!'

You soon found yourself in trouble if you began to dwell too much on the passage of time during your shift. For the first two or three hours there were plenty of things for a person – and especially an educated person – to think about in order to distract you from the mind-numbing tedium of the job. You might dwell on the books you were going to buy when you had the money, or the eccentric present you might get for your girlfriend or boyfriend on returning to civilisation. Five or six hours later and your thoughts were generally preoccupied with food. After eight or nine hours, however, it became a real struggle to find things to daydream about. You became oppressively tired of rolling the same thoughts over and over in your mind. As the afternoons wore on, you would see the young Romanian men looking furtively down the aisles in the hope of catching sight of one of the pretty girls who worked there. You would also see the disappointment etched on their faces when I stumbled clumsily around the corner. The sheer misery of the work left you craving cigarettes and alcohol and everything else that offered the promise of any kind of emotional kick.

A wretched and miserable job does not appal the middle classes so much as the behaviour exhibited by a person who does such a job – never mind that it is the dismal work that has often driven them to such behaviour in the first place. From the perspective of a middle-class professional cocooned in a London office, the belief that workers gorge themselves on stodge, grease and sugar because they are feckless and irresolute makes sense. After all, a middle-class person only indulges like this in a moment of weakness or as part of a rational cost/benefit calculation. He or she will 'treat themselves' to a chocolate bar or a slice of cake because they feel that they deserve it. It is the cherry placed on top of life itself; a rational decision representing a sugary pat on the back. A working-class person, on the other hand, will buy a greasy packet of chips as an emotional escape from the present. As Nirmal put it to me one afternoon, 'This work makes you want to drink.'

And it did. It was not only because it was physically exhausting, but because it was mentally deadening too. The job required an emotional palliative in the same sense that your burning and suppurating feet required sticking plasters at the end of the day. Unlike professional jobs, where there is usually some aspect of the work that is enjoyable, working on the bottom rung of the ladder at Amazon was no fun at all. Five pence on a can of Coke or a Mars bar is never likely to change that. Instead, it will simply make the lives of the people who float in and out of these jobs a little more miserable. When we walked through the door at midnight at the end of a shift, we kicked off our boots and collapsed onto our beds with a bag of McDonald's and a can of beer. We did not – and nor have I met anyone in a similar job who behaves in this way – come home and stand about in the kitchen for half an hour boiling broccoli. Regularity of dietary habit is simply incompatible with irregularity of work and income. As far as we were concerned the 'foodies' – those who appear on television to fetishise the over-intricacy of food made with expensive ingredients – could go to hell.

Rules, as I have already stated, were not really rules at all at Amazon. A good example of what I mean by this was the time allocated for break. Over the course of a normal day, workers were entitled to one break of half an hour and two ten-minute breaks. The half-hour break was unpaid but the shorter breaks were paid. The ten-minute breaks were actually fifteen minutes in total, but an extra five minutes (which you were not paid for) was tacked on to the ten in order to account for walking from the further reaches of the warehouse to the canteen. In practice it took around seven minutes to walk from the back of the warehouse (ten football pitches, remember) and through the airport-style security scanners to the break area. When the two minutes it took to get back to the pick desk at the end of the break were factored in, the 'fifteen-minute break' totalled about six minutes.

'The breaks are ridiculous,' said Claire. 'You obviously get your half an hour, because you get walking time for that. But on each break I'd say I'd get five minutes each time, because by the time I've got to my locker to get my fags or my phone and then gone outside it's time to go back in and walk back to pick.'

I never did receive an employment contract, so I have no idea as to my rights or anything else I might have been entitled to at work. Any knowledge I did possess was general and had been acquired beforehand. As for my Romanian co-workers, most of them lacked even a rudimentary understanding of the rights bestowed on a typical British worker. However harshly they were treated, in their minds such a regime was normal; it was simply what happened in England, a country where there were two types of people: those who wanted you to go home and those who wrote letters to liberal newspapers waxing colourfully about how wonderful and hard-working you were.

4

The Lea Hall Colliery, which opened in 1960, was the first modern coal mine opened by the National Coal Board. It closed on 25 January 1991, immediately throwing 1,250 men out of work. By the end it was losing £300,000 a week. The Cannock Chase coalfields once supported forty-eight mines. The last, Littleton, closed in 1993. Those working at the pit lost jobs that paid the equivalent of between £380 and £900 a week in today's money. In terms of the sheer numbers made redundant, there were also add-ons. Lea Hall had been the biggest colliery of its type in Europe. When the pit closed many people in the support industries also lost their jobs. The man who delivered ice-cold milk to the pit lost his franchise when the men stopped drinking gallons of it at the end of their shifts. In between the rows of blackened brick dwellings leading to the pit there once stood thriving little shops and tobacconists where the men would pick up newspapers, fags and packets of crisps during the early-morning shift changeovers. Gradually these disappeared too.

Following millions of pounds of investment old mining communities are being transformed, declared one headline in a local paper from 2011 when Amazon first came to the town.[24] The transition in Rugeley is one that is replicated across Britain. Amazon has other fulfilment centres in Hemel Hempstead,

Hertfordshire, Swansea, Doncaster and South Yorkshire – all former mining areas. Sports Direct's biggest warehouse, which was compared to a 'workhouse' and a 'gulag' by the trade union Unite,[25] is located in Shirebrook, Derbyshire, the site of the old Shirebrook Colliery, which closed in 1993. The UK's former mining areas are home to around 5.5 million people – about 9 per cent of the population. Typically, the pits there would close, a period of time would elapse where people were expected to survive on benefits, and when economic 'regeneration' eventually arrived it often came in the form of multinational companies offering precarious and low-paid work. Perhaps more humiliating for the communities in question was the fact that they were expected to bow and scrape to companies like Amazon because they needed the jobs.

Alex, a former pit mechanic and member of the rescue service at Lea Hall Colliery, told me that Rugeley had 'never recovered'[26] from the closure of the pit.

'There are no jobs. Or they're minimum-wage jobs and they're jobs based on short-term contracts and fear.'

I met Alex one evening when I stopped at Lea Hall Miners' Social Club,[27] a box-shaped, sandy-coloured building with a large conservatory incongruently jutting out of its front. The club was situated 400 yards up the road from the Globe Island roundabout, where four nine-foot, 2,000-kilogram concrete statues were erected in 2015 to commemorate 115 miners who had died at the Lea Hall and Brereton collieries during the working lives of the two pits. A modest plinth engraved with the names of the men stood nearby. One drinker told me that Rugeley's local Tory MP attended the miners' march for the old statues only to vote for anti-trade union legislation in parliament the very next day. While I was cocooned in Amazon's warehouse, the government was trying to push through legislation that would have lifted the ban on companies using agency workers during strikes and made it compulsory for strike leaders to wear special armbands or risk a £20,000 fine.

The club had a mixed crowd, though a handful of former miners drank their beer there every night. The atmosphere of a social club is much friendlier than that of an ordinary pub. You can imagine being in there on a crisp Saturday afternoon in November, sinking into one of the mauve chairs with a pint and a packet of crisps with the heating turned up while mist envelops everything outside and a reassuring voice on the radio reels off the football results from the three o'clock kick-offs. Everyone knows everyone else and you are never short of conversation. To paraphrase George Orwell's description of working-class interiors, you breathe a warm, decent, deeply human atmosphere that it is difficult to find elsewhere. It is the socialism of leisure time: the elites had their private members' clubs and so working men wanted their own private spaces too. Fittingly, there was a 'do it yourself' feel about most working men's clubs and the profit motive was largely absent. Unlike a pub, where you get a pint and perhaps a bite to eat before being ushered out onto the street after last orders, twentieth-century working men's clubs offered various self-improvement opportunities to members, such as lectures and keep-fit classes. Today, however, clubland is in its death throes. More than 2,000 working men's clubs have closed their doors since the mid-1970s, and more are shutting up shop every year.[28]

'People actually say, "I'm only at Amazon," and in the past they would've never said, "I'm only at the pit,"' Alex told me. 'You'd have said, "I'm a collier," because that's what you were and you were proud of it.'

The largest employers in Rugeley today are Amazon and Tesco – as well as what remains of the power station. In 1986 the main employers had been Lea Hall Colliery, the two power stations, Armitage Shanks, Thorn Automation and Celcon.[29] The excitement when Amazon first came to the town had long since dissipated by the time I arrived. Now the company was forced to bus in people – predominantly Eastern Europeans – from places like Wolverhampton, Walsall and Birmingham.

The fact that a growing number of British people are unwilling to be treated like animals by unscrupulous employers is often viewed as shameful, when it really ought to be considered a sign of progress. British workers have minimum standards with respect to what they will put up with – standards that many of the precarious and poorly paid jobs our economy now relies upon fail to satisfy.

'I wouldn't do that work. I'll make no bones about it,' Alex said of the work I was doing at Amazon. 'I wouldn't do it because I'd fall out with them [the managers] over how they treat people.' Instead, you had to commute out of towns like Rugeley to find decent work.

Drinking in the social club one evening was Jeff Winter, a local Labour councillor. Jeff was a big gregarious man in his mid-fifties whose long hair and check shirt made him look more like an ageing rock star than a councillor. He stood me a drink and started to reminisce about the Rugeley of old.[30]

'I mean, what is a decent job today? What have these former mining companies become? The warehouse was empty for about two years before Amazon came here. But are we grovelling then? Are we grovelling by saying yes, we'll accept anything [i.e. Amazon]? Because we're desperate for our people. The other thing is, you're not going to buy houses and you're not going to help your families on that, up there [at Amazon]. The uncertainty – can you get a mortgage on a zero-hours contract? What can you get?'

While we talked, the television suspended high up on the wall of the club was showing football. Liverpool were playing in the European Cup. It could almost have been the 1970s. As you moved a little closer to the screen, however, the generational transformation dawned on you. The names of the sponsors were garishly emblazoned across shirts and boots and all over the stadium in luminous colours. Gladiatorial music boomed over the loudspeakers at half-time. Money had saturated the game, and former miners who once sweated their guts out so that those above ground could heat their homes sat passively and watched these preened and primped working-class heroes kick a ball about. Today the common man is celebrated so long as he is no longer common. Respect isn't automatically granted to people who do working-class jobs. Instead, it goes to those who grab the slippery levers of social mobility and climb out on the backs of those they leave behind.

'I work around Stoke-on-Trent and you see a lot of people working on checkouts,' said Jeff. 'In Tesco and that ... You see a lot of older guys who have been made redundant, and they're not reaching retirement, they're having to work, they're having to go on checkouts and that. You never saw that years ago. I know it's changed, and I can accept it's changed, but that doesn't make it right.'

According to a 2016 report from Royal London, workers in some parts of the UK will have to work into their eighties in order to maintain a decent standard of living when they retire.[31] Between 1993 and 2012, the number of people working beyond the state pension age increased by 85 per cent.[32]

'If you went back forty years, and I know you can't, but you had a pit which employed a lot of skilled men, and a lot of people providing good machinery to that pit as well ... there was [sic] mechanics; there were electricians. There were labouring jobs at the pit ... but they were *still good jobs*. You had the power station with the skilled men. You had Thorn EMI over the road. That employed hundreds and hundreds and they were good, good jobs ... In the sixties we were rich – in proportion, you know. Working class and vote Labour yes, but we were rich. This was a happening place.'

And then, like steam from a kettle, the skilled jobs began to disappear. Together with the closure of the collieries, manufacturing jobs have disappeared right across the Midlands over the last thirty years, as firms have relocated their production lines to countries with fewer scruples about workers' rights. One in five working people had a job in manufacturing in Britain in the mid-1980s. By 2013 that figure had fallen to just one in twelve.[33] Thus when Amazon came to Rugeley in 2011 the local excitement was palpable. There was a sense that the town was about to regain its dignity. The local *Express & Star* newspaper reported shortly before it opened that the new depot was 'swamped' with applicants.[34] It was a 'massive thing for the community', as the lady in the cafe had told me wistfully. The creation of 900 jobs by Amazon also fitted neatly into the political narrative of economic regeneration: Britain's former industrial areas were going to be invigorated and twenty years of decline were going to be arrested. Yet this sunny optimism rested on a faulty assumption: that all jobs were created equal, and that, because an area had got back to work, the work itself was on a par with the jobs lost during the 1980s and early '90s.

It is easy to stray too far down the path of nostalgia, conjuring up a lost world of robust men in shirtsleeves going off to work happy while at home a dog curls up on a hearth rug and contented wives send the rich smell of Yorkshire puddings and gravy piping out of every kitchen on a Sunday. There are political tendencies of both left and right that yearn for this supposedly happy era. The most obvious objection to wistful romanticism of this sort is the advances in safety at work over recent decades (not to mention women's liberation from the shackles of the stove). I would have to be incredibly unlucky or foolish to be killed in an Amazon warehouse, whereas horrific injuries and sometimes death occurred regularly down the pit. The mania for the past is usually the preserve of those who know it won't be their sons who may end up buried under several tons of rock while the wife slaves away at home.

In some parts of the country the benefits of recent 'regeneration' projects have been obvious. With the creation of high-skilled tech jobs, cities like Manchester and Leeds have thrived in recent times. However, towns like Rugeley have 'merely replicated their economies', as a 2015 report by the Centre for Cities put it. 'They have replaced jobs in declining industries with lower-skilled, more routinised jobs, swapping cotton mills for call centres and dock yards for distribution sheds.'[35]

Nor were the respectable jobs the only thing that disappeared at the tail end of the twentieth century. The in-work training and the value afforded to the learning of skills vanished too. The academically gifted were encouraged to move away to university, while those without qualifications could do little more than stay put and take whatever was on offer locally.

'I mean, if you want good employment you've got to become a commuter,' said Jeff as he took a sip of his pint. 'You've got to commute out of this town to find the real jobs, whatever the real jobs are. If [you're] Romanian ... you can cross the border [and] you can come to work. And you know something, they love it these business people, don't they? You go to Stafford and you see the fruit-picking farms. All Eastern Europeans there. It's all around you ... Is that what you've got to compete against?'

Most of the men I spoke to that evening planned to vote Leave in the forthcoming European Referendum, though almost all of them had voted Labour all their adult lives. It was the noticeable decline of Rugeley that seemed to bother them more than the presence of Eastern European immigrants, however.

'The thing is, you go from pit to power station, you're talking about skilled men, apprenticeships, and all this,' said Jeff. 'This town has had this since the sixties, you know: the power station, good jobs, good money. And in 2016 what are we becoming as a town? Realistically we're becoming poorer as a town than we were forty, fifty years ago ... What does this [Amazon] provide? And someone mentioned [this] to me earlier today: capitalism relies on debt. You don't want these jobs so you go to university and take on £30,000 worth of debt. Fuelling capitalism. You buy the car on hire purchase. Fuelling capitalism. That's how it survives. And so you're living with your parents because you can't get a house. There's no social housing. Is that what we've accepted? It's a total wotsit from what happened in this town forty years ago when there was good jobs and this and that. All these clubs were full every night; the pubs were full every night. You know, there was people about, there was people doing things. Now it's a totally different society. And kids obviously don't know because they've never been part of that. But it don't make it *right*; it don't make what we've come to *right*.'

Later on that evening Alex, the ex-pit mechanic, told me the story of a friend of his who had lost his job when the pit closed. He managed to find occasional work but nothing regular. He was unemployed for around seven years before he eventually found something.

'He was desperate; I mean, he was *down*, and Tesco opened two or three years ago. And he got taken on. He works on nights, filling shelves. And he was over the moon, because he got a full-time job. All right, minimum wage and what have you, and it's not good, but that's the way the country is.'

Alex was happy for him. His old friend had got some of his dignity and self-respect back. He seemed to have a sense of purpose again. But then, ominously, Tesco began to cut his hours and the old fear reared its head again almost as before.

'He worked about nine months and then they reduced his hours from thirty-eight down to thirty-two,' Alex said in the cynical tone I was growing accustomed to hearing. 'But that's what they do.'

5

For me at least life soon settled into a routine. I spent each morning before my shift eating a hideous ready meal in my room. Sausage and mash from the Co-op. Beef lasagne. Macaroni cheese. Once I even ate a Birds Eye traditional chicken dinner thirty minutes after waking. I stopped buying milk and bread because they went off before I had the chance to eat them. 'The difference ... between the man with money and the man without is simply this,' the downtrodden novelist Edward Reardon declared in George Gissing's novel *New Grub Street,* 'the one thinks, "How shall I use my life?" and the other, "How shall I keep myself alive?"'

It is easy to slip into an unhealthy regime like this. You get up each morning at eleven, you have breakfast, shower and prepare your feet for the day ahead – several sticking plasters, two pairs of socks – and then you drag yourself out of the door by twelve thirty. You return home at midnight and you are usually in bed by one. Wash, rinse, repeat. Fastidiousness rapidly goes out the window. You have two meals a day and it is incumbent on you to get as much food inside you as possible at each sitting because it is impossible to know when you will next get the chance to eat a proper meal. Some snare-up in the security line on your lunch break could easily result in you missing out on a hot meal that day. 'I feel like I'm getting more and more tired,' my housemate Chris said to me on the first morning I met him in the kitchen. I soon understood why.

Managing on the salary paid by Amazon was theoretically feasible in a town like Rugeley. My salary worked out at £245 per week for thirty-five hours before tax (at £7p/h). It was tough, but it was possible to keep your head above water. In London you would pay £500 a month for a functional box-room like mine, whereas in Rugeley I paid £300, which included all of the bills.

In theory, then, I ought to have had a fairly ample sum to put towards food and other necessities – over £100 a week. Yet things rarely panned out like that. For one thing, at the end of my first week instead of being paid £245 I was paid £185.20. I expected to be taxed but not as heavily as £60 on a wage of less than £250. On seeking out a Transline rep to speak to about the discrepancy, I was pre-empted by a 'Yeah, yeah, we know about that',[36] as soon as I opened my mouth. I had been put on an emergency tax code along with several others. For some reason this had only happened to my British co-workers – all the Romanians had been paid the full and proper amount (or at least they had for that week).

At the end of week two I was underpaid again. This time I received just £150: almost £100 short. It turned out that I had again been taxed at a higher rate; however, Transline had also underpaid me along with every other picker, including the migrant workers. The sense of a shambles was reinforced by the fact that Transline refused to give out payslips that week.

The pieces of paper we finally received a week later were plastered with byzantine additions and subtractions, making it impossible to calculate whether or not we had been remunerated properly. After my weekly rent had been subtracted, the remaining £75 I had at the end of my second week was a good deal less than I had envisioned when I first got the job. I was confidently told by a Transline rep at my induction that I would see '£240–250 a week, easy'. I also earned less that week because on the Friday an Amazon rep had informed us[37] at extremely short notice that the warehouse would be closed the next day for 'maintenance'.

We were given the chance to work the following Wednesday to make up the shortfall; however, I had already made plans to visit my grandmother that day and was thus unable to do it. Others who I chatted to were in the same boat. Had they been given more than twenty-four hours' notice, they might conceivably have changed their shifts. As things stood, their wage packets were short by some £72 that week with little in the way of forewarning.

As to the difficulty of living on £75 a week, I am reminded of an article in the *Daily Mail* about a woman who survived on £1 a day. 'Frugal Kath Kelly, 51, ate at free buffets, shopped at church jumble sales and scrounged leftovers from grocery stores and restaurants,' ran the story.[38] This woman reportedly amassed a further £117 by rooting among the cigarette butts and dog mess, picking up loose change dropped in the street. This sort of thriftiness is typically jumped on by people who have always wanted to ration the poor. It is held up as the final 'proof' that poverty is really not as bad as all that: as long as you have a bit of middle-class pluck and ingenuity tucked away in reserve. If you are too useless to be able to survive on such a lowly amount, it is put down to some piteous deficiency in one's character.

In reality, most people could, I suspect, survive on, if not £1 a day, then certainly £50, £60 or £70 a week if they really had to. But the trouble with bold proclamations of this sort is that they are nearly always made from the standpoint of people with professional jobs and a regular income. Put another way, if you are at home or sat in an office for all or part of the day, you *can* survive on a fairly small sum. However, as soon as you enter the cheerless world of low-paid work you might as well be comparing oranges with pears. As I have already mentioned, the need to offset the physical and emotional drain of manual work is one thing – fags, booze and junk food are some of the few pleasures left to you. But time is another.

The speedy efficiency which characterises middle-class life is non-existent in many working-class homes. Poverty is the thief of time. You wait around for buses and landlords. You are forced to do overtime at the drop of a hat. You hang around for an eternity waiting for the person who has told you they will sort out the administrative error in your payslip. You go searching for a shop to print the wad of documents you need to start work. You must traipse around the supermarket looking for special offers with the diligence of a librarian searching for that rare first edition. You have to walk home afterwards. And so on and so forth. The point is that you are constantly wasting time, and it nearly always ends up costing you money: eventually it seems almost to melt off you wherever you go. Whereas a middle-class person will spend their Sunday afternoons eating a roast dinner before cooking another huge meal and putting it into little containers for the week ahead, a worker at the bottom of the economy will either be winding down or chasing down one of the company bureaucrats who seem to exist in order to thwart the smooth running of their life.

My typical budget over seven days was as follows:

Rent incl. bills	£75.00
Meals in the Amazon cafeteria x 4	£16.40
Snacks at work	£4.00
Tea	£0.50
Cereals and milk	£5.00
McDonald's x 2	£9.98
Ready meals x 4	£6.00
Other provisions (coffee, cheese, butter, etc.)	£10.00
Rolling tobacco	£4.89
Beer	£10.00
Public transport*	£6.00
Total	£147.77

*(The cost of public transport would have been considerably higher had I lived somewhere further away like Wolverhampton.)

There are of course items here that any middle-class person will immediately say ought to be cut out. Neither the beer nor the tobacco was absolutely necessary to my survival. However, I wanted to convey an idea of the sorts of things that the average person doing a job like this is *likely* to spend money on (as opposed to what he or she might theoretically spend it on). It is all very well crossing luxuries like alcohol and cigarettes off the list when you yourself are not oppressed by the same forces that drive people to take up such things in the first place. Anyone can do that, just as any middle-class person who starts at the gym can draw up a programme to strip almost every ounce of fat from their body inside of six months. I am more interested in how human beings *actually behave in practice*. The above list best represents my typical expenditure over the course of a week. I might have been *more* extravagant, yet still I burned through £150. I also probably spent more than this each week due to depreciated monthly expenses. For example, one week I got my hair cut and another week I had to buy a train ticket to Somerset (£70) to visit family. Broken down over a year, this is sure to add several pounds here and there.

Deducting £150 from the Amazon take-home figure of £227 (£245 a week minus tax) left a sum of £77. Emergency expenditure such as a visit to the dentist would undoubtedly have required overtime or some sort of loan; but on the whole there was a bit of elbow room. However, the gap between this and those at the very bottom is probably diminishing. Many of those I met in Rugeley and Cannock already had one foot in this subterranean world of dirt and fear. Life was characterised by the constant circling presence of an ominous grey cloud of landlords and capricious employers. A missed pay cheque, a debtor or some trivial misdemeanour at work were often all it took for a once respectable individual to be kicked down from a modicum of freedom and security into the hole of a soggy cardboard box on a street corner. Stopping there also fails to do justice to the reality of living on this amount of money. For one thing, the cost of living in Rugeley was relatively inexpensive, whereas in Hemel Hempstead, where Amazon had another of its warehouses, the cheapest rent for a room of comparable size was £112 a week. This is one of the reasons why the Joseph Rowntree Foundation calculated in 2015 that a single person needed £17,100 a year before tax to achieve a minimum standard of living.[39] My annual salary at Amazon before tax was £12,740.

There was also the small matter of not being paid correctly. It is just about possible to live tolerably provided there are no unexpected catastrophes. But in life there sometimes are, and they were occasionally a product of the incompetency of one of the agencies. When you bring home just £150 because of an administrative error (and such errors were common) you were left, after my budgeting, with £2.23 at the end of the week. In parts of the country where your rent costs more, it is at this point that you invariably sink deep into the red. A twenty-year-old Amazon employee called Lydia told me that she and many of her friends had all been underpaid at some point by the agencies employed by Amazon.

'I was expecting to wake up to a nice healthy bank balance, but it wasn't there,' she said. 'My friend ... she still hasn't been paid ... she's got £160 now in total but they still owe her like £200-ish. And the lady that I give lifts to, she hasn't been paid properly either.'

It is also worth asking what living on a paltry income does to a person's long-term health. When I started at Amazon I was a slim twelve-and-a-half stone. Despite walking around ten miles a day, by the end of the month I had put on a stone in fat. I was smoking again too: cigarettes were another of the vices that provided a momentary morale boost, like chocolate bars and cups of strong tea.

Norbert, a twenty-five-year-old man from Alesd, in western Romania, was one of the first migrants I had spoken to after being taken on by Amazon. He had approached me in the canteen one day and randomly blurted out that he liked cars, girls and Vladimir Putin. He was evidently lonely, and had seen me watching the news in the canteen and used it as a pretext for swaggering over and starting a conversation.

'Putin, he's a great guy. You like Putin? Strong. Fights judo. Good, strong leader.'

I asked him if he was interested in politics.

'Yes, a little; though I don't watch TV. It's bullshit, you know. For the sheep.'

We went for a drink one day in Wolverhampton where Norbert was living. We met in a bar called the Royal London,[40] a soulless modern establishment with The Smiths blaring from the stereo and St George's Day posters proclaiming '£1 drinks all night' pinned to every wall. Random decor hung from various spots on the ceiling – a flower pot, a child's bike and a selection of kitchen utensils, among other things.

'It was very fucked up,' Norbert said as he related to me how he ended up living in the Midlands and working for Amazon. They were told they were being brought to London. And so on a frost-bitten January morning, he and a friend had stepped blinking out of a Romanian bedsit and into the early-morning English sunshine. Where were the skyscrapers? Where was the River

Thames or Big Ben? And why was it so quiet?

'When I wake up I ask, "Where are we?" You know? "Where are we?" "Wol-Wol-Wolver-ham-ton." "Where is this?" Then we say, "OK, we will stay here for one month." It's a lot of Russians who have flats, but we find Romanian. Because we want to go to London, and when we [first] arrived at Luton, they [the people from the agency that brought us here] picked us up, and they come here [to Wolverhampton] with us.'

Like a lot of the Romanians I met, Norbert saw himself as a cut above his fellow countrymen. *They* had come to England out of desperation, whereas *he* had travelled here just for fun. Others came from a 'bullshit life', he said, whereas he wanted to take home some extra spending money for booze and cars.

'I look at all the Romanians at Amazon, and everybody is here just for money,' Norbert told me. 'I don't feel what they feel, you know. I don't know how it is not to have. When I quit from Amazon tomorrow I don't care, you know. Their situation is fucked up, that's why they come here. [In Romania] there is a good life for us, but you need money. For us is not problem, but for others it's a problem. For 90 per cent it's difficult.'

In 1935, George Dangerfield wrote of the 'uncouth toilers' who 'sweated and starved to bring to some comfortable little householder in Upper Tooting his pleasant five per cent'. The middle classes have long accepted the necessity of the working classes 'sweating and starving' for the sake of life's little luxuries. Yet many British workers are no longer inclined to play their allotted role. There exists a hypothetical floor, below which they will not allow themselves to sink. However benighted they may be, and however much those situated above might curse them as idle and impetuous, they appear to understand that in a civilised country they should no longer have to bow and scrape before so-called captains of industry. The conventional response is to disparage and ridicule the very idea of the English working class having any standards at all. There is apparently some mysterious virtue in people (always other people) being exploited by wealthy employers. In contrast, liberals will often lionise migrant workers for putting up with exploitative conditions, as if there really were no more to life than filling somebody else's pockets.

It was, at the end of the day, men and women like Norbert who kept Amazon going. If they found a good job in Britain they would stay because, as Norbert kept telling me, life at home was 'bullshit'. Life for many had become a treadmill in which they came to Britain and worked like dogs, took the money home, then came back again a few months later. Others treated it as a sort of working holiday.

'They [the others] will go back home, maybe stay one or two months, and then come back; because they'll just spend the money.'

For Norbert, the worst part of the work was the indignity of how the agencies treated you.

'They talk to us like we are slaves, you know. If you are a banker in England and you come to Romania, you will be a nobody. That's like me here – I am a nothing here. But you will come to Romania and you will be a nothing too. You're English people, but who cares, you know? Here, [we] are slaves; there you will be the slaves, because that's the world.'

This seemed somewhat delusional – realistically, a banker could live like a king in Romania – but I understood why Norbert might want to tell himself a story like this. It was hardly cheering to acknowledge that you could be treated the way you were for no other reason than your nationality.

Norbert was a gregarious man who looked younger than his twenty-five years. He was tall and muscular yet softly spoken. Since arriving in England he had found it difficult to make friends. He had one Romanian friend – 'Johnny', who had accompanied him to the UK – plus a few acquaintances he had made at work. Apart from that he was on his own. Most of the locals in Wolverhampton didn't want to know. Back in Romania life was more fun – there was more laughter. You may have been poor, but you knew how to have a good time.

'Here you can't have friends ... everybody look another way, you know. There [in Romania] you can have friends. You need help, you can call somebody and they will come to help, and they don't want anything, they don't want something; they just want to help and that's it. The English, they try to be friendly, but they're not. They don't make friends; everybody is just quiet, you know. But people, they try to smile, they try to be friendly but they're not. They don't know how to be friendly to us.'

Whereas in the past the men of the Lea Hall working men's club worked so the middle classes could enjoy more prosperous lives, today it is people like Norbert who sweat and starve to fill the pockets of some and deliver consumer goods to the rest of us on the cheap. Yet Norbert and others like him lack even the rudimentary political rights bestowed on their British working-class forefathers. At Amazon it was largely the task of this invisible army of downtrodden migrant labour, hidden in a rural warehouse away from any centre of civilisation, to process the internet shopping of Britain's burgeoning middle class – a middle class that would, unlike the Eastern Europeans further down the ladder, get a vote on who governed them and made the laws when a general election came around. In this respect Britain was re-shoring a slightly more tolerable version of the backwater sweatshop. Life at companies like Amazon increasingly resembles the separation of the Eloi and the Morlocks in H. G. Wells's *The Time Machine*: 'Above ground you must have the Haves, pursuing pleasure and comfort and beauty, and below ground the Have Nots, the Workers getting continually adapted to the conditions of their labour.'

You can, if you like, punch your credit card details into Amazon's website without ever having to see what goes on in this idyllic little corner of Staffordshire. It suits the English to have some anonymous foreign drudge, invisible to the outside world, tucked away in an enormous warehouse carting stuff back and forth with perspiration dripping from his brow. In truth, we want to ignore it as our grandparents turned contentedly away from what went on 4,000 miles away in an Indian sweatshop. It is in some ways easier today to wall yourself off from the outside world. You can sit, feet up and kettle on, turn on the computer and order something to arrive the next day with a mere click of the mouse. We have grown accustomed to cheap products that are cheap precisely because they have been produced in conditions such as I have described here. Our standard of living has come to depend on it. The people in this warehouse may as well not exist to the outside world, just as the coolies who broke their backs in the red splodges on the map did not exist in the minds of those who quaffed sherry in England's drawing rooms a century ago. *Plus ça change, plus c'est la même chose.*

PART II

—

BLACKPOOL

6

I finally left Amazon after someone from the company had come sniffing around the top floor of the warehouse one afternoon waving a non-disclosure agreement in my face. On their insisting it was something I needed to sign I decided straightaway to hand my notice in.

I had planned to make Blackpool my next stop after landing an interview with a care provider in the town. Once this seed had been planted in my head the place started to exert a pull all of its own. As the nights began to draw out, the prospect of luxuriating like a cat under a warm sun on the town's famous promenade had a good deal more appeal than sitting forlornly in a dingy Midlands flat that reeked of noxious paint.

I also grew up by the sea, and when you do there are things that stay with you so that you never feel truly comfortable setting down roots too far away from the coast. These are of course genuine memories, but also a mixture of clichés and half-remembered scraps: a panoply of long childhood days mashed together against a backdrop of carousels, shabby Edwardian shelters, seagulls zooming around as though attached to the strings of children's kites, poorly made cricket bats and an exhilarating range of ice creams and candy flosses. And of course the sand still emerging from your shoes weeks after your last visit to the beach.

This creates an image that, like much else in these islands, is about fifty years out of date. It plasters a layer of kitsch over the reality of life lived on the coast, which is often a struggle in the winter months when work becomes scarce.

I awoke after my first night in Blackpool with a physical sensation commonly associated with the town: a crippling hangover. A glorious evening in the bars along the seafront had turned sour overnight, like gone-off milk or meat left uncovered in the sun. I had a mouth as dry as cork and, further down, legs hanging there like lead weights. An evil fog sat malignantly at the front of my brain and was reluctant to shift even with the imbibing of paracetamol. It felt as if I had hardly slept at all.

The bright and hazy sunlight that flooded in through the gaps between the dusty blinds disclosed the prospect of a forlorn day drifting around the town waiting for a phone call from my new job. It may have been the height of the Blackpool summer, but beyond the dirty hotel walls a chill wind was whipping off the lead-grey sea, blowing grubby sheets of newspapers around and suspending pedestrians mid-step. Up above the sky was as clear as steel.

I spent my first night in a cheap hotel in the town's South Shore area. It was a large hotel in the Edwardian style, with a spider's web of dirty black scaffolding climbing precipitously up its side. This museum piece of faded grandeur ruefully bore down on neglected streets which would once have teemed with crowds amidst a clatter of buckets and spades under stormy English skies. A little way down from the hotel a handful of ragged men were torpidly going through their daily ritual, which involved pacing up and down a small stretch of street looking furtively for the pale orange tint of discarded cigarette butts hidden in the dirty cracks between the road and the pavement. This performance went on throughout the day, though always with a greater degree of agitation in the very early mornings, for it was then that the richest pickings could be uncovered from the night before.

From where I was staying you could see, peering out over the tops of the terraced Georgian houses, the rusty red tip of the famous Blackpool Tower. Illuminated at night, it dominated the town like a huge glowing torch driven up through the concrete. Yet the brassy and brightly painted seaside England of the promenade may as well have been a thousand miles away from this part of town with its flee-ridden hotels, roaming drunks, surreptitious cannabis dealers, boarded-up shops and, after dark, toothless prostitutes who loitered next to the cash machines touting for trade. This was Central Drive, the most deprived area of Blackpool and one of the most deprived areas in England. What would once have been prime properties situated within walking distance of the town's most popular attractions lay forlornly empty because 'nobody wants to touch them with a barge pole', as one local cab driver told me.

I had landed an interview here as a home/domiciliary care worker with a company called Carewatch UK. The company was founded in 1993 in Brighton. Today it has 150 offices all over the country, employs 3,500 care workers and is 'supposed to be one of the best'[1] as one of my co-workers put it to me. My own experiences would lead me to question this assessment.

It was not the first position I had applied for in Blackpool. But after spending two weeks chasing up online ads, it was the first that I'd managed to land an interview for. I soon learned that many of the employment agencies kept their job adverts up online long after the vacancy in question had been filled in order to get more people onto their books. It was apparently a familiar scam: you phoned up to enquire after a job you had seen advertised; the person on the other end of the line briskly informed you that there was no work at the present time; but could you possibly leave a name and contact number? The company would then get back to you if something came up. And if you passed over your details it usually did; however, the work eventually offered tended to bear little relation to what had originally been advertised – i.e., the very reason you contacted the company in the first place! The genuine vacancies – as opposed to the jobs that existed solely on paper – almost always offered fewer hours, involved more onerous tasks, and came with fewer guarantees. Positions you stumbled across on jobs websites that had been there for thirty or more days were invariably part of the same racket.

Getting a job as a home care worker – often called a domiciliary care worker – was extraordinarily easy. You simply phoned up the number in the job advert, answered a few rudimentary questions – *Do you have a car?* (Yes) *Do you live in the area?* (I've just moved here) *Do you have any experience of working in care?* (No, but I looked after a friend of my grandmother's for a little while when he had dementia) – and then you were summoned in for an interview. I had to present a few documents – some ID, the details of a willing referee and agree to undergo a criminal record check – and at the end of the interview I was offered a job and given a start date for my induction. During the ten minutes or so it took for the lady to rattle off a list of straightforward interview questions, it felt like all I really had to do was convey a basic level of common sense. The only moment of colour occurred when I casually mentioned that I wanted the job because I had 'heard good things about the company'. 'Some of the online reviews I have come across were good,' I added in the obsequious tones of someone desperately trying to ingratiate themselves with a superior. This was untrue, of course – I was simply trying to make small talk and demonstrate that I had made some effort to find out a bit about the company. But apparently it was a mistake on my part. The young lady promptly stood up, arms akimbo, dismissively shook her head and said curtly that I 'didn't ought to pay attention to *everything*' I read online.

A glance at the indeed.co.uk website made clear why my remarks had provoked such a prickly response. As well as hosting job advertisements, indeed.co.uk allows users to post employee reviews – giving each company a rating of between one and five stars – and write a short comment. It isn't an exact science, but most of the reviews seem to give a general picture of what it is like to work for a particular employer. Companies with a good overall reputation tend to do well in terms of ratings, and vice versa. After 477 employee reviews, the well-respected department store chain John Lewis had, at the time of writing, an overall rating of 4.2 stars out of 5. Even McDonald's, the archetypal capitalist demon regularly summoned by workers' rights activists, achieved a respectable 3.6 stars based on over 60,000 reviews. Carewatch, on the other hand, scored a lowly 2.6 stars overall based on 157 employee reviews. Reading through some of the reviews was like perusing the testimonies of nineteenth-century factory hands. *Office staff absolutely vile and only slightly civil when they need extra calls covering; Rubbish company to work for. I was there six weeks before I even got a weekend off even then they rang; All the management are nothing but liars and over run you with calls then drop you so your [sic] not earning; The pay isnt [sic] good travelling far for less than the minimum wage; You didn't get paid for the time you were travelling between service users' homes and that took quite a lot unpaid time,* etc., etc., etc.

All of this might have been highly unfair, of course. And there were a few positive glimmers amidst the shower of negativity. Overall, though, there were around three times as many one-star reviews as there were five-star reviews.

What was certainly true was that the care sector as a whole was desperate for staff. In Britain today, an ageing population co-exists alongside a harried and stressed-out working-age population. The pressure on the latter to make ends meet by toiling away for longer and longer hours makes it increasingly difficult to take the time out to look after parents and grandparents, who are living for longer. Around one in three babies born after 2013 will live to be 100. Meanwhile, British employees work some of the longest hours in Europe. Thus very often Britain's elderly resemble 'units parcelled up and sold to the lowest bidder', as one care worker from another company would phrase it to me.[2]

An illustration of just how straightforward it is to walk into a job in domiciliary care greeted me in the reception area outside the makeshift room in the single-floor office where my interview took place. Several young women sat nervously awaiting their turn in the brightly lit interview room. They were ready to get on a treadmill which had more than likely just thrown a similar number of young women off it. The churn rate in the home care sector is extraordinary. During my first week out working, one carer told me that Carewatch was 'crying out for people'. Yet the reason companies like this were so desperate for staff was that few of the people who started ever stuck around for long. The turnover rate in the care sector was 25.4 per cent, meaning that around 300,000 care workers left their positions every year.[3] That figure was higher in the private sector and among home care workers. 'People leave,' I was told by the same member of staff, 'because it's the living wage and [they] get sick of it.'

At the end of my interview I was invited in first thing on the following Monday to undergo four days' training. Aside from a few demonstrations as to how to use a hoist to lift and move an elderly person around, which was shown to us on the final day, the training largely involved classroom instruction and form filling. There were eight of us (two men and six women) who started on the Monday and by Friday a couple of the women had dropped out. Overall it was a tedious affair, and largely involved sitting listlessly in a classroom while the supervisor shuffled bits of paper around and talked us through the company's handbook and reference guide. We were quickly taught how to empty and change a catheter without covering ourselves in urine, how to administer medication, and what to do if we turned up at someone's house and discovered them lying flat out on the floor (i.e. phone 999 and do not pick them up!). We ought in theory to have learned a lot, yet the process of acquiring the knowledge resembled cramming in the lead-up to a school exam. All the information was telescoped into such a short space of time that beyond a certain point everything which went in invariably pushed out something we had been told earlier, like rice spilling out of a hole in a sack. I went home on the final afternoon tired and unclear about several important procedural matters involved in a typical care visit.

Our supervisor – Vicky – was patient with us throughout the training process, and derived an obvious pleasure from the thought that she might be doing some good in the world. She gave off none of the schoolmarmish and joyless air which had characterised so many of those in minor positions of authority at Amazon and Transline. Supervisors in Rugeley had often given us short shrift, possibly because they would like to have felt themselves to be further away from us than they really were. A care worker herself, Vicky was my first contact with someone who had years of experience in the sector. She talked about the customers – that was what we were told to call the people in our care – 'customers' – with genuine compassion and affection, which came as something of a surprise to me. I had grown so accustomed to reading media exposés of negligent care workers that I half expected case-hardened abusers to be lurking around every corner. I was constantly on the lookout for the 'bad eggs' one is forever hearing about. Yet I soon learned that they were to some extent a convenient scapegoat for the failures of how work in the sector was commissioned and the problems that often occurred as a consequence.

Every care worker had at least one hair-curling story of neglect, but on the whole the vast majority of carers I met viewed the job as a vocation and did their very best for those in need. When things did go wrong it was nearly always a consequence of staff having unrealistic expectations imposed on them by the company bureaucracy. Thus my positive opinion of Vicky was tempered ever so slightly when she implied that Carewatch's reputation was largely down to the performance of its carers. 'It's you carers that give us a bad name,'[4] she told us sternly, which was only half the story.

During our induction we were given contracts to sign. In bold grey lettering on the front of these were the dreaded but predictable words: 'Zero Hours'. At the time of writing, the number of people in Britain on zero-hours contracts sits at almost one million (903,000) – up 21 per cent in the year to June 2016. Almost a quarter of the jobs in the adult social care sector are offered on zero-hours contracts.[5] A few pages in, our contracts set out in stark terms exactly what this meant: *There may be times when no work is available for you and Carewatch has no duty to provide you with any work at such times or any payment in respect of such times.*

The company could send us out on a job at any given moment; but a brief phone call could just as easily inform us that there was nothing available for that week. This, increasingly, was what work entailed, and the insecurity it had the potential to generate was accepted by my co-workers as just another part of everyday life, like the daily commute. 'That's just how it is,' staff said to me fatalistically. In a similar vein, the contract also informed us that the work was *conditional* [upon our] *agreement to work flexible hours.* If any of us had got another job as well – say, for example, if we had felt we needed more hours – we would have to inform

87

the company about it, and Carewatch would *not have to provide you with any work if we reasonably feel ... that it may conflict with work you would be doing for Carewatch*. It felt like the company owned us to some degree.

There were other aspects of the contract that also caught the eye, not least the tone of unbridled hostility with which the words jumped off the page at you. A strong whiff of contempt leapt off the document like heat haze rising from scorching tarmac. *There are no Collective Agreements applicable to this employment. Carewatch does not recognise any trade union for the purpose of its provision of service.*

And so it went on.

One care worker I spoke to – she didn't work for Carewatch but had been employed by a number of similar care companies in Scotland – told me that she 'had to hide [the fact that] I'm a member of Unison' from everywhere she'd worked. She added that if the companies ever found out they would never take her on.

'We used to have to talk about it quietly and secretly between ourselves as colleagues,' she told me, 'and it was a colleague of mine who told me, "Get yourself into Unison, quick."[6] I raised the question in a training session, and I raised it in a very neutral fashion, and the response I got was quite alarming. They much prefer ... ignorance is bliss.'

The final hurdle before we were allowed out 'shadowing' – the three-day process in which you followed another carer around while they worked – was the check against the police's Disclosure and Barring Service (DBS), which we were all required to do. Previously known as the Criminal Records Bureau (CRB), a DBS check is something that only employers and licensing bodies can request. The purpose of the check is reasonable enough: it is to prevent unsuitable people – abusers, paedophiles, those with criminal records – from gaining access to vulnerable adults and children. What complicates matters are the delays that a DBS check can sometimes cause in the recruitment process. Due to swingeing cuts to police budgets imposed by central government in recent years, many workers who undergo the check are left in limbo for months on end while they wait to be given the all-clear by overstretched police forces. The average wait for a check to come through in the summer of 2016 was seventy-seven days – more than two months. Nor does the length of time it takes bear any relation to whether the person in question has committed an offence.

The practical consequences of being left without a pay cheque coming in for several months are obvious enough: you end up frittering away any savings you might have built up or you are forced to find something else which pays a sufficient amount to live on. You take whatever keeps your head above water. In many instances, when a clear DBS check does eventually come back the job in question has gone. Few employers are happy to wait around for two or three months after the initial interview before filling a vacancy. Most firms want staff who can start straight away. Like salmon swimming upstream, some workers make it through the DBS process while others are left stranded in a perpetual state of suspense.

And so our own round of DBS checks vanished into a deep black hole of bureaucracy. It was then just a case of waiting.

Some people were given the all-clear within a few days, while the forms belonging to others vanished for months on end. Unfortunately, I fell into the second camp. I had previously lived at a London address, which made a long wait inevitable: the London Metropolitan Police had one of the largest backlogs of any police force in the country. Only around 45 per cent of cases were being completed by Scotland Yard within the official target of sixty days. I was thrown into this penurious limbo of tedium and uncertainty – I had a job but was prevented from going out to work – not by my own idleness, irresponsibility or poor decision making, but by the incompetence of a state which was being cut to the bone.

7

While I waited for that elusive telephone call from work I had some time to kill – several weeks, as it would turn out. I intended to use this time wisely, which first of all meant escaping the cheap hotel I was closeted in and finding a reasonably priced room to rent. My room at the hotel was a pastel-pink box the size of a ship's cabin, with two single beds jammed tightly together at a right angle. It was as spartan as a prison cell, and apocryphal stories were rife among guests at the hotel that when it rained the fixtures in the bathrooms emitted sinister rusty-coloured water. It was the sort of room that was only tolerable if you never ventured outside, for it was when you re-entered that the musty smell of the place truly hit you.

I spent most of my second night in Blackpool listlessly drifting around the town. I took in a route from the promenade, with its penny slot machines and aromas of fried food piping out of the greasy cafes and chippies, to the shabby back streets where crisp packets and dog mess defiled the pavement. Hordes of children swarmed in and out of these terraced houses throwing little white bangers on the ground. This was the England of washing lines and poky back-to-backs, a variegated patchwork of red and orange bricks and front doors that opened out onto the street. You could lose yourself in the labyrinths of terraces as easily as in a dense wood.

A few hundred yards away on the seafront it was high tourist season. Drinkers from the bars and clubs spilled out onto the pavement in high spirits like a swarm of ants. When I ventured into his shop to buy a lighter, a man selling rock on the promenade informed me gravely and out of the blue that he 'hated the lot of them'.

'They come in and they'll barter with you. So it's six sticks of rock for a pound. "I give you 50p." I don't want 50p, I want a pound. "I give you 50p." And they throw their money at you so I throw it back. "There's your money, now get out the shop."'

There are several layers of English life on display when the sun goes down in Blackpool. On the one hand, it's the place where an ever-diminishing section of the English working class still come for their stag and hen parties. On any given night you are liable to encounter a roaming band of men dressed in golf gear or women decked out in frilly nurses' outfits. Despite the deteriorating economic fortunes of the British seaside, places like Blackpool have retained a healthy allure of indecency which continues to draw the crowds year after year (albeit far smaller crowds than the town attracted during its heyday). Inhibitions are cast off in Blackpool as naturally as a snake sheds its skin. If the upper classes jet off to Tuscany and the French Alps for their vacations, Blackpool represents the garish colour of life below stairs, where indulgence and revelry are ranked on a par with all the aesthetic pleasures of high European culture.

England remains a different world beyond the River Trent. Blackpool – like football as mass entertainment, music halls and plates piled high with greasy fish and chips – is a product of a mass working-class culture that developed in England during the late Victorian and early Edwardian period. Older working-class holidaymakers still come here to relax, while for the young it is a place to go for a drink, a smoke and a shag. As the writer Travis Elborough has written, there is something unpatriotic about going to the English seaside and not engaging in some sort of debauchery. In a few of the shops you could still find the Donald McGill-style postcards with their brightly coloured and timeless toilet humour: fat-bottomed wives, hen-pecked husbands and double entendres galore – 'I thought she had all her rooms carpeted last year?' 'Oh yes, but that's going up her back passage.' Meanwhile, from nearly every poster in nearly every glass window or wooden hoarding the giant face of a bouffanted, perma-tanned crooner seems to bear down on you with a tantalising promise to 'take you back to the good times'.

And this is a feeling that stays with you once your cigarette has gone out, your glass is empty and the last battered cod has been dispatched over the counter into the hands of the last inebriated customer in the early hours of a Sunday morning. Nostalgia is hardly a feeling confined to working-class towns, but its pull is invariably stronger in places like Blackpool, which feel somehow as if they are in precipitous decline. Many people come to Blackpool on holiday because they have always come here. But others come to *go back*, or at least to feel as if they are going back. To what exactly it is difficult to set down on paper. But there is an anxious sense among people of a certain age that beyond this bubble of 99p Flakes and lager-tops, of crooners and whisky-voiced stand-up comedians with their gratifying, straight-forward punchlines, and the venues where the older men still don suits when they head out for a drink, they are being swept away by the tide of progress. They are the hares on the marshes as the developers move in. This is felt just as keenly among locals. As in towns like Rugeley, the economic transformation of the previous half-century has taken away one source of income (in this case tourist revenue) without satisfactorily replacing it with anything else. If the twentieth century was the century of the common man, with his beer, social club and, like Arthur Seaton, his boring but steady job in the local factory, the twenty-first century is a world in which the working class are either maligned caricatures or venerated saints. With their supposedly innate xenophobia and stubborn inability to grasp the infallible theories of the salaried professor, it is as if they exist in order to perpetually disappoint the modern liberal. In contrast, the contemporary conservative reaches the opposite conclusion: the beer-swilling caricature of the working-class man – the football hooligan who gives his wife a black eye and loudly advertises his hatred of anything foreign – has suddenly become an 'authentic' representative of everything that is democratic and solid.

Many people looking for work are still drawn to Blackpool from the surrounding areas like moths fluttering around a burning flame. At one time the town was, after all, a vibrant and happening place. One local drinker in the Litten Tree pub just off the promenade explained the process to me as follows: 'You've got everyone coming here saying, "It's Blackpool, we'll make it, we'll make it." So they give up their flat in, say, Rochdale, come up here, stay in a B&B for the first week, can't get any work, but they've given up the flat in Rochdale, and so they're out on the street. There's only so much room in the hostels, and if they're all full, what you going to do with them? They're gonna be out begging on the street.'

You remember conversations like this because it's clear that Blackpool has a terrible problem with homelessness. As soon as the sun goes down this defeated army emerges from the shadows like the foxes and cats do in the city. Things have become so bad that it sometimes feels as if there is a bundle of rags propping itself up in nearly every shop and restaurant doorway. On arriving in town, I had spotted a pile of washing discarded outside of a local launderette and made to alert the owner. It turned out to be an old man buried under a pile of corrugated cardboard and bin liners. Occasionally you would see someone labouring under the effects of the drug 'spice', a crumbly green mixture of synthetic chemicals and herbs that resembled cannabis and which could be procured locally for as little as £10 a bag. 'Spice,' said a local barman, contempt dripping from his voice as he pointed a wagging finger accusingly in the direction of a young man lying prostrate outside a chicken shop with a streak of mud down his back. 'They're all fucking on it.'

That is a human being, you have to remind yourself as you stroll past trying awkwardly not to look too intently. The number of homeless people in Blackpool is higher than in some London boroughs. According to a report I came across in the local paper, each year around 2,500 households in the town seek help from the council because they have either lost their accommodation or are at risk of losing it.[7] There has been a big rise in recent years right across the country of private landlords throwing families out once their Assured Shorthold Tenancy period had expired.[8] Outside Blackpool library I met a father and son who the previous day had presented themselves to the council as homeless because their landlord had disappeared. They were recipients of housing benefit, but with the landlord's vanishing act there was no longer anywhere for the job centre to send the money.

'With the housing benefit cheque, who are you gonna pay it to?' the older man, John, asked me rhetorically. 'If there's no landlord, nobody is gonna get any money. It's what they class as intentional squatting ... [Then] they [the council] put us into what's called emergency housing. We were top of the list. Because with the landlord not accepting the rent, or being around for the rent, the windows were getting broke, the place getting smashed up outside [by kids].'

The bars and restaurants along the promenade come alive at night, but away from the bright lights and revelry, darkness is poverty's cloak. Gloomy-looking men and women will sidle up to groups of embarrassed smokers outside the bars to beg some spare change or a pinch of tobacco. The few hostels that do exist are typically full to bursting point. By around nine o'clock every evening many doorways and verandas in the centre of town will be procured by someone for a night out under the stars. Before bedding down, those who wish to retain a modicum of cleanliness will make their way to Blackpool's '20p hotel' – a toilet and washbasin located in the town's central library. It was outside here that I first met Gary – close to the dank and foul-smelling doorway where he usually slept.

A painter and decorator by trade, when I met Gary his paintbrushes and rollers had long gone and he carried his home and everything else he possessed around with him on his back the way a snail carries its shell. Gary was in his early forties, was completely bald and had protruding ears. In a certain light he looked much older, for the lines on his face were deep like the lines a child might trace in the sand with a stick. That day all Gary had eaten was a bread roll. He had drunk four cups of tea, bought for him by kindly passers-by.

As I intended to stay up through the night anyway – I wanted to see how the town changed after dark – I decided to sit up with Gary. We shared the doorway on Talbot Road with an older man who had wrapped himself up so tightly in plastic sheeting he resembled a caterpillar. It was a Saturday night and the dry August air was thick with the sound of shrieking and football chanting as drinkers and party-goers spilled out of the local pubs and poured into waiting taxis. Just down from us was a row of kebab shops – fuel for the drunken revellers – and Gary told me that it was here he usually made up his cardboard bed every night because of the reassuring presence of CCTV cameras.

'If a camera's there they can see anything that happens; they know what's going on. I know I'm OK then,' he confided in me plaintively.

An air of violence surrounds you in many English towns on a Saturday night. Everywhere it hangs in the air like the stench of drains, and far more so in the towns than in big cities like London or Manchester.

My initial feeling when Gary pointed reassuringly up at the

cameras was to wonder, naively, what he might be alluding to. Apart from the occasional hollow-cheeked, roving junkie looking for the next hit, what exactly was Gary afraid of? Several days later my initial naivety was driven home to me when I met a homeless woman with a badly swollen black eye – the result, she told me, of a violent boot to the face delivered by a drunken passer-by a couple of nights before. Her head had been kicked like a football or a piece of litter while she snatched some sleep. But what was worse than the violence itself, she told me, was the obscene laughter of the drunken perpetrators as they boorishly staggered away from the scene. 'Get a job,' one of the men had bellowed as the women shrieked and they had all tumbled into a kebab shop laughing like a rampaging fascist army.

'No one can begin to imagine what you get here,' Gary told me. 'People spitting on you, or people throwing bottles at you drunk at night. You just can't imagine it. I've had bottles thrown at me, I've been spat on, I've been attacked. They just don't see you. They just don't believe in you.'

Almost as bad were the passers-by who expected some show of contrition in exchange for their meagre generosity. 'Make sure you spend that on food!' they would instruct Gary, as if the very purpose of handing something over was in fact to squeeze the last bit of self-respect from the person they were glaring down at.

The night I met Gary, miserable rain had been steadily coming down for several hours. It would continue until sunrise, and caused the pavement to give off a musty and stale smell that you never really noticed from higher up. I was reluctant to sit too close to Gary for fear of infection. Like many 'civilised' people,

I had unconsciously imbibed the idea that the homeless were either drug addicts or squatting in some murderous aura of germs and disease. Mouthing platitudes about people like Gary was what you did in a warm pub among liberal friends. Wrapping yourself up in the same soggy cardboard box while a million new, not-altogether-pleasant sensations attacked your senses was something else entirely, and meant casting off everything you had ever consciously or unconsciously accepted about people living outside, which was in practice impossible.

But Gary was certainly ill: it was cancer that was ravaging his body. When he told me that, I felt a burning sense of shame. Gary had recently been diagnosed with aggressive type 2 Non-Hodgkin's Lymphoma, and once you grasped that, you soon realised what the lumps growing up his neck and into the back of his head were. You would occasionally catch sight of the dark red scarring where parts of the parasite had been cut out. Along with the regular doses of chemotherapy, Gary had to trek to the local chemist twice a day to collect liquid Oramorph, Demerol and Co-codamol. This cocktail of medication had to be taken with a tea or coffee procured from a generous stranger. The difference between Gary and most others who suffered with cancer was that Gary had to 'battle' the disease on a spartan diet of scraps and fitful sleep punctuated by noise, rain and, occasionally, lashes of violence meted out by drinkers. 'Rest' typically meant perching himself upright on a section of the pavement under a thousand miserly and hostile stares.

Shortly after Gary's cancer had first been diagnosed he had tried to kill himself. He'd trudged up the stairs of a huge local housing complex, found a window 80 feet up and looked down on the sprawling town and its celebrated coastline.

'I put my hands behind my back, I looked up to the sky, apologised to my parents, and the last thing I remember is putting my right foot off the roof. And that was it.'

And then he fell. Gary felt himself do several revolutions in the air and he waited – waited for the inevitable crack and thud and to be swallowed by the blackness. But instead of hitting the concrete, Gary bounced off something and was thrown around like a rag doll before he finally connected with the ground.

'Apparently what saved my life was three windows that opened on the levels. If they wouldn't have been opened, then I wouldn't be here now because they broke my fall on the way down.'

In Blackpool there were seventeen suicides for every 100,000 people according to a local paper in 2016 – almost twice the national average.[9] The town had the fourth highest number of suicides of anywhere in Britain. Nearby Preston topped the list. I was also going to be doing a job that had the highest rate of female suicides of any profession.

When Gary jumped he suffered life-threatening injuries and had to spend nearly a year in hospital. By the time he got out he had very little left: no job, no home and few prospects. He still had the cancer, though. He had been on the street for five weeks when I met him. He had another three weeks and two days to go until he could claim any form of social security. As Gary was over sixteen and with no children in his immediate care, he was also not classed as a 'priority' case for emergency accommodation. And so he existed in a sort of limbo: as well as falling from a window he believed he had dropped right through a gaping chasm in the social safety net. Gary was left counting the days until he could make a claim. 'Three weeks and two days,' he kept repeating to me. Until then he had to eat, sleep and do almost everything else outside.

'I never put a form in straight away when I came out of hospital because I didn't think I needed to. I'm supposed to be under social services, seeing healthcare [people] every day, twice a day ... And I thought I was automatically under them. And I guess they told me wrong, because it doesn't work like that nowadays. And I've never claimed benefits before so I don't know. And it's just left me no home, a heap. It's degrading ... It's gone from working from school, to *this*.'

Gary's eyes bored into me as he spoke. His skin had a clammy, matt look to it. He carried his clothes to the nearby Salvation Army hostel every third day to get them washed. This cost Gary £1, which was another sum he had to persuade passers-by to part with.

'You haven't got a clue how hard it is,' he told me. 'Sometimes I've got to have a drink just to sit down and ask people for money. I've worked all my life and it's absolutely degrading. I'm not putting myself down, but those people who've not had anywhere to live for years and years and years, *phwooar*, them people must be 100 feet above me because how they do that I don't know.'

The remarkable thing about Gary was that until relatively recently he had lived a life that most of us would immediately recognise as respectable. He had a roof over his head, a wage of £400 a week coming in and food on the table. Yet all of that had slipped away like water rushing down a plughole. Now Gary was 'a heap', as he put it.

Overhearing our conversation, the man who slept nearby would occasionally pop his head out of the plastic sheeting to reveal a long brown beard and a wispy half-head of hair. The man had deep-set eyes and a face so badly pitted with acne it resembled a close-up shot of the craters on the moon. Underneath the sleeping bag you could see the filthy remnant of a T-shirt, and underneath that, when this man stood up, you would catch sight of an emaciated brown body that resembled a bag of broken twigs dipped in treacle. The man was exactly the sort of gnarled veteran of the street that Gary admired. On hearing Gary lamenting the overcrowded state of the local hostels, he began to reel off his own list of complaints.

'When I go to the council they want to put me in one of them hostels. But then you end up having to pay an extra forty pound,' he said through a thick cloud of tobacco smoke.

'Forty pound out of your own benefit every week just to stay in the hostel, you know what I mean? I need to go to the doctors and get me sick note.'

The man told us proudly that he had the lungs of a 100-year-old, a condition apparently caused, not by smoking dark, pungent tobacco, but by the strong-smelling paints he came into contact with years before working as a decorator. He still carried a paintbrush around with him today – along with three strips of debauched corrugated cardboard – and used the brush to sweep the areas parallel to where he would place the card on the floor. That was done so that dirt and bugs would not find their way into his plastic sleeping bag during the night. The man relayed to us how, after a rare wash and shave, he was able to walk into a local cafe unnoticed, order a meal and walk back out again. It was, he said in a shredded rag of a voice, 'a darn sight better than being kept awake all night with an empty belly'. He offered up his open tobacco tin to me as if he were a museum guide holding the prize exhibit.

The discomfort of sleeping on a dirty fifteen-inch wedge of wafer-thin cardboard was almost as bad as the cold that stalked you after a soaking in the rain. If you lay flat on your back your coccyx bone dug into the hard concrete; if you lay on your side your hip bone would do the same. Sleep, when it did come and if you could accurately call it that, was characterised by a fitful dream-like state. You were neither conscious nor unconscious, but trapped in a fuddled grey purgatory where you were always faintly aware of your surroundings – the gnawing wind creeping in through the stitching in your clothes, the boorish and throaty laughter emanating from the nearby bars, the tumultuous movements of passers-by whose pinched and hard faces swam blearily past your half-shut eyes as gloomy smudges. You floated there, occasionally succumbing to that sickly nightmare where you are tumbling suddenly off a ledge. Sleeping outside for any length of time would, I imagine, have the power to turn even the most straight-edge individual to anything which quickly induced chemical oblivion.

We rose early as the first light of morning swept over the town to the rushing sound of the approaching tide. The bearded man had already vanished. The battered hotels disgorged the rumbling clatter of cutlery and the smell of bacon and eggs as breakfasts were prepared for the guests. A tortoiseshell cat slunk tentatively out from behind some nearby milk bottles. England was waking up. We must have slept for no more than three hours in total. I said goodbye to Gary, whose mood was a little more optimistic this morning. He told me cheerfully before we parted that he was 'blessed'.

'I've still got a few sets of clothes,' he said proudly. 'I don't proclaim I've got nothing, because I've still got a few sets of clothes and I'm better off than some people.'

I had decided to stay out because I wanted to find out just how big the gap was between life on the street and what you might call a conventional life of a job, a wage, a full stomach and a place to live with a roof on the top of it. An August 2016 report[10] by the homeless charity Shelter claimed that one in three families in England could not afford to pay their rent or mortgage for more than a month if they lost their job. There had been a huge rise in the number of people living on the streets since the recession. Homelessness had increased almost every year since 2009/2010.[11] It is most visible in the cities, but the rise is really noticeable in small provincial towns, where the homeless have returned with a vengeance after decades of being a problem 'they get down there in London'. The sight of a man or woman sat cross-legged on the pavement looking up with a dog-like expression into the faces of passers-by has become a feature of almost every high street. Local councils are typically approaching the problem as one of law enforcement rather than compassion: a notice on the front page of a copy of the *Lancashire Evening Post* that I got my hands on, dated 20 August 2016, proudly boasted of: *the moment police officers issued their first warning notice to a man caught begging on Preston's streets*. This sentence sat below the bellicose headline, *On Your Way*, along with a picture of the beggar in question, whose face was so hollowed out and emaciated it resembled a waxwork skeleton.

There is always a risk of adopting a paternalistic attitude towards people like Gary, and of transforming the poor into 'the downtrodden' – an almost heavenly class of people with all their vices removed. Like every social class, those with nothing still have their warts – the drinkers who languidly roamed up and down Gary's street were 'the poor' just as much as any earnest lead in a Ken Loach picture. The real mistake would be to entirely discount the material factors that could turn 'deserving' people like Gary into the bundles of rags who walk the streets swigging from cans draped in tatty brown paper bags. Several strokes of bad luck could conspire and pile on top of a person like layers of rubble until it became next to impossible to extricate yourself. As for those who doled out bursts of sudden violence to the men and women who bedded down under the decaying grandeur of Blackpool's doorways and verandas – 'This is not a human being,' they must have told themselves as they climbed into their waiting taxis and slipped home to hot showers, warm beds and plates full of food, averting their eyes from the smoke that came from other people's fires.

8

Care workers form part of the backdrop to life in any civilised country. They are a flash of cobalt darting up garden paths and through porches at midday on a Wednesday when most people are at the office, just as the postman or woman is a clatter of the letterbox and a red reflection through the frosted glass of the front door on a winter's morning. You only really notice them when you have to rely on a carer yourself, or if you have ever worked in the profession, in which case you will know exactly what that habitual blue blur is as it charges from one house to the next. You may also be aware that this harassed and browbeaten individual will probably have recently cleaned up a pile of sick or wiped a person's bottom. On a particularly difficult day, they might even have been the last human being another person will have spoken to as they have slipped off this mortal coil. Yet as a society we treat carers like dirt – or as 'glorified cleaners', as one care worker would phrase it to me.

In 1979, 64 per cent of residential and nursing-home beds were provided by the NHS and local authorities. By 2012 that figure had plummeted to just 6 per cent. Today the private sector employs over two-thirds of all adult social care workers. Around half work in care homes, while 38 per cent are employed in domiciliary care.[12] Currently, around 300,000 people live in residential care homes in the UK, while some 500,000 older and disabled people rely on home care visits for things like washing and dressing. Estimates predict that 1.7 million more adults will require social care over the next fifteen years[13] as the population ages.

Most care workers are paid the minimum wage. Home care visits typically take place within twenty-minute windows. On the completion of each home visit *she* – for 80 per cent of adult social care workers are female – will charge out of the house, down the drive and into her car, racing off to the next house and the next appointment.[14] The company she works for will usually be the one that can do all of this for the local authority at the lowest price. Therefore the most cost-effective company invariably empties the most catheters and changes the most medical pads.

Competition between care providers for a slice of the shrinking social care budget has resulted in a race to the bottom: care staff are often paid peanuts and employed on precarious zero-hours contracts, while in domiciliary care, lightning-fast home visits are increasingly the norm.

A substandard level of care has been exacerbated by cuts to local authority budgets. This has had a knock-on effect on the employment conditions of care staff and, inevitably, on the vulnerable people they are charged with looking after. According to a 2014 report by the Public Accounts Committee, local authorities have cut costs 'partly by paying lower fees to providers of care, which has led to very low pay for care workers, low skill levels within the workforce, and inevitably poorer levels of service for users'.[15] Around a third of the workforce were on zero-hours contracts and 'in some areas', the report went on, 'whilst local authorities might pay private providers £13 an hour, the worker only earns the minimum wage of around £6 per hour [now £7.20]'. Austerity – and the resultant cuts to local authority budgets – had resulted in some local authorities spending considerably less than the £554 per week minimum amount recommended for the residential care of older people.[16] Meanwhile, some private care providers are demanding a return on their investment of as much as 12 per cent.[17]

It would be easy to make this purely about local authority budgets, but the privatisation of social care has cloaked the profession in a profit-making penumbra which at times seems to trump the welfare of those the sector is supposed to serve. For many of the companies that vie with each other for business, elderly people are first and foremost pound symbols on a balance sheet. The corporate jargon which permeates the sector reflects this avaricious *raison d'être*. Elderly people are 'clients', 'customers' and 'service users'. 'Patients' are a separate category of people for whom the NHS has to send an ambulance in emergencies.

The National Institute for Health and Care Excellence's (NICE) official guidance states that a home care visit should last at least thirty minutes.[18] Visits ought to be long enough, the guidance says, 'for home care workers to complete their work without compromising the quality of their work or the dignity of the person'. Yet this is merely guidance, and is thus an advisory nudge rather than a mandatory direction. Unsurprisingly perhaps, it is regularly flouted. According to Unison, three-quarters of English councils commissioned visits of fifteen minutes in 2014, up from 69 per cent the previous year.[19] Half a million (593,000) care visits between 2010 and 2013 lasted five minutes or less.[20] When the five-minute figure made national headlines in 2013, the care minister at the time, Liberal Democrat MP Norman Lamb, lamented the findings as 'totally inappropriate and unacceptable'. Yet so-called 'clock-watch care' was arguably the logical conclusion of both the privatisation of social care and the swingeing cuts to council budgets which the 2010–15 coalition government (of which Norman Lamb was an integral part) implemented with gusto.

Prior to the 2015 General Election, Labour leader Ed Miliband promised to ban care visits lasting a quarter of an hour if he became Prime Minister. Ironically, it was older voters who were the deciding factor in ensuring that Miliband was locked out of Number 10. Only 23 per cent of over-sixty-fives voted Labour in 2015, compared to 47 per cent who chose the Conservatives. As a Fabian Society pamphlet put it after Labour's unexpected defeat: 'The reason that Ed Miliband is not Prime Minister today is because Labour was rejected by older people.'[21]

Several weeks after my initial induction with Carewatch, I was finally given the chance to go out and do some home visits. A receptionist telephoned me out of the blue to ask if I was ready to begin work shadowing another carer. She reassured me that I would be paid for any shadowing work I did. I was still waiting for my DBS check to come back; however, I was to be allowed to go out provided I worked alongside someone else. For certain care jobs – for example, using a hoist to move a customer around – you needed two carers present by law to carry out the procedure safely. But for more run-of-the-mill care, the company were legally within their rights to send you out before your DBS check had come back; the buck simply stopped with them if anything went wrong. Such was the ineptitude of the DBS system that I only ever went out for Carewatch shadowing someone else – even at the end of my six-week stay in Blackpool my DBS application was still uselessly marooned in 'processing' at the dreaded stage 4 (the stage at which it was dealt with by overstretched and under-budgeted local police forces).

As for the length of the visits I went on, the typical care visit was pencilled into my rota for thirty minutes. That included all travel time to and from the customer, which typically took around ten minutes. This left around 20 minutes per visit. However, some visits lasted for as little as five or ten minutes. This was due to the fact that appointments were packed into a carer's schedule like sardines crammed into a tin. So if one appointment took longer for whatever reason – say, a customer was feeling unwell – it would invariably spill over into your other scheduled appointments, resulting in you spending the rest of the day racing around town cutting visits short in a desperate attempt to make up the time. If you were unable to do this you could end up working entire days non-stop – from seven or eight in the morning until ten or eleven o'clock at night – without so much as a tea or coffee break. By contrast, a lot of unpaid time was sometimes spent sitting morosely in car parks waiting for the next call.

Hazel,[22] a fifty-two-year-old Edinburgh-based home carer, relayed her typical day to me as follows: 'So you're working from seven in the morning till two in the afternoon, and if you overrun at any point that's your two-hour break gone because you're back on duty at four and working till ten thirty at night. I mean, in reality ten thirty at night is eleven – plus you've got your journey home.'

It was not uncommon to get to bed between twelve and one o'clock in the morning. You were up again at six. On an average day I would meet another carer early in the morning – between six and eight o'clock – and would work right through until around two o'clock. I would then go on my break from two until around four or five o'clock in the afternoon, when I would come back on shift until about ten o'clock in the evening. I was lucky if I got any breaks at all, for it was completely incumbent on everything running like clockwork during the shift, which was far from certain in a job that involved looking after old and, in many cases, extremely poorly individuals. On one of my usual visits I would enter a customer's house and begin by checking their custom-made care plan to understand exactly what they needed. With another carer I would then, to use a fairly typical example, help the customer to get out of bed to go to the toilet. This would involve walking them to the bathroom, cleaning them up after and changing their nappy or sanitary pad. Once that had been done we would usually help that person to get dressed before administering any medication they required. The final task would involve preparing the customer's breakfast, lunch or dinner along with a tea or coffee.

You could be on your feet for long hours at a time. One colleague I spoke to told me he was working eighty hours a week to help support a disabled spouse. Another said she would 'get home at eleven, got to be back in at seven. Legally you're supposed to have twelve hours' [rest] ... I wish someone would tell our firm that. We don't get that, we get seven or eight.'[23]

One of my younger colleagues had a second job in a fast-food restaurant. She would finish working with us at ten o'clock at night and then be at the restaurant for 3 a.m. You suspected that if care work was a little better remunerated she might have preferred to stay in bed rather than get up and head out in the middle of the night to serve people takeaway meals.

As well as the physical side of it, care visits were often emotionally draining. It was challenging enough cleaning up the bodily fluids ('You just get used to it,' one carer reassured me), but it would take a heart of stone not to be moved by some of the situations you encountered. I saw instances of very elderly customers being left on their own by relatives with no food in the house, necessitating an unscheduled trip to the local shops on our part to pick up essentials like milk or bread. Due to the sheer speed at which everything had to be done, not all carers would carry out 'extras' like this. On one occasion, I gave a blind man a bath, which took more than twenty minutes – the entire scheduled length of the visit. There were other times when it was a case of staying with the customer longer than the allotted twenty minutes or else leaving them at risk of neglect. Almost every carer had at least one story of an elderly person being left unfed or uncovered in a cold house. If you were late – and sometimes you were through no fault of your own – a customer could be left sitting in a urine-soaked pad for hours at a time, causing nasty sores. The list of potential indignities was endless. But you couldn't beat the clock. Time was constantly working against you. The carers I worked with would sometimes deploy a series of loaded questions in order to speed visits along – 'You don't need any shopping today, do you, Ethel?' or, 'You're not hungry, are you, Brian?' Not wishing to cause any trouble, the customer would invariably say no. A colleague of mine had noticed this going on and relayed to me what typically happened: 'There's one carer, and the actual service user … she has her pad changed this lady; she can't walk – and this carer will go in and say, "You don't need your pad changing, do you?" So the client will sometimes say "no" when she really does. It's framing it … So I've been before and said, "Are you sure?" and she's said, "Oh, I will." You know, so it's like making sure that people get what they want. Because if this lady doesn't need her pad changed, you could be there ten minutes rather than forty, so some people wanna rush. And it's really naughty.'[24]

The trouble is you are performing every task in the knowledge that you are probably keeping someone else waiting. This works against any bond you might form with the person you are caring for. According to research carried out in 2016 by the charity Age UK, half a million over-sixties spent every day alone, with no interaction with others. Nearly the same number would not see a living soul for five or six days at a time.[25] Often that was all people wanted once we'd taken them to the toilet or made them a cup of tea: a bit of company. I would see the disappointment etched on their faces as we dashed out of their front door: the realisation that even a brief chat was too much to ask. We were racing against the clock and it was the customer who lost out. That, after all, was what they were – a *customer*, engaged in a frigid transaction with you, a representative of *the business*.

The spectre of death lurked in the background too like a dark shadow. There were the sweet old men and women you inevitably become close to – you saw them almost every day, sometimes for years on end. And then you might check your rota one day and, where previously there was a familiar name, there was a blank space. Death was a blank sheet of paper and you were moved on.

The haste that dominated every aspect of the job could carry graver risks with it too: I saw several instances of MAR (Medication Administration Record) sheets being left blank when medicine had already been administered to the customer. This could easily have resulted in a poisoning. Another carer might have turned up later that day, noticed that the column on the sheet was empty, and proceeded to give the customer a second dose of medication. Hazel told me over the phone that she had in the past been sent to look after someone who 'had been given the wrong drugs on so many occasions that it's surprising she wasn't poisoned'.

She attributed this partly to the poor English-language skills of some care workers: 'Because a lot of the carers, their English wasn't good enough to read what she should be having, and when.'

A growing proportion of migrants from Eastern Europe work in the care sector. Like their British colleagues, the majority are compassionate and hard-working. Yet, similar to at Amazon, you got a sense from speaking to British care workers that the care companies knew they could extract a level of fearful compliance out of Eastern European workers that they would not necessarily expect from their indigenous equivalents. The threat of being replaced by an acquiescent migrant from Eastern Europe, hard up and therefore willing to put up with almost everything that management threw at them, was, according to care workers from other companies I spoke to, permanently there in the background, and sometimes darkly referenced in a nudge-nudge-wink-wink manner by the companies.

'I think the attitude [is] ... well, if you don't like it, bog off because we'll get ten other people from other countries who will happily do it,' Hazel said.

Hazel had been a migrant worker herself in Switzerland, and told me that she meant 'no disrespect to migrant workers because many of them have a good heart'. But she worried about the mistakes that she said kept cropping up in her customers' care notes.

'You know ... some of the migrant workers can't even read the instructions on the food to cook it correctly. And I have no problem with migrant workers, but they should have to take some kind of degree or an English exam at least that shows they can competently read and write ... It's like in Switzerland. My French isn't bad but it's nowhere near ... I wouldn't be comfortable writing a record in French that could become a legal document.'

That, ultimately, was what the Medication Administration Record sheets were: they could be used both in clinical investigations and in court cases. A 2012 study of care homes around England found that 90 per cent of residents had been exposed to at least one medication error.[26]

The situation might have been improved by better provision of English classes for migrant workers. Yet the Tory–Liberal Democrat coalition government of 2010–15 cut vast sums of money from the ESOL (English for Speakers of Other Languages) programmes. Between 2010 and 2016 ESOL participation fell from almost 180,000 to just over 100,000.[27] At the same time the government was regularly extolling the virtue of migrants integrating into British society.

Very often, when well-intentioned people expressed their concerns relating to immigration to me, I could sense the tremulous fear in their voices – the fear of being bracketed, at least loosely, with the reactionaries who *really did* want to slam the door on most immigration. Conversations were always parenthetically adorned with adamant protestations as to how liberal and broad-minded the speaker was. It would have been easy to mock and dismiss this sort of thing, or associate it with the clichéd and sinister qualifier 'I'm not racist, but ...' that preceded any hostile statement about foreigners. Yet it would have been unfair to characterise the care workers I spoke to in this way. These were real problems.

Besides, at some of the other care companies even if you did blow the whistle on mistreatment or medicine errors, there would be no guarantee the problem would ever be resolved.

'If you try to fill out an incident or accident form ... they push you out,' Hazel said of a company she previously worked for. 'They send you on all the worst cases so you get fed up and leave.'

They could also cut your hours down to nothing, which was one of the benefits for the company of employing staff on zero-hours contracts. You didn't need to sack people; you just didn't give them any work.

One of the hardest things to get used to were the stomach-churning human smells that would invariably waft through some of the houses you visited. It sounds awful when written down like this, but it was unquestionably the aspect of the job that I found the most difficult to deal with. Everyone had their own phobias, and that was mine. 'Extra Strong Mints are the best thing to get rid of the smell of poo and sick,' Hazel told me matter-of-factly. Yet more than the terror summoned by the bodily functions, I felt a sense of admiration for the people who just got on with the job without my own pathetic scruples. Everything I struggled desperately to get to grips with was accepted uncomplainingly by others, and in exchange for a pathetically low salary. There is no glory in this sort of public service any more. A lot of the time there isn't much respect, either.

'I had a lady, a lovely lady, I really liked her ... she'd been a botanist and she had a prolapse,' Hazel told me.

Prolapses occur when part of the large intestine hangs out through the anus. They are typically triggered by a bowel movement. To an experienced care professional, they are nothing unusual or shocking. But a prolapse is quite a traumatic thing to have to deal with for a new recruit.

'I arrived in her apartment my very first time of meeting her and she was on the toilet with basically her bowels hanging out. And I had to shove them back in and call for help. And I rang the office and said, "I can't possibly make my next appointment." You know, I'm literally holding this lady together, waiting for help. And they knew this had happened and they said [casually], "Oh, has it happened again?" I mean ... I'm fifty-two so I'm fairly worldly wise, but had I been ... younger ... that could've been really frightening.'

Rochelle,[28] a forty-year-old home care worker from Newcastle, had in the past worked for one of the largest care providers in the UK. It operated on the same kind of model as Carewatch. Rochelle had put in twelve-day fortnights, working each day from half past seven in the morning until ten o'clock at night.

'I regularly worked [at least] sixty hours a week ... And I worked nine weeks when I first started without a day off, and if you kick up a stink they'll cut your hours right down,' she told me resignedly.

Rochelle knew one girl who 'was getting £62 for a twenty-four-hour shift'. This is because sleep-in carers are paid a flat overnight rate which excludes hours slept, and so often comes in at below the minimum wage for total hours spent on the job.

Rochelle suspected that it was not just the staff who were being impacted by the exhausting scheduling.

'For me, terms and conditions of employment directly impact on quality of care. So the care workers [are] working for way less than national minimum wage, no travel time, fifteen to twenty two-minute calls back-to-back, rushing in and out, and not actually having the knowledge and skills required to deal with particular situations because you were thrown into places.'

As well as being paid effectively less than the minimum wage, there was also the cost of the petrol to travel between appointments. Carewatch paid 15p per mile and you were entitled to claim another 30p per mile back out of your tax. Yet you could not claim for your journey to the first client of the day. Nor, typically, did what you claimed cover the amount of petrol you actually used.

'I even calculated on occasions getting paid £4.30 an hour,' said Rochelle. 'When you work out you're getting paid for, say, three twenty-two-minute calls, put them into spaces of two hours; but those calls can be five to ten miles apart. You haven't finished work [and] you've got to rush to get to the next job. And the only way you could ever make up would be to cut call times, and that's just stealing time off vulnerable people. And that's what those organisations encouraged you to do. "Oh, you can just get that done a little bit quicker."'

Looking in from the outside, the sheer turnover of staff in the care sector might seem incredible. The care sector is expected to face a staffing shortfall of a million people in twenty years' time. A poll commissioned in 2016 by domiciliary care provider Home Instead found that, when questioned, 60 per cent of people said they would not want to become a home carer due to some of the unpleasant and menial tasks involved.

'Oh God,' the customers would say to Rochelle, 'another face. I had such and such last week, and you're here today and I had somebody else last night.' From the inside it seemed more obvious why people rarely stick around. I too was desperate to finish in a way that I had not been in Rugeley, trying though the work at Amazon had been. What seemed to make it worse as a home carer was the way the treatment meted out to us had the potential to rebound on the people we were charged with looking after.

'And it's so sad, because these [customers] are lovely people,' said Hazel. '[They] quite often gave so much of themselves through conflicts like the Second World War and Korea and stuff like that, and are intelligent, valuable human beings who get treated like dirt really.'

It was one thing to see products damaged or delayed because an order picker has been rubbed up the wrong way, but it was quite another for the consequences of skinflint management to fall on fellow human beings, especially when they were as frail and vulnerable as those relying on social care often were.

As for where things stood as a worker, I suppose I ought to have considered myself lucky to have a job at all. One day, as I slipped off my blue uniform and stepped out onto Blackpool's Central Drive, it was obvious that simply having a job was a minor blessing in a place like this. Granted, we could not be sure if our hours would soon be reduced to a level where we could no longer afford to pay the rent on our dismal rooms, but for the time being there would be money coming in, and that was something.

9

A large proportion of the work in Blackpool is seasonal. The recent recession seems to have exacerbated the highs and lows of summer and winter. Rather than the rolling hills of the past, they have gradually become modest peaks and precipitous troughs. Between 2008 and 2012 the level of peak winter claimant unemployment in Blackpool doubled.[29] According to local hairdresser Alan Wade,[30] many of those who have managed to find work since the national economy started to pick up are 'frightened to death' of their employers.

'The stories you get told in here are unbelievable,' he said of those who came into his modest salon on Ansdell Road.

'I had one in here last week and he was nearly crying. He'd worked [on a building site] for three months and he thought he was doing well. He started at six, and I think it was six till two; and at ten to two they said, "Right, we don't need you any more." He said, "When, till Monday?" And they said, "No, we don't need you any more full stop, don't come back." So basically they said we've got to sack you. He said, "What for? What have I done?" They said, "Oh nothing wrong, really." They wouldn't give him an excuse, you know. And he was in his early twenties, nearly crying.'

It wasn't hard to find more examples like this. Along the so-called Golden Mile – the stretch of promenade between the town's north and south piers – you would often see unemployed men traipsing back and forth trying to sell a little magazine. The publication – named *Gag Mag* and going for £3 – operated on a principle similar to that of the more famous *The Big Issue*, with a percentage of the cover price retained by each vendor. Gaz, a seller I bought a copy from near the famous Pleasure Beach complex, told me Blackpool was a 'different town from summer to winter'.

'People struggle here, it's a long old winter, mate, you know what I mean. People come here for the day and think, "Oh, what a nice place; everyone must be buzzing" ... All it is [is] zero-hours contracts.'

Gaz was 'a talker', he said, who would take 'anything that earns me money really'. He worried about his mum, who he said 'wanted a full-time job but she couldn't find one'.

'All she could find was part time. They won't give out full-time contracts ... very, very difficult to get a full-time job with a contract as well. Everyone seems to be a number now. It's not like a workforce any more or a family. I mean, she worked at Marks and Spencers [and] they used to do their hair for them and everything. You know, look after their staff. But [with other firms], you're a number now ... [The zero-hours' contracts they use] are just to cover their arse, aren't they? And when you've finished they'll sack you off and bring new ones in ... It's wicked what they're doing. They're arseholes.'[31]

In the 1970s Britain was branded the 'sick man of Europe' by her critics. The 1973 oil crisis created a huge increase in the rate of inflation, which in turn created tumult in the trade unions as fears grew that wages were not keeping pace. The economic medicine administered by Margaret Thatcher's government in the following decade resulted in a large short-term increase in unemployment and over a longer period a discernible transfer of power in the workplace. Today Britain is, comparatively speaking, a far richer country than in the 1970s. Yet much of that wealth depends on a permanent class of people who live a fearful and tumultuous existence characterised by an almost total subservience to the whims of their employers. Thanks to the expansion of university education, more young people can go off and get a degree – a far greater number of working-class young people go to university today than, say, forty or fifty years ago. Yet what of those left behind? It's no longer so easy to be the 'self-made man' who works his or her way up from the shop floor to the boardroom. This is strikingly apparent at Britain's top companies. In 2014, 41 per cent of British-educated FTSE 350 CEOs were products of the private school system.[32]

'You go back – well, I know you can't – but we can go back donkey's years to the 1960s, it wasn't like this,' said Alan the hairdresser, echoing some of the conversations in the social club back in Rugeley.

'It might've been on farms down in the south-east, but not up here or anywhere else. We had unions, and unions protected you. But when Thatcher came in they got rid of the unions. And you've got no rights any more. You've got some rights, but you haven't got the money to carry it out, you know, to take your bosses to court. So these bosses are laughing their heads off.'

As with a lot of the older people I spoke to, there was a sense that younger generations either didn't care or had no fight left in them.

'It's so unfair. But your generation, and the generation that's after you, they don't know any better, they don't know any history ... I'm getting on me soap box now ... One guy, he's come in here since he was about six or seven; he's twenty-one now and he's got grey hair, and you think, "You're old before your time."'

The day I met Alan I managed to secure a cabin-like room in a small semi-detached house a few streets away from the hairdressing salon. The rent was £60 per week inclusive of bills, which seemed reasonable. My housemate was a young Englishman called Steven, who had lived in Blackpool for most of his life. Steven was thin and had cropped dark brown hair. He had pointed features, sallow cheeks and would often wear loose, long-sleeved T-shirts which made his shoulder blades jut out. He was about the same age as me but he was a better-travelled veteran of the world I was eagerly trying to penetrate. Steven had done all sorts of jobs – from shop and factory work to heavier labour on local building sites and farms. A few years back, when he was out of work, he had got a job at the local B&M Bargains warehouse as an order picker. B&M, which employed around 22,500 workers at the time, started life in Blackpool and had four giant distribution centres and more than 500 stores spread across the UK.[33] On the front of every store was a distinctive bright orange and blue sunburst fascia. Founded as Billington & Mayman in 1978, B&M was acquired in 2004 by the British entrepreneurs Simon and Bobby Arora, who together with another brother (Robin) turned the loss-making company into a profitable one. Today the brothers have a net worth of £2.2 billion.[34] 'How one family has transformed the high street and plans to conquer Britain,' declared an unctuous article in the *Daily*

Express in 2012.[35] The Arora brothers came fourth in the Asian Rich List 2015, and their wealth increased by £170 million in the twelve months prior to publication of the *Sunday Times Rich List* 2016.[36] Born in Manchester to Indian parents, the brothers are one of the contemporary success stories of liberal identity politics. This is a philosophy which asserts that tuning up elites by making them 'representative' is a more urgent task than doing away with those elites altogether. It is OK if your boss makes 100 times as much as you do – as long as the chances of being the boss are divided up along the appropriate demographic and social lines.

B&M is one of those stores that has thrived on the back of the British public's appetite for a bargain in hard times. Discount stores grew at a rate of 52 per cent between 2010 and 2015, while traditional supermarkets grew by 33 per cent over the same period.[37] The 2008 financial crash and subsequent recession drove many people to shop at discount stores simply to keep their heads above water. The rapid growth of B&M was described by some retail pundits as the 'second coming' of the now-defunct brand Woolworths, at one time one of the best-known high-street names in Britain. When the last Woolworths store closed in 2009, 27,000 jobs were axed, marking the end of its ninety-nine-year presence on the high street. What did for Woolworths was the 2008 credit crunch and the shop's inability to compete with supermarkets and a new generation of discount stores.

The void on Britain's high streets was quickly filled by pound stores and discount retailers. A year after the closure of the last of the famous stores, almost 40 per cent of Woolworths' former premises that were being let or were under offer had gone to discount stores.[38] The biggest takers of the old stores were, respectively, Iceland, B&M, 99p Stores and Poundland. A year after Woolworths closed its doors, B&M had moved into thirty-eight of its former premises. The former Woolworths store in Blackpool, which sat almost directly under the famous tower, is now a Poundland.

Over a pint in a pub near the house, Steven[39] told me about his time working for B&M. He had worked in the Blackpool warehouse for three years in total and had done similar jobs in the past.

There was no music in the pub but about five television screens spread about the large open-plan lounge area. Every screen was showing the same Sky Sports News channel, which was eagerly reporting the multi-million-pound transfers prior to the kick-off of the forthcoming football season. We took our drinks out to one of the picnic benches in the concrete beer garden. The August weather had been a mixed bag but on this day it was balmy, even at seven o'clock in the evening.

'You shouldn't enjoy yourself going to work, you know, you're there for nine, ten hours a day; but you shouldn't have to work in fear. You shouldn't have to start a shift at six o'clock in the morning and think, you know, am I getting sent home at quarter past six? You know, am I gonna make one box wrong out of 2,000 and get sacked for it?'

When he'd started at B&M Steven had recently moved back to the area after the break-up of a relationship, and was looking for something to tide him over. He'd heard about the openings at B&M and so had decided to give it a go.

'I started off with an agency – so there were two big agencies, which then merged into one agency; then all of a sudden B&M got rid of the agency, and no one really told us what was going on; and it was literally having to go into the office and beg for a job there, which is what I did.'

When he started Steven had to go around the warehouse with a pick list of items to be sent off to Manchester or Lincoln or whichever store the stock was intended for. He picked the boxes, planted a sticker on the front and put them on a pallet ready to be sent out. As at Amazon, all of this took place in an enormous frigid warehouse which, in the case of B&M, was so big it covered two different postcodes.

'They're old airport hangars, about a five- to ten-minute walk from here. They used to make Wellington Bombers [here] in the Second World War. [It's a] massive, massive warehouse.'

Eventually Steven worked his way up into one of the coveted managerial positions. Thus he could, he said, 'see it from both sides because I ended up becoming part of the management team'.

'What I always found and noticed was that if people were getting up to the twelve months where they then said in their own handbook that we will have to give you a contract, they'd be sacking them for all sorts of different reasons, or telling them that there was no work.'

The staff hierarchy at B&M resembled that at Amazon: the yellow-coats were the lowest rank, picking and pulling pump trucks around; while the orange-coats were the management.

'It was an us and them mentality ... Even when I was a manager, I was still fearful of my job and whether, you know, the company was going to relocate to Liverpool ... There'd be a big pile [of application forms] in my inbox tray in HR, and then they'd go, "Right, get the next lot." And you'd see it as a manager; you'd hear in the office and stuff like that: "Get the next twenty in, get the next twenty in." That's what the main bosses would say. Just turning [staff] over constantly, constantly.'

Some of the distances you put in on an average shift were comparable to those I walked in my job at Amazon.

'One day, we were talking about what kind of miles you walk per day, and we were guessing. And we were talking to this army guy, and [he] said he's done army training regimes and stuff, and he says this matches it ... Every worker agreed on the same thing. You'd finish at two o'clock, and by three o'clock in the afternoon you'd go home, sit on the couch and you'd be asleep for two hours. You were just absolutely shattered.'

According to Steven, in 2010 many Polish, Latvian and Lithuanian workers arrived in Blackpool – six years after the accession of ten new member states on 1 May 2004.

'All of a sudden I went to B&M and there was a massive [influx]. It happened obviously all over the country ... It was a massive culture shock going in and working with these people.'

There was a great deal of tension between the migrant workers and the predominantly English workforce, Steven said.

'The Polish and English despised each other ... Everyone would sit with their own tables. I suppose if we went to Poland we'd probably do the same: you'd stick [with] your own ... There was a few Polish lads I tried to make conversation with, it was like, "You know, why is there hostility between English and Polish?"

And the only thing I could ever get out of the Polish lads was that England didn't give Poland recognition during the Second World War for the Battle of Britain. And that was the only reason they *ever said*. I mean really, guys, come on ... They [the Eastern Europeans] really hated you. They always played on the language barrier as well. "No, I don't understand ..."'

Steven believed that staff drug and alcohol tests B&M introduced weren't stringent enough, and could have been used by the company to reduce staff numbers.

'Because so many people were just smoking weed or what have you, they could just go "Right, random drug test" and get rid of their ten, fifteen [staff members] every week ... So it was like, "Right, basically we need to do these random drugs tests" ... and their thing was like a list, with A up there and Z down there ... They closed their eyes, management, and they'd be, like, "That's random." And I kicked off one day, I said, "That's not random." I said if you want to go for someone called Aaron you're inclined to go top left corner [of the list]. If you want to go for Zakarius you go bottom right. Other times, management would come up to you and go, "Right, there's ten random drugs tests, find A, B, C, D and E." So you'd have to go looking round the warehouse for them. People would just do runners, because most people in Blackpool – well, not most people, but a lot – would do the odd joint and stuff. With you working so early in the morning as well if you'd had a drink the night before you'd get done for that.'

A few of the staff at B&M eventually got organised. The final straw was finding out that those doing the same job at B&M's Liverpool warehouse were being paid more because it was classed as a city. Yet the Liverpudlians who lived and worked in Blackpool said there was no practical difference between the cost of living in their home town and the cost of living in Blackpool, which was just an hour's drive up the M6.

'So we ended up contacting the union, which was USDAW,' Steven told me.

Eventually, Steven and the workers at B&M managed to recruit the 10 per cent of the workforce required for the company to recognise the trade union.

'[The union people] tried to canvass on the car parks here, and you know management would be running over: "Get off the land! Get off the land!" But we'd already got our quota anyway; people were so fed up of it. People were sneaking packs of application forms down their pants to get it into the warehouse to go further down to hand them out. It actually binded us together.'

Steven talked of a 'fear factor' among staff.

'Especially people with families. A lot of people wouldn't join up just because they were so scared … I mean, they [the Polish] were the hardest ones to get to sign up to the union. They were really bad for it – "No, I'm not interested, I'm not interested." And they were so scared. I suppose you would be, wouldn't you?'

Eventually USDAW received the legal recognition they were after, and things appear to have improved at the Blackpool warehouse since. The most important trade union work is typically quite dull. The best trade union leaders are also, by extension, interested in the boring stuff – the length of the toilet breaks, the rules governing agency workers, the quantity of the paid breaks a worker is entitled to, and so on and so forth. These are the things that matter when you work in a job at the bottom end of the labour market, not the rigid dogmas and slogans summoning a radiant utopian future, nor a new set of superiors booming at you in impenetrable jargon. It struck me talking to Steven that there would be far fewer workplaces like the one he described if the left was a bit less fixated on the romantic penumbra surrounding the word 'socialism' – the slogans, the thundering speeches and the whiff of 'revolution' – and a little more interested in the boring stuff.

'Unions are like Marmite, aren't they?' Steven said as we got up to leave the pub and started walking home. 'People either love them or hate them. They either love them because they think they're going to stick up against bullying, or they're just stirring little bastards that ruin companies ... I remember when I were seventeen, I was just like, "Yeah, I'm not interested. What's the point in giving them an extra £2 a week?" Ten, fifteen years later it's like, they're worth their weight in gold, they really are.'

10

A few customers of mine at Carewatch lived near to my room on Central Drive, and these were typically the hardest cases – alcoholics waiting for a space in rehab, penurious pensioners or those who simply lived in self-inflicted squalor. Central Drive is a long undulating road that starts near the promenade a few blocks from the famous Winter Gardens and runs for around a mile until it reaches just past the Bloomfield Road stadium, home to Blackpool FC. Central Drive would once have been classed as a working-class area, but according to local statistics, when I was there, almost twice as many people were on some form of unemployment benefit as were in full-time employment.[40] Half the children in this part of town lived in poverty.[41]

There was also an off-licence for every 250 residents and half the population smoked. Blackpool has changed a great deal since it was described in 1789 as an 'abode of health and amusement'.[42] As it got closer to midday you would see little groups of men slowly gathering outside the local betting shops and pubs. Some of the older men wore moth-eaten suits, which would hang from their limbs like crumpled old sacks. One bright summer morning, a roadside building was being demolished while a handful of bedraggled onlookers stood on the pavement nearby, drinking thirstily from black, can-shaped plastic bags. This was their morning's entertainment, and free of charge at that. A thin, weather-beaten man with an iron lung stuffed in his backpack stood alongside them, greedily drawing on what was left of a burning roll-up. It would have been harder to dream up a better cartoon strip of life at the bottom. As soon as the day got into its full swing this small group of street drinkers would migrate to the bus stop across the road so that it looked like they were waiting for a bus, rather than having can after can, one followed by another. When one of the group spotted a policeman or woman they would all rapidly dart into a doorway or down a side alley, only to re-emerge warily once the danger had passed. They would then totter back to the bus stop and anxiously bounce from leg to leg like a spring when the pressure is removed. 'A lot of them drink to escape the reality of the place,' was how one local cabby put it to me.

Every Wednesday in Blackpool's main library you would see the people who had been sent like badly behaved children to 'job club'. The Department for Work and Pensions removed public phones from job centres in 2014, and claimants were thereafter forced to phone expensive 0845 numbers – costing up to 51p a minute – for queries about their benefits. The computers were gone from the job centre too, so in Blackpool job seekers without an internet connection at home have to go across the road to the library to apply for work after signing on (most jobs are advertised online). If you need to print any application forms that can cost another 50p. Some of the men and women I spoke to had been sent on maths, English and IT courses in the hope that another piece of paper might make them more employable. Many of those who were sent on the courses also had no computer at home on which to practise their newly learned skills.

Elsewhere in the grand old library building were the somnolent pensioners who sat for hours on end waiting for their turn with the *Daily Mail* and its headlines booming about Europe. Arguments occasionally broke out over possession of the paper, with disproportionate anger directed towards anyone thought to be coveting it: 'Come on. Jack, you've had it long enough now, haven't you?' At the very bottom of the library's pecking order were the town's down-and-outs, who floated in and out between the walls of books throughout the day, holding filthy carrier bags which draped behind them like pieces of crêpe paper. They would very often perch in a chair in some gloomy recess with their legs pulled up like grasshoppers. Some fell asleep, the newspapers resting on their chests and slowly rising and falling with their breathing. A member of staff would eventually throw them back out onto the streets. The same men and women would invariably reappear later on for a wash in the '20p hotel'.

'You go in the job centre and they don't help you,' a chubby twenty-three-year-old man had told me one day as we smoked cigarettes together outside the library.

'They turn round to you and say things to you like, "Oh well, you're better off on benefits," or, "Oh, there is a job but you'll earn less than you do on benefits. Bye, come back next week" ... I mean, they're not even bothered. You're in there, like, five minutes: you just walk in and walk out. There's no help ... It's like they want an easy life, because they give you no advice ... I've been saying to them for ages that I want to do my English [GCSE], and they're just like, "That'll be nice, won't it?" ... Because the other thing is they treat you like scum. I mean, it's very hard to explain, but just the way they look at you and talk to you. They think they're like a higher being or something.'

During the two-week interregnum between my induction with Carewatch and finally being sent out on a job, I had managed to pick up some casual work on a building site. I'd spotted an advert scrawled on a piece of torn paper in marker pen and Sellotaped haphazardly to a bus stop near the house. A minimum-wage, cash-in-hand job. But the money would tide me over while I waited for a phone call from the job I was supposed to be doing. On calling the number I was told to wait near the town's football ground at half past eight the next morning for a man in a white van called 'Mick' who would swing by and pick me up.

The work itself was mainly labouring – dirty, back-breaking work digging trenches, carting materials to and fro and some painting. Despite it all happening under the radar (at least as far as our pay went), the boss was a stickler for routine: we always worked from nine in the morning until five in the afternoon, with an hour set aside every day for lunch. Each day was bookended with an on-the-dot pick-up and drop-off in an uncomfortable smoke-filled van with The Doors perennially playing on the CD player. Occasionally after work Mick would take us to the pub and buy us pints of fizzy lager. One of the workers who got the van with me was Polish and another two were locals. One of the younger English lads, a skinny kid called Aiden[43] who always wore a Blackpool football top under his dirty work clothes, was on benefits and worked on the site because he believed the job centre would take the money away if he told them.

'They've got this sixteen-hour thing,' he told me in the pub wearily. 'So I said to them [in the job centre], "What if I get sixteen hours?" "Oh well, you'll lose your benefits." I went: "So I'm no better off? What's the point?" I'm not thick, you know.'

The day after this conversation I received the call from Carewatch instructing me to go into the office the following day. I told Mick when he whizzed round in the van to pick me up the next morning that I would have to finish. I had expected him to get angry, but he didn't seem to mind. 'No worries, mate,' he said, drawing on a badly put-together roll-up. 'Used to it, innit? At least you had the decency to come in and tell me. Dunno what you wanna work with those *fossils* for, mind.'

I did one more day on the site, after which I regained my ability to bend down in the mornings and walk up the stairs without hamstrings like taut elastic bands that had been left out in the sun. I did have one unexpected memento besides a head full of indy rock tunes, however. Trying to shift a wheelbarrow full of hardcore a little too quickly on my final afternoon, I was hit by a sudden and inexplicable pushing sensation in my gut, just above the groin area on the right-hand side. I hurried home when the shift finished and the pain seemed to subside. However, it would reappear months later, resulting in me lying in hospital with a surgeon slicing my belly open and peering into my abdomen the way someone might open the corner of a parcel.

You can reel off statistics about the way people are living in Blackpool till the cows come home, but it was the things I saw that burrowed more deeply into my brain. One thing you soon notice is a preponderance of overweight people compared to further south. A significant proportion of the people strolling round outside the grubby fly-blown hotel I had stayed in looked as if, rather than pulling on their clothes, they had been melted and poured into them. Poverty has made them fat. Bloomfield is the unhealthiest district in Blackpool, which is England's unhealthiest town. The signs outside the local eateries clamour to tell you that everything on offer is fried and embalmed in a thick pool of grease: *deep-fried, pan-fried, stir-fried, sautéed*. As for smoking, lighting up is just something to do.

A few blocks away from the promenade, many of the former hotels and boarding houses that once served the holidaying mill workers and office clerks have been converted into cheap flats and bedsits. Owners typically sold up, families died off and a set of *nouveau riche* landlords took over the properties. Close behind were the poor and needy, who continued to be drawn in by Blackpool's historical allure of exuberance and prosperity. These penurious out-of-towners arrived and the landlords were only too happy to put them up. The guaranteed housing benefit the newcomers brought with them provided many landlords with a reliable income. The same thing seems to be going on in other local towns. One Saturday I travelled up the road to Morecambe, a town that faces economic challenges similar to Blackpool – deprivation caused by the diminishing allure of an English beach holiday and a predominance of insecure, seasonal work. When budget airlines made package holidays affordable for all, properties in towns like Morecambe began to empty out. It became increasingly difficult to fill the hotels without shipping in the destitute who, paradoxically, were the only people who could be sure to pay rent to the landlords who bought up the shuttered hotels. Speaking to the BBC in 2006, a journalist for a local newspaper described Morecambe as a 'B&B ghetto' for people on benefits.[44] Tony Vettesse, the owner of the cavern-like Old Pier Book Shop which stands out proudly on Morecambe's seafront, told me that there had been a tipping point twenty or thirty years ago when 'the only way to fill the hotels and guest houses was to bus in the unemployed'.

'That's what happened. Same as Bournemouth, all those kinds of places. Two local entrepreneurs used to take a minibus to places like Manchester and Birmingham, and load it up with the unemployed and homeless, mostly the homeless ... and stow them in their guest houses, fill out all the forms for them and the government pays for their benefits. The guy that did that died in a nasty motorbike accident. Not many people shed a tear.'

Britain's fastest growing cities between 1981 and 2013 were all (apart from Telford, a 1960s-built new town) in the south. The fastest shrinking towns were all in the north.[45] The jobless rate in the north-east was the highest in the UK in 2016.[46] This was in stark contrast to the industrialisation of the nineteenth century, when thousands of people poured into towns like Wigan and Preston in the hope of finding work, often living in unsanitary conditions in overcrowded alleys and yards. Charles Dickens based his mythical Coketown in *Hard Times* on Preston, which he visited in 1854 during a twenty-three-week strike by cotton workers. On the journey up to Preston, Dickens met a man on the train – 'Mr Snapper' – who insisted that the strikers ought to be 'ground' to 'bring 'em to their senses'. 'One must either be a friend to the Masters or a friend to the Hands,' added the man, to which Dickens retorted in characteristically liberal fashion that one 'may be a friend to both'.[47] One of Preston's biggest former cotton mills had been turned into a call centre by the time I visited.

Before finally leaving Blackpool for good I spent a hot, late-summer day meandering about on the famous promenade. It had seemed almost perverse not to, considering the weather. A group of Muslim women in headscarves huddled around bags of chips as grey-haired pensioners stood patiently in line for 99 Flakes. An aggressive, drunken argument got underway outside the famous Merrie England bar and I moved away to sit in one of the Edwardian seafront shelters where I got chatting to an older middle-aged couple who had travelled down from Lancaster for the day.

'At one time Lancaster was full of work, between factories and that,' the husband told me as he bit into a rapidly melting cornet.

'It was far bigger than Blackpool ... You had quite a lot of railway workers there ... but they all went ... Lancaster you went to as a kid, you couldn't go wrong there. If you worked in the factories you couldn't go wrong with it. If you worked four shifts ... and you'd get people who would do it. And there was just no problem about jobs.'

There were still skilled jobs in the north-west. In 2014 manufacturing continued to provide more than an eighth of the total employment in the area.[48] Yet in towns like Blackpool people very often float from one precarious job to the next, or else find themselves navigating the Kafkaesque world of the job centre with its endless paper trails, vindictive jobsworths and automated telephone messages. You might, as I had managed to do, find work in social care. But after several weeks in the job, the only thing I wanted to do was quit. I was evidently not alone in feeling this way. I was part of the 47.8 per cent of care workers who would typically leave their posts within a year.[49] And besides, when I jacked it in, a month after my initial induction, I still hadn't been paid a penny by the company for the hours I had worked. I never did understand why. I phoned up the office a couple of times but was fobbed off – so and so will call you, etc. There was still no sign of the money months later, when this corner of England had become a diminishing haze of cigarette smoke, alcohol, sandcastles and row after endless row of rock shops.

PART III

—

SOUTH WALES VALLEYS

11

Wales for me has always been synonymous with a man called Len: my step-grandfather, as I suppose I ought to call him. Len was originally from Cwmbran, a new town established in 1949 to provide employment to the South Wales coalfield. Its name means *Crow Valley* in Welsh; the word *Wales* itself comes from the Old English word *wealh*, meaning foreigner. Len, with his unusual accent, which to my maturing ear was musical and filled with unusual epithets and inflections, was initially a foreigner in my family. But spending the greater part of my childhood with him and my grandmother, I was too in a way.

It fell to Len to do the job of both my father, whom I had never met, and my grandfather, who passed away before I was born. As such, like the *Beano* and a battered old cricket bat, Len was a permanent and reliable fixture throughout my childhood. It was Len who would stoically sit next to me reading the *Daily Mirror* aloud as I was folded up in bed with crippling asthma during the long wintry afternoons. It was Len too who took me out for long summer walks in the green patchwork of the Somerset countryside, regaling me with stories of working-class life in the South Wales coalfield sixty years previously: of how he had slept three-to-a-bed with his brothers growing up and of how, later on, his cloth cap had been abruptly knocked off by a self-important foreman after he spoke up about an injustice at work.

Len was a lifelong socialist who revered Aneurin Bevan, Labour's 1945 minister for health and the founder of the National Health Service. As a young man Len had heard Bevan speak in a working men's club, and was for the rest of his life electrified at even the mention of his name. Growing up, Len had seen the desperation of the dole queues first hand. 'Struggle' to him was more than high-flown theory or a fashionable cause to be discarded later in life with the swelling of the bank balance and the expansion of one's waistline.

The first thing Len taught me – and a lesson I would learn again as a teenager when I started to take a proper interest in books and newspapers – was that Britain was several countries melded uncomfortably into one like different types of clay. Not so much in the geographic sense, but more in the way that people rubbed along side by side yet inhabited vastly different universes. We may have been an island of chinless Royals, mediocre dukes, privately educated self-made men and fatuous celebrities who puffed and pouted in the pages of glossy magazines, but these islands also had a radical democratic history, even if democracy today was something liberals sneered at and a resurgent right interpreted as *carte blanche* to whip up hatred against immigrants. England was Queen and flag but it was also Chartist and trade unionist. It was the angry diminutive man hunched over the steering wheel of a 4x4 in an identikit retail park, but it was also the person with nothing who offered you his last cigarette, or the wizened ex-miner who invited you into the snug of his home for a cup of strong tea and to reminisce about the old times. The working class go in and out of fashion in Britain like the cheap contents of a catalogue collection. Occasionally there will be an outbreak of charitable feeling towards 'the poor' – a sanctified group who exist as a sort of stage prop to make the *bien-pensant* feel better about themselves – but typically the contribution of the working class to Britain's economic progress is vastly undervalued, even by those who make a comfortable living pretending to speak on their behalf.

It is important here to recognise that 'the poor' and 'the working class' often mean different groups of people, though there is obviously some overlap. The former – the 'downtrodden' – are a sort of column and dining-table caricature – ragged mute creatures onto which liberals can project whichever virtues they wish. People of almost all political hues are decidedly uncomfortable with genuine working-class radicalism of the sort that rocked South Wales intermittently during the twentieth century.

Autumn rain streaked the windows of my car as I crossed the Second Severn Crossing and arrived in Wales. I soon reached Swansea, where I encountered a familiar sight: a huge grey and yellow Amazon warehouse sitting ominously at the end of 'Ffordd Amazon', a street purpose-built for the company by the Welsh government to the tune of £4.9 million. *Ffordd* is the Welsh word for 'road' or 'way' – the use of the traditional word presumably designed to display Amazon's cultural sensitivity. Winner-takes-all capitalism comes cloaked today in cultural specificities. Money for the *ffordd* came on top of the £8.8 million regional selective assistance grant given to Amazon for the cost of the warehouse to encourage the company to come to Swansea.[1] The year the purpose-built track was finally completed, Amazon racked up £4.3 billion of sales in the UK, yet paid just £2.4 million in tax – less than 0.1 per cent of its total revenue. As in Rugeley, it felt as if Amazon had been welcomed to South Wales out of desperation. The Welsh government had rolled out the red carpet as part of its 'regeneration' agenda, a drive to transform formerly industrial areas which also found expression at the other end of the supply chain in the huge out-of-town retail parks that were killing Britain's increasingly ghostly high streets. Whereas Margaret Thatcher had led an all-out assault on the working class, the hollowed-out response of Blairism was not to tame capitalism but to offer a palliative of consumerism to those who sweated to make the wheels turn. You may not have been able to exercise much democracy at work, but you could go out and buy a three-piece suite and a giant television set on the never-never – or as one young Welshman phrased it to me in another context, you could 'live a champagne lifestyle on a Panda Pop wage'.

Sneering at working-class materialism – and consumerism more generally – is typically a luxury afforded to those who have never had to want for anything. That said, at least some of the prosperity of recent decades has been illusory and built on a mountain of debt. GDP may have grown over the past thirty years, but labour's share of national income is back to where it was in the 1930s.[2] The resulting political backlash, underway with a fury as I type these words yet relatively dormant when I first set out on my journey, is attributed to everything from a philistine disregard for rational thinking to the innate 'intolerance' of working people to anyone who looks or sounds a little different from themselves.

The outside world slept as the battered old Volkswagen Golf I was driving snaked over and around the undulating roads and on into the Valleys. Nestled between the chartreuse-green bracken and the clusters of houses loomed the monuments to an industrial past of iron, coal and steel. Most of the slag heaps had been removed but the landscape remained dotted with mining paraphernalia, even though the last deep pit in Wales was closed for good in 2008. The sound of the miners' boots tramping on the gravel was no more, but if you closed your eyes you could still imagine the groups of men marching down the windy streets of towns like Cwm, Ebbw Vale or Merthyr, their voices ringing out musically and soaring up and over the little stuccoed terraced houses which clung to the wooded hillsides like dirty grey milk cartons. You could almost feel the rattle of steel-shod boots on the tarmac, smell the smoke of the steam trains and detect the movement of the winding gear.

Yet there is a danger in romanticising the past, both politically and with respect to one's own life. You can be overawed by the history of a place or a movement just as you can be swallowed up by the lingering recollections of childhood. A great flood tide of sentiment can then swim over you with its warm and reassuring certainties until the present is prostrate before some imaginary paradise lost. The answers to all present and future problems are henceforth found by excavating the past and wallowing among its ghosts. 'Happy we were then, for we had a good house, and good food, and good work,' as an aged Huw Morgan recounted wistfully in *How Green Was My Valley*, a moving (and nostalgic) novel about life in the South Wales collieries.

The majestic beauty of the Valleys is also misleading if treated as a sort of museum artefact. You might slip on a pair of walking boots and trudge along the breathtaking mountain tops on the way to Tredegar, but it is wise to keep in mind the socialist Welsh poet Idris Davies's admonition to seek out the people who live in such ostensibly pleasant locations before waxing romantically on the beauty of the thatches in the cottage roof. The Valleys contain the sort of picturesque landscapes that often serve today as fodder for the daytime TV property shows that violently assault the senses of the unemployed with their affluence. Yet as Davies put it almost 100 years ago, 'Any subject which has not man at its core is anathema to me. The meanest tramp on the road is ten times more interesting than the loveliest garden in the world.' When you see the beautiful house, do not stand like a lemon gazing at its majesty; seek out the occupant and listen to his or her story.

Davies's poetry typically dwelt on the air of melancholy and despair that stalked the Valleys during the years of the great depression, an echo of which has returned in recent times. During a four-year period on the dole, Davies wrote *Gwalia Deserta* (Wasteland of Wales), his first published work, the verses inspired by the 1926 General Strike and mining disasters at Cwm and elsewhere:

Who made the mineowner?
Say the black bells of Rhondda.
And who robbed the miner?
Cry the grim bells of Blaina.

The miners of Davies's era spent prolonged periods out of work, drawing when they could on an insubstantial social safety net to feed their families. In his 1939 mining memoir, *These Poor Hands* – a book that slotted into a genre once called 'proletarian literature' – the miner and writer B. L. Coombes, who moved to the South Wales coalfield from Hereford, relayed to middle-class readers a reality of 'continual slavery and dust; the poor clothes and bare living; the need for decent men to beg their bread ... the eviction from his home of some miner who has opened his mouth too wide or refused to be robbed of his wages when they were due.'

Idris Davies worked underground for seven years until the General Strike of 1926, when the pit he worked in closed and Davies was left without a job. Like many others in the Valleys, he turned to Christianity and socialism for the answers.

Wales has a radical history, even if today, as elsewhere, many of its working-class actors sit metaphorically slumped in a state of perpetual defeat. The ghosts of this rebellious past exist just beneath the surface wherever you turn, whether in the statues of local Labour Party heroes like Aneurin Bevan, or along the streets named after early pioneers of the trade union movement. A plaque in the Ebbw Vale Wetherspoons informed me of the legend of the local Chartists who were rumoured to be so militant they produced their own arms and ammunition up in the moorland beyond the village of Trefil. A portrait of the late former Labour leader Michael Foot hung on a pastel-coloured wall of the same pub, squeezed incongruously between two lurid and flashing fruit machines named Bankers' Birthday and Paddy's Payday. Capitalism co-opts every rebellion against it. You got the impression, however, that an identikit corporate beer chain would be more reluctant to embrace radical history if the Labour movement had any oomph left in it. Impertinence is celebrated as long as it remains at a safe distance from the present. Then it is repackaged and flogged in anodyne corporate packaging, its substance reduced to trite platitudes that are sold once again by content-free politicians – the 'shiny men', as one local called them.

In a stroke of good fortune, on the day of my arrival in Wales I managed to secure accommodation in Brynmill, a student area around two miles west of Swansea city centre. The room itself was pricey – £100 a week, inclusive of bills – but the necessity of securing a place to stay at short notice overrode most concerns about the cost. My prospective job hinged on my finding a place to live right away. I had got through the interview process at local car insurance company Admiral, and had been offered a position renewing customers' policies in one of its call centres. The company required immediate 'proof of address' in the local area. While none of the 'professional' jobs I have done have ever required this, at Admiral – as at Amazon and Carewatch – it was considered urgent. Thus I had to get a deposit down on a place right away – spending more money than I had intended to in the process – and chase up my bank for the ellusive statement with my new address on it.

Brynmill is a relatively affluent suburb adorned mostly with dirty white stuccoed terraces. Living there whilst working from eight till five in a call centre you soon come to realise just what vastly different worlds students and locals in university towns and cities often inhabit. Weekday parties blast out of some student pads until deep into the night, and sparsely furnished workmen's greasy spoons sit alongside organic cafes selling slices of cake for £2 – only slightly more than the cost of a full English in places 100 yards down the road. In one little down-at-heel cafe, three well-spoken students bustled in through the doors, ordering greasy breakfast baps to go. While they lingered, they quietly mocked the 'ironic' working-class décor out of earshot of the owner.

Despite the recent imposition of tuition fees, being a student remains a highly enviable existence. It also overwhelmingly remains the preserve of the comfortable classes. The bottom fifth of the population are 40 per cent less likely to go to university than the top fifth.[3] Students from less affluent backgrounds are also more likely to drop out and less likely to graduate with a good grade than their better-off peers.[4] Of course, many of today's university graduates will struggle to buy a home or clear the mountain of debt they will have accumulated by the time they have finished studying. But for all the hard-luck stories, you suspect the future bodes better for them than it does for those marooned in small towns toiling away in miserable jobs. I was once a student myself in Nottingham, and held a completely unrealistic image of the town until I took a part-time job as a postman for the Royal Mail in the depressed areas around Broxtowe and Gregory Boulevard. Predatory loan sharks would go from door to door on these estates, while I would follow closely behind with a bundle of letters – to be greeted tetchily by 10 a.m. drinkers enquiring eagerly over broken picket fences as to whether or not I had 'got the giro today, duck?'. The circular, inward-facing estates of Aspley, which I visited early on a Saturday morning, and the student union, where I was invariably found propping up the bar on a Saturday night, might as well have been Mercury and Pluto.

Some choose not to move away and study. Others have children young or are obliged to stay put and care for older relatives. But going to a *good* university remains something of a luxury. The gulf between a prestigious institution and an average one is an excellent example of the contemporary garb layered over the British class system. Privileged children still go to the top universities whereas poor kids, if they stay in higher education at all, typically attend the much less prestigious former polytechnics. Discrimination is frowned upon in theory but acquiesced in practice. Second-rate 'unis' are, if you like, the political elite's condescension to meritocracy – the utopian idea that opportunity in life can bear no relation to the prosperity enjoyed by one's parents.

12

At Admiral I would go on to meet quite a few university graduates – products, in most instances, of the former polytechnics. A 2015 report by the Chartered Institute of Personnel and Development found that more than half (58.8 per cent) of graduates were in jobs that did not require a degree.[5] In recent decades the UK economy has been creating low-skilled jobs at a faster rate than high-skilled jobs. Between 1996 and 2008, for every ten middle-skilled jobs that disappeared in the UK, around 4.5 of the replacement jobs were high-skilled whereas 5.5 were low-skilled.[6] Thus many students who were promised a leg-up into the professions find, on emerging from the glass-plated 'aspirational' production lines with a mountain of debt, that the ladder has been kicked away and the spaces at the top are already stuffed with those who went to more privileged universities. Britain's economic strategy these days seems to involve packing hordes of teenagers off to university while making occasional noises about apprenticeships and skills training for those left behind. Politicians no longer have much faith in the state to create work, and so you end up with thousands upon thousands of indebted university graduates sitting morosely at the end of production lines sticking Sellotape onto cardboard boxes or reading scripts down the phone to irritable consumers.

Predictably, of course, disappointed students are derided by the media for their 'unrealistic' expectations. A few years ago the millionaire television chef Jamie Oliver criticised young British workers for their unwillingness to knock out eighty-hour weeks in dead-end jobs. Unlike their desperate Eastern European counterparts, young Brits were 'wet behind the ears', Oliver proclaimed. Yet as a youth worker I would meet in Ebbw Vale told me: 'If you've studied and you've got a degree, do you *really* wanna be working in a call centre?'

Probably not, and you will notice that the celebrities and commentators who bleat on endlessly about graft and hard work rarely send their own children to toil away fruitlessly in call centres and scrabble around pulling vegetables out of the ground in the sodden fields of Kent.

In Wales I was working as a 'Renewals Consultant'. It was up to me to persuade customers who had found a cheaper car insurance quote elsewhere to stick with Admiral. There are around 5,000 call centres in the UK, employing around a million people.[7] As well as Swansea, Admiral has offices in Cardiff and Newport and is famously a 'good' company to work for. Or at least they are if you take any notice of the 'Best Companies to Work For' surveys published annually in the *Sunday Times*. Admiral is, in fact, the only company to have featured in the survey every year since 2001, and finished an impressive second place in 2014.

The UK's big four insurance companies spend around £100 million annually on advertising, and the industry is exceptionally good at making one of the most boring concepts imaginable appear wacky and fun. The most well-known example is the fictional meerkat Aleksandr, who has helped make a multi-million-pound fortune for Compare the Market. At Admiral, the clownish behaviour was not confined to the company's advertising campaigns. 'We like to have a laugh,'[8] the Admiral trainer assured us, David Brent-style, every five minutes.

And to be fair to them, the company did make a considerable effort to create a positive and, dare I say it, fun environment to work in, even if at times there was a strong whiff of a cult about proceedings. You were bombarded with positivity and contrived wackiness near enough as soon as you stepped through the doors of the company's glass-plated building near Swansea's maritime quarter next to the River Tawe. 'They [the company] try to do what they can to make your lives easier. People who like what they do do it better,' one of Admiral's trainers told us on the first day while we nodded along serenely. Progressive corporate generalisations like this were foisted on us the way political slogans might be delivered to an audience of young student radicals by a bearded ideologue.

I started working for Admiral at the beginning of November and was due to receive a couple of pay packets before Christmas. One thing that did get on my nerves was being told we would be paid on a *monthly* rather than *weekly* basis. This is not unusual for minimum-wage work, and there are advantages and disadvantages to both. Firstly, most bills arrive on a monthly basis, therefore it is often easier to pencil-in outgoings like rent and heating against a monthly income. But budgeting on a day-to-day basis is a good deal easier when the next pay packet is always, at most, seven days away, especially if you still rely on a pre-pay gas or electric meter, as many low-income households do. But by far the worst thing about a monthly salary is the initial wait from when your money from a previous job or your jobseekers' allowance dries up to when you get your first pay cheque. Waiting a week is bad enough; waiting an entire month is an intolerable burden that throws people into dire straits and only encourages the opportunists who prey on poverty's perpetual victims.

Because the job centre does not cover the period from when you get a job until the point at which you are actually paid, there is always a window in which getting hold of things 'on tick' is the only way to maintain a decent standard of living. It is this sort of thing which has fuelled the parasitic payday loan industry, the modern-day equivalent of the loan sharks who at one time would stalk ground-down estates in order to squeeze money out of their impoverished clients with an army of threatening enforcers. One of Britain's biggest payday lenders increased its profits thirty-two-fold in the years after the 2008 recession, while nine of the ten biggest payday lenders saw their turnover double in the three years after 2010.[9] Since then, the industry has been reined in somewhat by tighter legislation, but the desperation that leads many people to seek out high-interest loans in the first place remains.

I got chatting with the Morgans, a local family who lived in a poky house on the road to Merthyr Tydfil. The Morgans were what you might call a typical low-income family. Mr Morgan was a former miner who had silicosis of the lungs caused by the inhalation of coal dust over many years. He had received a small amount of compensation for this, and nowadays spent most of his time sat, taciturn and head bowed, in a tatty felt armchair which stood in the corner of the square living room near the gas fire.

Mrs Morgan worked part time in a local shop, while their son, who was in his early forties, was unemployed; although he did do occasional cash-in-hand work for an odd-jobbing friend. The son had recently brought home a new television for the family from one of the large rent-to-own companies after the old set had packed up. These shops sell sofas, televisions and hi-fis to those with bad credit scores at huge mark-ups. More than 400,000 households used the rent-to-own sector in 2016, a 131 per cent increase since 2008.[10] You buy now (at high interest and usually with a mandatory warranty) and very often regret later.

Mr Morgan, who had little else to occupy him, needed his 'news and rugby', his wife told me. The television set that Mr Morgan's son had purchased was worth around £150, yet by the time the repayments for it were finished it would have cost the family about £400.

On its own this may have been unfortunate, but it was fairly unexceptional. However, the set had a fault: when it was switched on it would flicker like the projector of a cine camera. The company had promised to send somebody out to look at it but nobody had ever come. I joined the family one evening for several cups of tea. The four of us sat down in front of this big television, which flickered violently as an announcer from the BBC read out the evening news. You went away afterwards cross-eyed and sharply aware of the fact that the family had paid £400 for this. For its part, the store was still demanding the weekly payments on time, and a member of staff from the local branch would phone up religiously each week to convey the importance of making the weekly payments promptly – or else risk incurring a 'penalty charge' that would be bolted on to an already exorbitant rate of interest.

What was striking about the whole episode was the helpless position of the family. The television set was really a side issue, but it neatly illustrated one of the fixes that many of the people I encountered found themselves in. Whether it was the employment agency underpaying you, the job centre messing you about or the rent-to-own store trying to bamboozle you, there was often this exhausting running battle with the authorities taking place behind the scenes. It was an accepted part of life, like bread and milk being on the shelf in the shops. Mrs Morgan, meanwhile, seemed almost entirely preoccupied with the security of the house.

'You've gotta be like a prison in the house; you've gotta make sure your security is high, because you just don't know who's who,' she said to me as she clambered unsteadily down the house's narrow staircase carrying a box of Christmas decorations for the small plastic tree in the window.

'My nephew put a big fence from the end of our building to the wall next door, with all the spikes along the top. Marvellous, best thing ever that was out there. But mind, touch wood, I've never had a problem with anybody in the garden. Nothing.'

At Admiral, when I finally received my first wage packet, three weeks after my start date, I was paid £936.44 after tax. It had by that point already cost me £800 to secure a place to live: £500 for rent, £200 for the damage deposit and £100 for the miscellaneous 'agent's fee'. This was not a full month's wage, as by that point I'd only worked three rather than four weeks; I would have to wait until just before Christmas before I received a full month's salary –

almost two months after starting work. For those who do not live with parents or partners who might be able to lend them money, it is hard to imagine how anyone could survive through that long period from the start of November to the middle of December with so little cash coming in. For those without children, the state is not a great deal of help either. For a single adult without children, my before-tax salary of £14,500 a year brought me in at just above the threshold for working tax credits, even though my take-home wage after deductions was a mere £13,027 – £4,000 less than the Joseph Rowntree Foundation's recommended amount for a minimum standard of living. The base rate of pay was also no better at Admiral than it had been at either Amazon or Carewatch, though I was earning slightly more now than earlier in the year thanks to the increase in the minimum wage from £6.50 to £7.20 for anyone aged twenty-five or over. The fact that the previous government had raised the Personal Allowance figure to £10,000 was also a big help.

The silver lining at Admiral was the fact that the basic salary was supplemented by a company share scheme and dividends, which were paid out bi-annually. 'If you're bringing in the profits you're bumping up your share price,' one of the trainers said to encourage us. Yet staff had to remain in employment for three years from the date of the award of the shares to see any benefit from them. Many didn't. The average staff turnover rate at Admiral was 19 per cent a year, compared to a UK average of 15 per cent. I suspected that most of us, even those who did plan on sticking around for the long term, would have preferred a decent basic salary rather than sweets, parties and dividends which may or may not pay out at some point in the future. I was subsequently told by a shop steward from the Unite union, someone who had previously worked in call centres, that it was normal for many companies to 'use all those tricks really as a way of circumventing actually paying people a living wage'.

At Admiral we had to work on the phones from eight in the morning until five in the afternoon, keeping us in the office for an hour longer than many similar jobs. We were entitled to an hour's break for lunch, which was bookended by two fifteen-minute breaks. The work itself resembled the job of Frits van Etgers, the sardonic youth who whittles his time away in an office in Gerard Reve's novel *The Evenings*: 'I work in an office. I take the cards out of a file. Once I have taken them out, I put them back in again. That is it.' In my case, I picked up the phone and I put it back again. I woke up at half past six in the morning, I showered, ate cereal, got dressed (you could wear what you wanted at work, which was nice), and I made my way to the office by eight o'clock. Or most of the time I did: I received a peremptory dressing-down – a brisk warning delivered in a side-office by two of the trainers – for being late during my second week. Paradoxically, it turned into a real effort to drag myself in to an environment where I knew I would be sitting down for the entire day. The tedium was severe, and can only compare with certain dreaded lessons back at school, though at least then there wasn't such an acute feeling that you were doing it all for the sake of someone else's bottom line.

During my training period I sat in the same place for about seven hours a day in a classroom behind a desktop computer. We were instructed how to use the customer database, given the various customer scripts that we had to memorise and taken through the ins and outs of the law in terms of selling insurance. We were occasionally summoned into the call centre itself – to listen in on calls initially and as the weeks passed to practise with each other and then with real customers. The call centre was huge, loud and boisterous. It contained banks of hundreds of lightly partitioned desks and there were whiteboards dotted about the place like road traffic signs. On each of the desks there were usually the customer scripts Blu-tacked to the backs of the partitions, along with a worker's personal effects such as photos of their children or spouses. Dotted about the office there was a mass of the saccharine tat you see nowadays in garden centres and in those 'quirky' and 'ironic' souvenir gift shops you only ever visit at Christmas. 'Keep Calm and Drink Prosecco'; 'Dream it, Live it, Love it'; 'Love is all you Need', etc. This thought-terminating cocktail of uplift seems to have spread like a particularly contagious disease in recent years, and it is hard not to view it as a soothing palliative churned out en masse with a particular end in mind. Religion no longer has much of a hold over young people in Britain, yet some of its fatalism has been cleverly appropriated by consumer capitalism. Of course, 'Life is crap so get drunk' is not a bad motto, but it is hardly an adequate way to live when someone else decides how much money you have in your pocket to go out drinking in the first place. This sort of thing is at root a call to stop thinking, a homely retreat to an isle of fatalism dressed up as liberation, whereas times like these demand one's full engagement with the world. There was an attempt to encourage worker participation in the call centre, but only in the sense of company-centric 'fun' and 'theme days', where staff were encouraged to wear fancy dress in to the office. One Friday afternoon we were told that the rest of the work day would be broken up by 'fun activities'. This involved everyone on our floor of the call centre being divided into groups of five or six people. One group at a time was then tasked with performing a five-minute play while the rest stood around watching and singing bizarre songs – more hypnotic recitals – about the company from scripts that were handed out by management. I wouldn't describe it as an enjoyable experience, despite the fact that it meant we were away from our desks – the songs had a definite whiff of the ode to the tyrant you sometimes hear in authoritarian countries. Nor was I alone in feeling slightly perturbed at being pressed into this company-ordained horseplay – most of my colleagues radiated a definite waiting air while the whole thing, which took around two hours, carried on. The entire performance represented a very specific form of 'participation' which seemed like an attempt, conscious or not, to undercut the fact that we had no real chance to participate in the running of the enterprise. We were almost – though not quite – the crowds bussed into the town square of the tin-pot dictatorship to smile, wave flags and sing ditties to the great and wise benefactor. The admonition to 'not take things too seriously' is not always as subversive as it sounds, though in recognising that one obviously has to be wary of turning into a sort of Marx-spouting Victor Meldrew.

The management in call centres are often very effective at winning workers over to their point of view – even as the company continues to exploit them. The giant carrot dangled in front of your eyes at Admiral was the chance to take home a healthy slice of commission. This was your incentive to sell insurance policies, but it was also the only way you were ever going to put any significant distance between yourself and all the people who wanted money from you for essentials like a bed, heating and things to eat. Estimates fluctuated wildly as to how much you could earn on top of the basic salary at Admiral depending on who one spoke to. 'One guy made £1,400 [in a month],' I was told by a young man whose calls I was instructed to listen in on during training. Typically, though, I believe that most people made an extra £200 or £400 a month if they did well. The 'average incentive', according to the company, was £3,000 a year, which worked out at around an extra £250 a month before tax. Doing well meant holding onto customers who phoned up wanting to cancel their policies. Every intake of employees formed part of a 'team', and these teams were encouraged to compete with one another in terms of who could retain the most customers.

It was all straightforward enough, yet there was a constant feeling that if you failed to hit your targets the mask of joviality would slip away to reveal a more hard-hearted capitalism. There was, the trainer told us, a 'very Big Brother eye' watching us at all times. 'They've got three eyes down there,'[11] he speculated sinisterly, gesticulating towards the ground floor of the building.

The worst aspect of the job – and the downside to most work of this kind – was the sheer tedium of it. You sat in a swivel chair from eight till five taking call after call after call from customers who were (somewhat predictably) unhappy with the amount of money leaving their bank accounts. Working with the public for any length of time always has the potential to turn even the most serene person into a bitter misanthrope. I took home very little money, and I was supposed to get through on sweets, chocolates, a few perks – discount rates at the gym, shares – and a big end-of-year party, where a free bar (not bad, granted) and cameos by second-rate celebrities would lift our hearts even if they could not pay our rent. In three years' time I might receive a pay-out from the shares, but that would depend on how they performed in the meantime, which I had very little power to affect.

Yet the attitude among my workmates towards politics of any kind was dismissive. 'The government loves to put taxes up. They've got to pay for all their expenses,' remarked a colleague during our first week. 'I don't get involved in debates because it's not worth it,' he later said with a shrug. Politics was for other people – a realm in which people like us did not belong. Another colleague asked if the Prime Minister was 'that MP woman'. To be actively interested in the affairs of the state would have marked you down as a bit of an oddball. It was something that was *done to you*, rather than a topic you took any real interest in. Political decisions were something others took, while you let the arguments wash over you along with everything else emitted by 'them' – politicians, the taxman, landlords, the men and women who read out the Six O'Clock News, the company that billed you for your mobile phone, the moth-eaten busybodies who turned up religiously to local council and Neighbourhood Watch meetings. Politicians were in it for themselves, and it was a sign of something worse if they were not – the mark of a fanatic. The tremendous effort that Admiral went to to make work fun was really an attempt to portray themselves as one of *us* rather than one of *them*.

13

The 'post-work' world has become a media talking point now that the jobs of affluent professionals are threatened with automation. Yet there are parts of Britain that have long inhabited something resembling a 'post-work' realm. Indeed, at times the Valleys look an awful lot like a precursor to an automated – and therefore jobless – future. Putting a little bit more money into people's pockets would have been welcome, certainly; but few here believed it would solve the myriad problems that stemmed from the loss of work. 'Flash' was seventy-two when I met him,[12] and had worked across the South Wales Valleys in four big state-owned pits and eighteen private mines over forty years. A short-ish, solidly built man with a kindly face, Flash had deep smile lines above a whitish grey moustache and a pinched mouth. Below a cropped head of hair of the same colour sat intelligent, piercing eyes. Flash's hands were dotted with miners' tattoos – the blue scars that adorn the flesh of every miner where coal dust had penetrated holes in the skin like sand after a day at the beach. He first went underground in 1959 when he was fifteen.

'That's all we wanted ... just come down here, and there was a bus, and just get off up by there and go to work.'

When you went down the pit in those days you went down with an older man, an experienced collier – or a 'butty' as they were called. They trained you up and stopped you getting yourself killed before you'd handed your first wage envelope to your mother. Some of the butties Flash worked with when he started were ex-soldiers who had been interned in the Burmese jungle during the Second World War. When they washed their backs in the pithead baths, you could still see the red scarring on their skin from the bayonets of the Japanese.

'And this was a land fit for heroes. And there they was being robbed down there on the coalface. By the governments, all governments.'

I met Flash at the South Wales Miners' Museum in Afan Argoed, which sits amid the winding roads and steep slopes of the Afan Valley above Port Talbot, where the hills are lined with a carpet of pines, oaks and Sitka spruce. We sat and drank tea in the museum's brightly lit visitors' cafe.

'I came down here [to the museum] because I enjoy doing it. I know a lot of boys who worked in the mines – well, lots of my mates are dead – but some of them [are] drinking, there's one or two stays in the house, you don't see them, they don't even wash. They don't do nothing and their wives have died and they [are] by themselves.'

We perched on soft chairs as a young waitress buzzed around us, busily picking up mugs and wiping down tables. Flash, who wore a moss-green jumper, was leaning forward, pulling scraps of information from his memory and unloading them in a soft, slightly throaty voice. His real name is Allan Price, but when he was a young lad he was given the nickname and it stuck.

'I was playing rugby on the wing. And I was running with the ball and I looked behind and I seen these two bloody monsters running at me, and that's why they call me Flash,' he said, emitting a chuckle. 'But you should've seen them; they had hair on their elbows.'

I went underground myself in Blaenavon at the Big Pit National Coal Museum. Five of us were tentatively lowered down the 300-foot-deep mineshaft into the pitch black and dripping caverns of the huge cave in a benign re-enactment of the miners' daily commute. Flicking off the light on my helmet, I experienced a darkness so total that it was impossible to see the two fingers I held up directly in front of my face. It was almost suffocating. Of course, descending into that preserved old mine could not compare with dragging yourself off in the middle of the night, going down below the hills in a filthy cage and digging out the black gold which allowed those above to sleep serenely in their beds. Our experience was more akin to a theme park – albeit one with a purpose beyond pure physical exhilaration.

'When I started in 1959 it was 800 yards deep ... And you're going down there twenty-two metres per second, you're dropping ... *whooosh* ... Your guts is in your mouth.'

Flash grinned mischievously as he told me about his shattered nerves on the very first day underground. He wore an ill-fitting helmet jammed down upon his head and a belt tucked tightly around his waist. His sandwiches were squeezed into a little tin box which protected them from vermin. One of the men gave the signal and the cage rapidly descended into the musty and fetid darkness of the pit.

'[I was] excited more than frightened. I think it was bravado ... We was getting there, looking at each other, didn't know what was gonna happen, didn't know if the bottom was gonna come off or you're gonna jump down on a parachute or what.'

Once inside the bowels of the mountain the colliers would usually have to walk – 'a mile, mile and a half, two miles' – along a black, narrow tunnel to reach the coal seam where they would begin the back-breaking work, ducking always in order to avoid the lumps of rock and metal that jutted menacingly out of the roof. The jagged teeth of the machine which cut the coal tore violently into the mountainside, ripping off shards of black rock and throwing up dirty great clouds of glistening dust which found its way into every orifice of your body. The miners would go home with blackened faces and dirty lungs, their irate wives engaging in a futile struggle to expel every particle from the house. The dust would eventually enter the men's airwaves and silt up their chests like the delta of a river. The body's immune system would then attack it, causing inflammation which gradually hardened the lungs until, over the years, it left you flat on your back gasping for breath. By the time Flash finished underground in 1999, he had lost 30 per cent of the capacity of his lungs. By 2014 only 30 per cent of his lungs were still healthy.

'It takes a hold on your lungs. It's there, it grows ...'

Flash would joke about it to visitors to the museum: 'I've left strict orders now to be cremated, and I'll be there [burning] all day. A ton of coal today must be [worth] a hundred and thirty-odd pound, good coal, black diamond as they say. They can put me there [and] I'll be there [burning] for three days.'

Pit life is often romanticised, but few miners wanted their own sons or daughters to go underground. Men toiled under the earth for twelve hours a day; and until the pits were nationalised, they were usually paid according to the amount of coal they dug out. In the nineteenth century, miners were not always paid in cash at all, but in tokens that could only be spent in the 'Truck Shops' owned by their bosses, where prices were invariably steeper than in the local markets.

Death stalked the underground tunnels and shafts of the pits. The chances of me dying on the job at Amazon or out visiting an elderly client in Blackpool were about as likely as Swansea City winning football's Premier League. In contrast, men frequently died underground. When George Orwell went down the pit in Wigan in 1936, there was an average of 134 deaths per 100,000 miners.[13] Prior to that, the figure was higher still. One former miner I spoke to in Rugeley told me that, during an eighteen-month period at a nearby pit, one man was dragged into the belt rollers and another was crushed by a runaway wagon, causing his thigh bone to be pushed up into his abdomen until it burst through the skin covering his stomach. Both men were killed. Just down the road from Rugeley, at the Hamstead Colliery in Great Barr, a total of 144 men perished during the period the pit produced coal between 1878 and 1965. Some died in explosions, flooding and mechanical errors, while others were buried under several hundredweight of earth after a sudden roof collapse. The worst disaster in British mining history occurred at Senghenydd, Glamorgan, in 1913, when an explosion wiped out 439 men and boys, devastating the local community. The disaster at Senghenydd typified the negligence of the private owners when it came to the safety of the men who dug out the black gold that lined their pockets. Another explosion caused by high levels of airborne coal dust had killed eighty-two men in the same pit twelve years earlier. Yet recommendations from an inquiry into the initial disaster were never implemented. After the second big explosion, the manager of the mine was charged with negligence and fined £24 – the equivalent of £2,500 in today's money. The life of a miner at the time was valued by the British establishment at five and a half pence.[14]

'There's holes in the ground where I've walked in and rats have been dragged swimming out, you know ... Very little oxygen, black bag full of air, breathe that,' Flash told me.

Most of the miners I spoke to said that conditions like this were more common in the private mines, which continued to exist in pockets even after nationalisation. Ron, one of the ex-miners I went underground with in Blaenavon, told me that the manager of a private mine he worked in as late as the 1990s used to smoke underground, despite the obvious risk of an explosion with all the noxious gases swirling around.

'When I was working in the NCB [National Coal Board] there was an inspector in our face once a month, and if he thought something was wrong he'd say, "I'll give you a week to put that right, and if I come back in a week and it's not done I'll close the pit." So everything was kept up to date, you know what I mean? I was in the private mine for three years. I seen the inspector *twice*.'

But the National Coal Board could be just as bungling and inept as any private owner: it was the criminal negligence of the NCB in failing to remove a dangerous spoil-tip which led to the disaster at Aberfan in 1966, when 116 children and twenty-eight adults were killed as 360,000 tons of thick black slurry cascaded down the mountainside and crashed into a farm, houses and Pantglas Junior School, suffocating those inside. In the aftermath of the tragedy, the NCB resisted the elimination of what remained of the tip and when Harold Wilson's government eventually gave in to pressure from the residents of Aberfan to remove it, they raided the disaster fund to pay for it.

On Friday 2 February 1990, Flash was working alongside three other men at Cefn Mawr No. 2, a small mine in the Afan Valley. They'd started work first thing and by midday had filled thirteen drams, the containers that carried the coal out of the mine. They returned to the surface for a twenty-minute tea break before going back down. Two of the men made their way to the coalface while Flash and another miner, Terry, bored holes in the heading to open new sections of the face.

'Next thing, whoosh, I felt air coming back,' Flash said. 'The top had come down in there ... And I could hear somebody shouting, "Flash, Flash, Flash."'

Flash and Terry crawled into the hole and found one of the men – David – screaming in pain. A huge boulder had fallen from somewhere in the roof and lacerated his skin. But it was Raymond that the stone had fallen directly on top of.

'His head was just out, and all [his body] was covered. So I had this young guy pass this steel railing, like a lever so I could lever it ... So I was trying to lever it up, but you gotta watch [the roof]. So I thought if I [get it up] just a little bit I'd get him out, pull him out.'

But the boulder was too heavy.

'[The roof] started coming down then, so I crouched over him like that [to shelter him] ... but he died then. I crouched over him until he died.'

More men arrived with a car jack and Flash used it to dislodge the boulder and pull Raymond out. He was placed on a stretcher and taken to the surface. Raymond was the last miner killed in the last working mine in the Afan Valley. Flash had to break the news to his distraught mother.

'Single boy he was ... She was *old* and ... broke her heart, didn't it? When I went out there I looked at him then, opened the sock to have a look at him. [He had] cut his eye, nothing much, because I stopped the bleeding underground, put my finger on it, you know.'

Flash was back at work the next morning and had a memorial plaque placed at the entrance of the mine. On the anniversary of Raymond's death he visited the site of the accident with a bouquet of flowers. He brought the plaque with him when he started volunteering at the museum, and today he shows it to visitors as he takes them round.

After the First World War the collieries had been denationalised by the government of David Lloyd George. Investment in mechanised cutting and conveying subsequently dried up, resulting in a long period of stagnation in the industry. Colliery owners blamed the slump on the miners themselves, and in 1925 announced plans to cut miners' pay and lay men off as their dividends shrank. As a result, unemployment in the industrial areas never fell below a million in the 1920s, and continued to ravage many areas throughout the 1930s. Between 1928 and 1936,

24 per cent of miners were either wholly or partly out of work.[15] This prompted a wave of worker unrest. By 1920 the Miners' Federation of Great Britain (MFGB) had grown to 900,000 men – 45 per cent of mineworkers belonged to a trade union by this point. The growing unrest among the miners resulted in a nine-day General Strike in 1926 and the deployment of the full force of the state against them. The BBC refused to broadcast anything on behalf of either the trade unions or the Labour Party. Leading socialists and communists were thrown in jail. The army was sent out to patrol the streets. The TUC eventually capitulated to the government on the basis of assurances (later disowned) that talks over miners' pay and conditions would resume if they went back to work.

The miners had lost the strike, but their demands gradually fed into the Parliamentary Labour Party. A walk-out by 100,000 Welsh miners in 1944 won an increase in the minimum wage for miners that had first been secured by the 1912 Coal Mines Act.[16] The Coal Industry Nationalisation Act 1946, enacted by the newly elected government of Clement Attlee, brought the industry into public ownership for the first time during peacetime. Subsequent investment in modern machinery improved productivity, as did the amalgamation – or 'rationalisation', as it was called at the time – of smaller pits into economies of scale where more than a thousand men worked.

But the golden age would not last long. As coal was supplanted by cheaper fuels such as North Sea oil and gas, the industry slipped into the decline from which it has never recovered. Domestic demand withered with the switch to diesel and electric in place of steam power on the railways and the modernisation of central heating systems. It also became cheaper to import coal from countries with weak trade unions and fewer scruples about sending children underground and paying poverty wages.

'There's nine-year-old boys dragging it out in sacks in Colombia,' Flash told me matter-of-factly when I asked him about the loss of the industry.

Between 1957 and 1964, 264 collieries closed. Following that some 300 pits were closed by the first Labour government of Harold Wilson. At its peak the coal industry employed over a million men, but by the 1980s Britain's state-owned coal industry had contracted so that it employed 171,000 miners at 170 collieries around the country. Its total workforce (including white-collar staff) was around 221,000.[17]

Yet even with the workforce much-depleted, government ministers in the 1980s knew that the sudden closure of the pits would destroy communities, for most of the jobs in the industry were concentrated in a dozen or so areas. Thus while the pit closures of the 1980s were the culmination of a larger trend, Margaret Thatcher saw them as a way to hobble the trade unions and to avenge the NUM, in particular, for its role in bringing down the previous Tory government. During the subsequent strike of 1984–5, Britain's press showered the miners with invective in a way reminiscent of the 'cowardly scribblers' depicted by the poet Idris Davies in his 1926 poem 'The Angry Summer':

> *Here is Arthur Cook, a red rose in his lapel ...*
> *And tomorrow in all the hostile papers*
> *there will be sneers at Cook and all his capers*

Arthur Scargill was no Arthur Cook, and was still dividing opinion among the miners when I was in South Wales. 'I thought he was all right, to be honest with you. I thought he was doing good,' said Aiden[18], an ex-miner at the Merthyr Tydfil Labour Club. Another former miner, Selwyn,[19] believed that neither Mrs Thatcher nor Arthur Scargill 'gave a shit for anybody'.

'She didn't worry about the miners and I don't think he worried about the miners as well. He's doing all right now; he'd always have done all right, mind, Arthur Scargill. It's all right and very well for him to get up and say "don't go to work" and this and that.'

During the strike the miners were transformed almost overnight by the media from 'the best men in the world, who beat the Kaiser's and Hitler's armies and never gave in',[20] to the 'diluted human residues', as one commentator described them in the *Sunday Times* in August 1984.[21] As the twentieth century edged towards its close, being working class was going out of fashion faster than flared trousers and big hair. During the stand-off with Mrs Thatcher, the police were deployed as a political force against the miners as they had been in the 1920s, administering beatings and questioning those they arrested about their political views and which newspapers they read.

'I was in Aberavon ... and we was having a nice friendly chat with a policeman,' Flash told me, 'and this one is lovely. I thought, "There's a nice guy." I seen him an hour later [and] he was beating this blimin' picket down the line, on the floor. Since then I've never trusted the police. One minute he was laughing with us, the next he was beating a boy on the floor.'

The South Wales miners had initially voted to continue working, but Flash says striking miners from Kent came down and persuaded them to walk out too.

'On the Monday morning when I was going to work we seen there was some boys there, from Kent, on the picket line. Well, we all looked at each other like this and one of the men then tipped his water out, and that's it, we wouldn't cross the line ... we've gotta support them. We wouldn't cross a picket line and that's for sure.'

Flash soon found himself taking part in what one local newspaper described as 'one of the most spectacular industrial actions ever seen'. Along with a hundred other men, he scaled a 300-foot-high crane at Port Talbot to stop 30,000 tons of American coal being unloaded to keep the local steelworks in production and undermine the strike.[22]

'I drove a van up there with men in, a hundred and one of us was there, and when it was unloading we ran up the cranes and all the steelworkers was running off, and as we was going up we put barbed wire right around the legs of the three of them [cranes], commando-style.'

Flash was so high up that when he looked down he could see a police helicopter flying below. He was eventually coaxed down with the other men after the NUM managed to negotiate for them to have a hot meal in their cells before questioning by the police. The men subsequently appeared in court in Swansea in what made history as the largest number of people to be charged with a single offence at the same time.

'Hundred and one of us, and we had two policemen each to guide us ... We was there, and the laugh was that there was this guy there, you know, lag, and he had done three months or something in jail [before]. And the judge sends him another three months. And he [the judge] said, "What do you say?" And he said, "Beam me up, Scotty." And we all burst out laughing.'

The judge gave Flash and the other men suspended sentences. Flash was still worried, though.

'I was worried about my job. Thirty years in so far, and if I was going now they were not going to pay me my redundancy or nothing ... But I was all right ... We had our redundancy money, we didn't care a damn. Thirty grand in our pockets, some of us, because we'd been there a long time. But you know, I'd rather have a job.'

After the strike finished Flash decided he had had enough. The times were changing, and what it meant to be working class was changing too.

'I couldn't really wait to finish. I knew [it was closing], it wasn't the same. There was bosses there that thought coal was white. They didn't talk the same as us. I think they come off a different planet, you know. I call it the year of the nasty men. And that's what they were. It wasn't like the old managers, who'd have a laugh and "all right, boy" and all that ... A laugh and decency, and that's on both sides, you know.'

Flash said he always tried to go to work happy.

'Work is a lot easier [like that]. Because once you're facing seven and a half yards of coal every morning it's like a nightmare. Be happy, get on with it ... and that's the way to do it, otherwise it's not worth it and you may as well stay in the house. That's all I was there for: to fill my coal, put my timber up, [make] where I work safe. And it's there for the following day, and that's the right way to be, you know.'

The decline of deep mining was probably inevitable, but in those places where the industry was wound down almost overnight, the market failed to see enough potential profit in the people left behind to replace it with anything.

'Years ago around here, anything wrong up in our valley the women and kids would be marching down the road, stop the buses, this and that, they'd soon have something ... Today the youngsters are not like us. I was a communist when I was fourteen.'

Flash told me the worst legacy of the pit closures was still unemployment as well as drug and alcohol abuse.

'There's a lot on social, there's a lot ill and everything else. It's sad, you know ... And everybody in my village will tell you they know them, they're out seven days a week drinking whatever ... Before they go to the doctor they drink two cans ... And lots of them come from good men, and good families, hard-working ... Some of my family have moved away to Swansea, Neath.'

Life underground, where death was omnipresent, potentially lurking in the next roof cavity or pit shaft, had the power to bind men together like the braiding of a copper cable. Selwyn told me emphatically that given the chance he would 'go back tomorrow' because 'everybody stuck together, no matter what'.

You were physically safer in many of the jobs in the new economy – only middle-class pseudo revolutionaries pined for the children of the men I met in Merthyr Tydfil to be sent back down beneath the mountains. Yet the jobs in the town today often lacked the solidarity and support networks of the past, let alone the stability propitious to family life.

Selwyn told me how his nephew had lost his job at a local factory. He had been looking for something else 'for months and months'.

'And then I seen him in town one day and he was excited. "I got a job, I got a job, Selwyn!" he said. I said, "What's that doing?" "In B&Q; sixteen hours a week." But it was eight till twelve of a day. They phoned him up and they said, "Come in for four hours today."'

Flash told me before I left that every day he still thought about life underground. 'The comradeship, the laughter. Sad times, mind, but good days. It was a good, good comradeship. You wouldn't get better than that, I think, because you didn't know if you turn your back you're dead. So you just as well as say we lived for today, or we lived for the moment. You know, I really enjoyed it. The Valleys are a lot poorer without them guys ... Education is everything, but you've still got to have somebody to use a shovel ... a pen is no good for clearing clay out or anything.'

14

The equivalent of a shovel in South Wales today is arguably a telephone headset.[23]

Across the UK as a whole, more than a million people work in call centres. In Wales there are more than 200 call centres employing around 30,000 people and contributing £650 million to the economy. [24]

The sorts of jobs that once gave local communities their identities are gone. Or at least most of them are – there is still an ongoing fight to save what is left of Wales's steel industry. The disappearance of dirty and physical industry has had positive effects too: the Valleys were a lot cleaner when I was there than they were a few decades ago. The surrounding countryside looked something like it must have done before belching chimneys and giant filthy mounds of black took over and came to symbolise the might of the industrialised world. Many of the threatening and unsightly spoil-tips have long been removed or reshaped, and the streams run clear and contain life.

You are also much safer in a call centre. You can turn up at the office, sit at your desk and switch to robot mode. Then you go home again. Today, you fight your greatest battles with a wall of boredom rather than a threatening coal seam.

And aside from the paucity of the salary, Admiral could be an enjoyable place to work. It did not resemble the battery farm or 'dark satanic mill' that call centres – or customer contact centres, as they now liked to call themselves – have been melodramatically labelled by some. The contrived culture of 'fun' may have eventually grown tiresome, but I had worked in worse places. The main thing to note about the generosity on display at Admiral was its essential precarity. The most sustainable employer benefits have historically been squeezed out of companies by their workers, typically through the activity of trade unions. Benevolent companies, where kind-hearted bosses shower perks on their staff like confetti, have existed as long as capitalism itself. Yet this is comparable perhaps to life under a benevolent dictator: a usurper might just as easily come along and sweep everything away. The benefits the company lavished on us could easily have been got rid of if doing so was thought to improve 'productivity'. Also, I suspect that most of my colleagues would have happily eschewed the sweets and chocolates and parties for a modest increase in their basic salary. Being treated well at work was nice; however, we would surely have been on firmer ground had we wrung those benefits out of the company ourselves. Then it would have been within our power to resist had the company tried to snatch anything back.

The situation in some call centres is, of course, worse than anything I experienced at Admiral. In order to coax firms to keep their call centres in Wales – rather than relocate offshore to places like India – companies have trumpeted the purported 'flexibility' of the workforce (see: part-time, casual, poorly paid). Cardiff houses many of Wales's biggest call centres, and a lady called June, who worked at another outsourcing call centre, relayed to me just how stressful this sort of environment could sometimes be.

'[The staff] get stressed because the targets for sales and all that ... And there's other things in the job that you gotta promote, so I still have to promote, and I still have to be on target, and sometimes that can be stressful ... people stay home ill and different things because they just fed up or end up leaving.'

Some call centres operate a system of overarching surveillance that has been compared by the academics Sue Fernie and David Metcalf to the 'electronic panopticon'[25] – a system of management in which every action is monitored, tracked and logged. The panopticon was a model of prison devised in the eighteenth century by the philosopher Jeremy Bentham, in which surveillance was absolute. Because inmates of Bentham's imaginary prison believed they were being observed at all times, they internalised the objectives of their gaolers, behaving in line with management prerogatives as if they were being watched – even when they were not.

'The team leader listens to your call and marks your call, marks your performance and that ... if your ACW is too high, [or] if you stay too long on the call, it will lead to you having a disciplinary.'

ACW stood for After-Call Work, the various tasks a worker had to perform during and after the call, such as logging any details passed on by the customer or recording the outcome of the call. Making too much small talk with a customer or spending too long recording the outcome of the call could at some companies result in a disciplinary.

'I haven't had a disciplinary, thanks be to God, but ... it looks to me like a threat, you know. And sometimes you can't help that because sometimes the customer wants to talk, and it's hard then to really ... you can't cut in and you have to listen to them and sometimes they take longer than usual, and, you know, you'll be stuck, and that's what they [the company] don't like.'

Even at Admiral there were league tables based on the performances of staff on the phones, making clear who was doing well and not so well in terms of customer retention. The system of mutual competition could be very stressful for some workers, while others thrived under it. June told me that some of her younger colleagues, the men especially, could get ultra-competitive over sales, which in turn spurred them on to increase the firm's bottom line.

None of this, though, resembled a world of fully 'augmented' human beings. Looming over the horizon may be a future in which employees are monitored around the clock so that their bosses can keep track of things like mental state, sleeping patterns and workplace conversations. The Chinese government is already in the process of creating a huge system which gives every citizen a social credit score. If dystopia is in our future it is almost certainly found here, in the creed of meritocratic productivism, rather than in the nightmares of Philip Roth or Sinclair Lewis, who envisioned a return to racialised fascism. You already get a sense that certain tech corporations are working towards this kind of beehive society in which a citizen's merit is calculated on the basis of their contribution to the growth of the nation's economy or the balance sheet of the firm. But while the future may look more like the *Rise of the Meritocracy* than *Nineteen Eighty-Four*, it had not arrived in South Wales when I was there.

The reality was more prosaic. The level of surveillance we were subjected to did not preclude trade union activity or worker resistance. Indeed, some element of monitoring is inevitable in any business where the majority of the interactions take place over the phone. The real struggle was to confine such monitoring to the workplace, whether by refusing to answer work-related emails and telephone calls outside of hours or resisting broader attempts to turn workers into mere tools of the company in their free time. The problems experienced by workers in call centres are typically more dull than dystopian, and revolve around things like toilet breaks and management bullying. For example, most of June's problems seemed to be concerned with the company's reluctance to accommodate her disabilities and the lengths of the breaks.

'I'm anaemic and I'm diabetic as well ... they [the company] were being very funny with me before, that's why I tried to get the union involved ... and it's just that I have to rush to eat and it's hard ... and you can't eat at your desk ... You have to go to the break room and by the time you do all that and get back to your desk sometimes it's not feasible, you know.'

In truth, the greatest impediment to collective organisation in a call centre environment is probably the apathy of the workforce, especially among younger workers, who often do not know even what a trade union is. Society is far more broken down and atomised than it was, say, forty or fifty years ago. The idea of collective strength is an alien concept for many; problems are solved in isolation or through managerialism masquerading as 'teamwork'. There are also the practical challenges that have seen trade unions reduced to rump organisations increasingly confined to the public sector. Back at somewhere like Amazon, organising workers who often intended only to stay in Britain for as little as a month presented an obvious challenge. Why bother giving up even a few pounds when, by the time your union forms have come back, you would be on the coach home? And unless the union had a worker in the factory already, it can be very hard to organise from the inside – you are reduced to standing outside the premises sheepishly handing out leaflets. Most of the workers I spoke to also believed that the companies they worked for would punish them if they got wind of trade union activity.

Besides this, at Admiral there was a layer of staff who were paid slightly more than us but who had the ear of the management. It was very hard to get away from these people. They were a constant, lingering presence, like wasps around an open pot of jam. The way in which authority descended in a slow gradient was a stroke of genius. On the one hand, it made it easier to get any concerns you might have dealt with – there was always someone there to pass any concerns up the chain. But the ubiquitous presence of a team leader could also thwart any collective action on the part of the workforce. I had to be far more careful at Admiral in terms of revealing my identity than in previous jobs, for the simple reason that we were rarely separated from a member of staff who was in direct contact with those above us. He or she was your colleague and your mate; but they were something else, too. You were not quite equal, and your interests were not quite the same.

I suppose what I learned at Admiral was that even dull jobs could be made bearable for the workforce without any real cost to employers. Working in the retentions department of a car insurance firm was as dull as I had expected it to be. Yet the company did make a serious effort to ensure that it was not the sort of workplace that, sat at home watching *Coronation Street* in the evening, you dreaded returning to the next day. It was tolerable, and most of the staff I spoke to seemed if not to enjoy it then at least not to find it too oppressive, even if *I* thought they should be paid more. But even at 'good' companies like Admiral there were, for the most part, few trade unions in sight, meaning that there was nothing in place to stop a good company at some point metamorphosing into a bad one. Everything we enjoyed could be whisked away at short notice, like a dummy yanked from the mouth of a helpless child.

15

The crash de-industrialisation of the 1980s left a grim legacy in parts of South Wales. This sense of defeat seeped into your veins in certain towns like the injection of an intravenous drug. This was especially true in Ebbw Vale, the largest town in Blaenau Gwent.

The town took its name from the Ebbw River, which ran almost parallel to the town of Cwm, three miles to the south. As in the north-east, at one time families had flooded into the Valleys from the surrounding areas as industry sprang up and provided plenty of work. In the old parish of Bedwellty, which included Rhymney, Tredegar and parts of Ebbw Vale, the census of 1801 recorded just 619 inhabitants. Yet after the Ebbw Vale Iron Works was founded in 1778, it began to rapidly expand. By the end of the Napoleonic Wars in 1815 the number of inhabitants had trebled to 2,200. By 1891 there were 17,341 people living in Bedwellty. Today in Ebbw Vale alone there are around 33,000 residents.

My first impression of the town was of a forlorn place which, while not squalid in the sense that parts of Blackpool were squalid – there were not homeless people seemingly lurching around every corner – nonetheless had an air of torpor hanging over it which felt as foreboding as the winter fog that clung to the surrounding hills and mountains. These mountains were at one time synonymous with a modest prosperity. But now, the dark December afternoons seemed to exacerbate the prevailing mood.

'All this coal we've got here, you know, [we've] got the steel company by there ... Across the M4 motorway by there, there's multi-million tons of coal, the best coking coal in the world,' Flash had told me. 'Two good colliers could throw that coal over the M4 and into the furnaces.'

But that no longer happens, thanks to the wild fluctuations of the market. And so like many other little towns across the Valleys, Ebbw Vale remains trapped in limbo between an industrial past and a future that has yet to arrive. The first thing to collapse after industry was the general health of the local population. In 2013 it was reported that 10,000 residents of Blaenau Gwent were on some kind of anti-depressant medication. The total population is fewer than 60,000, meaning that one in every six adults was collecting a prescription for drugs like Doxepin, Prozac and Trazodone. When this story first came to light, sections of the media, quick to apportion blame, predictably jumped on the purported generosity of the benefits system and the moral laxity of local GPs. The latter were accused by the *Daily Mail* of handing out anti-depressant tablets 'like sweets'.[26] That said, the newspaper did find one (in its eyes) morally upright local GP who had the right idea in terms of weaning people off the 'happy pills'.

'A very common reason for people wanting to stay on anti-depressants [unnecessarily] is to remain off work,' the doctor told the newspaper confidently. 'They don't want to go to work. If it meant you were going to starve, it would be different. That doesn't happen in this country.'

Put another way, poverty is a moral failing. Rich people will only work if you give them money whereas poor people will only do so if you starve them. The sudden collapse in people's health does not derive from the collapse of industry, but from their own moral laxity. Never mind that many of the social problems seen in the Valleys today were virtually non-existent a few generations ago when local industries were thriving. Very often there simply aren't enough jobs to go around. In 2012, the number of jobs in the South Wales coalfield area per 100 residents of working age was estimated at forty-one. The UK national average at the time was sixty-seven.[27]

'There's no work,' said Geoff, an old former collier who sat wrapped up in a green cardigan out the front of a little cafe on Ebbw Vale high street. We both drew on roll-ups and drank hot tea in the bitter cold while shoppers sauntered past.

'I have always lived here. I worked in the pit, and then from the pit, when it closed, I was in the steelworks,' Geoff rasped between drags.

'As regard to work, there's nothing about here. Have a look in Wetherspoons. Go and have a look. That's where you'll find everybody.'

The first thing I wanted to know upon arriving in the Valleys was how things had changed, not just in the last ten or twenty years, but going back further than that to the middle of the previous century. The picture painted by Geoff rang true when I looked in on the office of the local PMP recruitment agency on the high street. I was familiar with PMP already – they were one of the agencies that sent workers to Amazon. Almost all the jobs advertised in the window were for minimum-wage warehouse skivvies or cleaning jobs on zero-hours contracts.

'I've had the best growing up, let me tell you that,' Geoff told me as we smoked. 'I've had the best growing up of anybody. Everybody my age would say they've had the best growing up because there was plenty of work about. You could jump from one job to the next. Oh aye, no trouble at all. But we had the steelworks going. When they went [the] pit was going, Cwm pit was going, that's only four mile away. There was plenty of work; everything was thriving about here.'

When I visited, the future of the nearby steelworks in Port Talbot was hanging in the balance as the owners, Tata Steel, had recently announced plans to sell up. Fifteen thousand jobs were up in the air: 4,000 workers at the plant itself and thousands more contractors and workers employed in various parts of the supply chain.[28] At one time, steel from the Ebbw Vale works was used to construct the Sydney Harbour Bridge, the Stockton and Darlington railway lines and, rumour has it, the Empire State Building. Blaenau Gwent was the beating heart of British industry, envied the world over. How many schoolchildren in London would believe you if you told them that today?

Locally, of course, the presence of the old industries is still felt, like a deceased relative whose portrait stares down at you ominously from the mantelpiece. The Ebbw Vale steelworks closed for good in 2002. The nearby Marine Colliery in Cwm was the last big deep mine to work in the Ebbw Valley and closed in March 1989. Today the direction of travel is often in the opposite direction to B. L. Coombes's day: you have to leave the Valleys to find a secure and well-paying job.

'Well, it hasn't recovered,' Geoff's younger friend chipped in as we talked about this vanished world. 'A lot of the jobs about here [today] are usually on zero contracts. It's the hassle of sign off the dole, maybe get some hours, [and] if you don't you gotta sign back on the dole. And [when] you sign back on the dole the hassle involved, people don't wanna know ... you gotta have a regular wage coming in, or a certain amount of money coming in, to pay rent and everything.'

'You can't earn it, man; they ain't paying it!' Geoff interposed emphatically as he got up and shuffled towards the cafe's door to go in and get his lunch. 'I got a carer coming to me, he's out the house at six o'clock in the morning. He don't get back till five in the night and he don't earn £30. Now then, how can he keep a family? How can he do it?'

The high street was littered with the sort of fare I had come to expect in small towns like this: pound shops, pawnbrokers, arcades and bookies. I counted three pawnbrokers on the short walk from one end of the street to the other. It seemed strange to think that the thriving city of Bristol sat just thirty-five miles away. Most of those walking around the town looked over fifty, as did almost all the customers sat inside the little cafe when I went back there later on that day and ordered a corned beef and onion sandwich for £2.70. I thought it a curse to be born in a place like Ebbw Vale in the twenty-first century. This may seem harsh, and if it sounds like a judgement on the people who do stay in places like Ebbw Vale to make a life, it isn't meant to.

After my sandwich I went to the pub that Geoff had urged me to visit. A woman overheard me talking to someone and approached to drum home a point that I would hear again and again: *there is no work.*

'All my kids moved away because of the bloody work,' she said emphatically. 'One lives in Northampton and one lives in Cardiff!'

There was work, of course. I had managed to find a job, after all. But some people had an incredibly difficult time of it when it came to customer-facing jobs such as those in the call centre. If you don't have a certain manner and confidence that it's hard to teach, the companies will never take you on. Some young people are raised by parents who did not value education because they never felt they'd needed it themselves. An attitude that believed that you could 'walk into any job' had travelled with them to a future where it is no longer possible to march out of the gates of one factory with your P45 in the morning and have a similar job elsewhere by teatime. But they had imparted that attitude onto their kids, who now found themselves in a professionalised economy where qualifications are everything.

The democratic socialists of the previous century argued primarily for human beings to be put to work. A job could give life a sense of direction and purpose. Unemployment was an evil scourge which could be countered by the arms of the state if people wanted it badly enough. This was not progress in the liberal sense in which tender-hearted elites suddenly noticed the existence of the poor and felt the pangs of conscience. Working-class gains still had to be fought for. Nor was there envisioned a final victory, whether in heavenly paradise or earthly utopia. 'Progress is not the elimination of struggle but a change in its terms,' as Tredegar's most influential son Aneurin Bevan – himself the son of a local miner – had once phrased it. Margaret Thatcher understood this, which is why she set out unwaveringly to smash the power of the trade unions and tip the balance firmly back in favour of the bosses. Rather than being able to 'jump from one job to the next', as Geoff had wistfully put it, the aim was to have ten people chasing each position – all the better to keep wages low and workers on their toes. But Thatcherism's greatest success was probably in the gradual erosion of class solidarity.

'I reckon there's jobs out there for people and they don't wanna work,' one retired drinker told me in the bar in Wetherspoons as I sat next to him nursing a pint of Guinness. 'They're quite happy, they're living with the parents, they're getting the dole money once a fortnight, giving their mam a couple of bob, and the rest is theirs.'

I asked the man what he would do about the people he was talking about, and he demanded irritably that the government take their social security away and 'make them fucking work'.

'Do something, painting fences, anywhere. Don't let them sit in the house with their feet up watching telly ... I left school in 1961 and I worked all my life. I worked all my life. And I had some stinking jobs.'

Quite a few of the conversations in Ebbw Vale developed along these lines. They typically revolved around a contradiction: the person calling for some draconian punishment to be meted out to the unemployed would, in the next breath, remonstrate passionately with me about how difficult it was for the person *he or she* was acquainted with to find work. *Then* it was different, and as with the men who had complained to me in the pubs of Rugeley about migrants, a sense of fear had taken hold which was wildly disproportionate to the reality. The statistics bear this out. Rather than a multi-generational epidemic of worklessness, just 1 per cent of workless households in Britain have two generations who have never worked. Meanwhile, around 4.3 million *working* families are in receipt of benefits or tax credits.[29] Most people living in poverty in Britain today *are going out to work*. Most of the people I met tended to grasp this once you cut through the hearsay gleaned in fragments from the newspapers.

'There's a young lad who comes in on a Saturday and he breaks his heart,' the man continued in a new tone of understanding as we ordered more beer. 'He's working for an agency and ... come this time of the year agency workers are out [laid off]. Or you take Amazon ... all year they've just employed another 3,000 people, or, you know, I'm just saying that as a figure. Come December twenty-second they're gone ... You take my son-in-law, right, he works for a cleaning company, and he travels all over the country. *All over the country.* He might be working three or four days. All of a sudden, now, there's no work coming in. He likes doing that job; the problem is the company he's working for.'

To really understand unemployment – or in this case *underemployment* – you have to go out and talk to the people who are buffeted from pillar to post by its volatility. You have to leave the comfortable realm of 'freedom, equality, property and Bentham' – or Twitter and Facebook, as Marx might have added today. It is no good simply looking at the figures released by the Office of National Statistics once a month, for this alone tells you little about the struggling woman who is working on a checkout for three hours a week, or the man packing boxes for thirty hours one week and two hours the next. The post-2008 crash years have been characterised by a huge rise in the number of people on zero-hours contracts and in temporary work. No politician waxing optimistic about record levels of employment would be likely to get a hearing among the people I met in Ebbw Vale.

After spending a short amount of time in South Wales I was unsurprised to learn that most people here had voted to leave the European Union in the referendum earlier in the year. All around there were reasons to want to 'take back control', as the anti-EU slogan had urged people to do. The European Union had, to many people, become a surrogate for the loss of industry and subsequent sense of hopelessness and defeat. I heard tales of disgruntlement with Europe wherever I went, whether in the subdued streets of Ebbw Vale or along the quiet, snake-like terraces of Cwm. But others saw the decision to leave the EU as a grave mistake.

'I mean, we saw this sign coming down, didn't we? "This road is funded by the EU,"' said Ron, a miner I had been down the pit with in Blaenavon. He was incredulous that local people had opted at the ballot box to puncture the lifejacket which, in his opinion, was keeping the region afloat.

'And you think the people here voted against it, against staying in the EU! And the projects that are around here, in Merthyr ... every project ... is *funded* by the EU!'

But for others Europe was an identifiable target for the pain inflicted over recent decades. The decline of many former industrial communities roughly coincided with Britain joining the European Economic Community – the precursor to the European Union – in 1973.

'My own personal view,' said Brian, a former miner at Bryn Colliery who volunteered in the South Wales Miners' Museum in Port Talbot – the place I had first met Flash – 'is that it all started [to go downhill] as soon as we joined the EU ... Look at this country, and look how it was thriving in the fifties, sixties, even up to the seventies, but since we joined the EU it's just gone down ... I believe a lot of it is to do with the EU ... I mean, Germany, are they closing mines? They still got coal mines producing? You know, their steelworks are thriving ... One thing I'll take my hat off to Merkel for: that she took over Europe without firing a bullet. You know, fair play to her.'

'It was hustle and bustle, steam trains and trucks clanking and shuntings and buffers, it was a hive of industry,' sighed Jack, an eighty-five-year-old former collier who now spent his days helping Brian at the museum. 'Colliery just up the road – two here. Just up the road couple of hundred yards. There was a thousand men working in one of them. Aye, there was a couple of hundred working in this one. Now that the coal's gone everything's disappeared ... It's amazing how we're surviving, put it that way ... It's only because of our pride that's keeping our heads afloat. We're living on our wits, more or less, aren't we?'

I heard similar complaints in Cwm. I asked an elderly man about local politics as he stood waiting for a bus on the long terraced high street. 'I know [it's] very anti-EU,' said the man whose name was Robin. 'I think it's probably because they lost their steelworks here, and they see Port Talbot under threat as well, and I think it's just a backlash from that.'

Over the years the Chinese state has massively over-invested in steel, and its domestic market has been unable to absorb the surplus. And so the Chinese elite have dumped masses of cheap steel on the world market. Yet it had been governments in Westminster, wedded to a black-and-white interpretation of the free market and keen to attract Chinese investment in the nuclear industry, that had vociferously resisted attempts at a European level to tighten up 'unfair trading practices' which might have prevented it.[30]

But whatever the reason, Cwm had 'stagnated' in recent years, Robin said, and you had to travel out of town to find work, which could be a challenge in itself.

'Public transport is not that brilliant here. For me now I have to go to Ebbw Vale to get the train back to Cardiff. But sometimes I get to Ebbw Vale and the train's just gone – I got another hour to wait. And Sundays, forget it, there's no transport at all on a Sunday. Fortunately, I've got a good few friends around here [with transport].'

'The thing about the Valleys is they are small, tight-knit communities, not like places like Swansea or Cardiff,' a librarian in Cwm told me.

Others complained that the community was seeing its identity slowly washed away because of immigration. 'There's a lot of people coming in now,' said Anne,[31] a pensioner who had popped out to buy milk. 'Polish people coming in here and all sort of people that they're rehousing and [renting] accommodations to, so nothing is like it used to be.' But again, the migrants Anne knew personally were 'no bother'. 'Speak as you find, I got a [Polish] family next door to me in the front part of the house here and I don't know they're in there, don't hear a peep. That's what you want … About six years ago the [Welsh] boys here now was all out there … they had wild parties from Fridays till Mondays and they'd throw all the bits over to my garden, cans and all wot nots. So I used to get my shovel, and fling it back over. We got the Polish here [now], and the Polish down the bottom block, and the neighbour said the same thing, she don't know they're there. No problems with them at all.'

Many of the grumbles about Europe reminded me of the complaints one frequently hears on the other side of the Severn Crossing about a creeping loss of English cultural identity. The blame for this is typically placed on newcomers. 'We're losing our culture' has for many years been the plaintive cry of those opposed to the movement of migrants to British shores. And sometimes the complaints are rooted in something real – it is untrue to say that a distinct English culture does not exist and, ultimately, that an English people do not exist either. Those who engage in this kind of self-flagellating talk would be in your face if you ever suggested that, say, Jamaica or India did not have their own distinct cultures and ways of life. It is hardly surprising that the English should resent being disparaged in this manner. Yet it is capitalism that has truly lost its patriotic element, preferring instead the global marketplace in which cultural sameness is mistaken for genuine diversity. It is odd in a way that anger at the slow erosion of British culture should be directed so overwhelmingly at migrants rather than at the companies whose identikit stores plaster a bland façade of monotonous homogeneity upon every high street throughout the world. But it is a question of proximity, I suppose: the immigrant, or the drinker next door who you suspect of robbing the social to pay for his beer, is a lot more solid – a lot more *real* – than the shadowy multinational that serves up trash under a slick and anodyne fascia.

What those hoping for change do have is politics. It has become a cliché to say that politicians have become mere managers, yet large swathes of the people I met in Wales seemed to genuinely believe that little could be done to bring about any sort of change in circumstances beyond brandishing a big stick and waving it in the faces of a few tabloid pariahs. All politics seems to offer places like Ebbw Vale is the defeatist idea of 'social mobility', a philosophy in which a golden ticket is available to a lucky few. Those unable to reach the handle of the oar are left to fall through the rotten boat and sink. The market decides if jobs come to places like this, not the smiley men and women in suits who turn up every five years to ask you to tick a box on their behalf. There is worse work out there than that found in a call centre, but it is an atomised existence that grants you none of the respect and little of the solidarity of the industries of old.

It is perhaps this gradual transformation in the role played by the state, rather than a sudden outbreak of 'post-truth' discourse – the fashionable *bête noire* singled out by liberal commentators to explain political turmoil – which helps explain why the door has swung so invitingly open to demagogues and blowhards. The latter are some of the last people willing to stand up and propose solutions to society's ills, even if the remedies they offer are ugly, cynical and violent. The autocrat derives his appeal from his promise to replace anonymous power with the visible power of the infallible leader, while grinding anything that stands in his way to dust. The fewer things that our managerial political elite believe they can change, the bigger the chasm for these small men writ large to swagger into.

PART IV

—

LONDON

16

An alarm clock pierced the silence in the dark flat like a firework going off in a churchyard. It was 4:40 a.m., and the harsh sound cut through the damp stuffy air like a scythe. After a few days this noise would drill down into your subconscious like a tick burrowing into the fleshy part of an exposed leg. Wherever you were, upon hearing any sound like it you would be momentarily teleported back to the pitch-black room in the dreary block a few streets from some of the landmarks of affluent London.

Not long after the wailing of the alarm clock had abated, a crack of sickly orange light flooded beneath the cardboard partition that separated me from the person in the next bed. Cigarette smoke soon followed, drifting through the gaps in the makeshift wall together with a veritable chorus of coughing and wheezing. This poorly chest belonged to one of the Romanian men. Outside in the thick dawn the barking of faraway dogs would pile on top of these inner stirrings like the rhythm section of an orchestra joining at the third bar. It was unlikely you were going back to sleep.

The flat contained a curious array of people. The cigarette smoke belonged to Dorothy, an elderly English woman in rooms that were for the most part filled with young Eastern Europeans. She too had been woken by the alarm, which belonged to Lili, a Hungarian lady who went out in the gloom each morning to sweep the floors and mop the toilets of the city's office blocks. Not long after the alarm had sounded Dorothy would begin to loudly reel off a list of familiar complaints in a forlorn and croaky voice. 'I can't really explain it. It's too much to explain,' she began one morning when Lili, who was busy making the tea, asked her what she was grumbling about. A minute or two later Dorothy was ready to explain precisely what the matter was and at great length, much to the exasperation of the others who longed to snatch some sleep before stepping out into the bitterly cold day with its brisk thudding wind.

'It's me son, actually. We was always together. And then lately he's been tearing off and going elsewhere. I think he's got somebody else,' Dorothy complained on my first morning in the flat.

The diminutive old lady, her body bent over and ensconced in a tatty cardigan like a poorly wrapped Christmas present, must have been nearly eighty years old. Her much-lamented son had run off suddenly and 'took all my money', she told us. And so here she was, floating from one set of cramped digs to another with what little money she still possessed. Occasionally, landlords let her stay on for free because they felt sorry for her. She spent much of her time sitting in the flat nursing a stray black cat, which I suppose was the only real egalitarian among us in that it never seemed perturbed by the rambling of this poor old woman.

'It's not the food part, it's having the money to do things you want to do … I've got no money to do anything,' she lamented. 'I've got a poor cat in there that's got a sling on its neck, and I don't know how long it's been on it and it's a lovely little thing.'

Listening to Dorothy talk while I gazed up at the ceiling under the dim electric lights, I felt as if I were in some cramped and cold dungeon, sequestered away for ever in a city where millions of people were peacefully sleeping. On the wall behind my head the phrase *C'est la vie* was carefully written in small black letters, the light flickering off the heart that stood in for the apostrophe.

I had arrived back in London from Swansea shortly before Christmas. The capital at this time of the year has an almost magical feel to it: the familiar Christmas tunes spill out of garrulous pubs which disgorge crowds of dolled-up and besuited revellers. The historic buildings are decorated with their own array of dazzling illuminations, under which excitable children drag reluctant parents into shops to pick out what they want from Father Christmas. It is the type of scene to which every journalist feels compelled to attach the epithet 'Dickensian'. London has of course changed a great deal since its panoply of life was captured in the stories of Charles Dickens – and later in the reporting of researchers and writers like Henry Mayhew and William Booth. A thousand ragged cockney wretches no longer throng the streets of the East End. Nor are those same streets 'filled with a new and different race of people, short of stature, and of wretched or beer-sodden appearance', as Jack London observed more than a century ago. Many of the workers who contribute to the capital's prosperity today are migrants whose voices are no more audible from under the metaphorical boot of a new generation of exploiters than the characters which shocked middle-class readers in the London of old. Whereas yesterday's urban poor were represented by painters like William Hogarth as slum-dwelling grotesques, their faces and bodies bent and twisted by the harsh conditions under which they lived, today's migrant poor remain for the most part out of sight. The same attention is simply not paid to the grievances of Romanian labourers or Bangladeshi cab drivers as it is to English workers. They lack a voice just as their comrades did in the past, but it is their lack of the literal voice – an *English voice* – which often results in their complaints travelling no further than the walls of a filthy bedsit in Plaistow or a dosshouse in Barking.

Or in our case in London Bridge. The garret-like flat I was sleeping in was situated in a former social-housing block – all brick and soot and age – which had been sold off many years before. Since then it had passed through the hands of several owners while its market value – along with practically every other property in and around central London – had skyrocketed. The current landlord – who I never did get to meet face to face – had not, I was told, owned the property for long. The rent was £80 a week and in exchange for that you were given a rectangular bed the shape of one of those pink wafer biscuits you get at children's birthday parties. This bed was nestled within four cardboard walls measuring around 6 feet by 10. It was rather like living inside a shoebox, but a shoebox lined up alongside six other shoeboxes, each of which contained another human being rather than something you put your feet in.

The present housing situation is far worse in London than elsewhere in the country for several important reasons. Over the last twenty years the number of people living in the capital has increased by 25 per cent, while the number of homes has increased by only 15 per cent. In 2016 there was another sharp drop in the number of new builds.[1] Just 13 per cent of new homes approved in London in 2014–15 were classed as 'affordable', and the rising cost of rent means that workers are gradually fanning out towards the periphery of the city like ripples in a pool of water. Even some of the properties deemed 'affordable' could command rents of as much as 80 per cent of the market rate. From 2005 to 2016, average rents in London increased by 38 per cent, while earnings rose by just 21 per cent.[2] Any prospective escape from the treadmill of private renting – in 2017 one in seven tenants were frittering away more than half their income in rent[3] – was becoming increasingly difficult as rising house prices far outstripped wage increases. The average house price in London in August 2016 was £489,000,[4] which worked out at around thirteen and a half times the average annual wage in the capital.[5]

In practical terms, this left large numbers of people bedding down each night in poky dwellings a few streets away from enclaves of tremendous wealth. Those were certainly the sorts of places you often ended up in if you were, say, driving an Uber or cleaning the offices of Thatcherism's 'Masters of the Universe' over at Canary Wharf. Either you lived in a place like this and put up with it, or you moved out further east and burned through your money commuting back in to work each day.

You stumbled across accidental juxtapositions of rich and poor at every juncture in London, and they found solid expression in the data put out by various charities, think tanks and government bodies. According to an analysis of the 2010–12 Wealth and Assets Survey, the most affluent fifth of Londoners owned an average of £1.78 million in wealth, compared to the poorest fifth who owned an average of just £4,000.[6] Homelessness in London increased by 134 per cent between 2010 and 2017,[7] while a 2014 investigation by the *Evening Standard* found that 740 'ghost mansions'[8] were sitting empty because super-rich investors were treating potential living spaces as Monopoly pieces to bump up their wealth. If you pulled aside the plastic curtain in our little set of rooms you could look out on the glowing point of the Shard sticking out from behind some rusty gates and an ashen-coloured office block. Just down the road from us was a grotty pub, where moth-eaten men would whittle away long hours in a musty-smelling lounge, hunched over drinks while a fire occasionally threw out orange sparks onto a scuffed and dirty carpet. A few blocks down again was one of those trendy eateries, where a portion of food the size of the palm of your hand costs an arm and a leg.

Yet it felt important to be located centrally in order that wherever I was working in the city I would never be *that* far from something resembling a base camp. You wanted to get out early in the morning and then come home late at night, with the day parenthetically broken up by a period of rest in the afternoon when the streets were quieter. It was in the afternoons, so I had been told by others who did the job I was about to take on, that the pinging of the app on my phone – which was effectively my new boss – happened more infrequently.

I had arrived back in London because I was about to join the 'gig' economy, a growing portion of the labour market characterised by freelance work and 'gigs' – flexible jobs often paid at a piece rate and usually – though not always – delivered to workers via mobile-phone apps. The name of this growing domain summons up images of fame and insouciant swagger – like a guitar-wielding megastar bestriding the stage, you could roll lazily out of bed and turn up to a 'gig' whenever it suited you. Similarly, you might just as quickly drop off the radar again once you were done. The words 'freedom' and 'autonomy' are bandied around in this pseudo-subversive universe like confetti at a wedding. An algorithm rather than the bars in the verse of a song is your master. You may have waived away your rights; but, dude, you're gigging, and in this brave new tech-utopia you could (in theory, at least) retain your freedom and autonomy while bringing home the bacon.

The 'gig' economy operates in a sector of the economy that has been expanding rapidly in recent years. Much of the increase has occurred since the global financial crisis of 2008. In 2008 there were 3.8 million self-employed workers in the UK. By early 2016 that number had risen to a record high of 4.7 million.[9] Back in 2008, 12 per cent of the workforce officially worked for themselves.[10] In 2017 that figure stood close to 16 per cent – an increase of almost a million people since the start of the crisis. Optimistic assessments put this down to a rising number of entrepreneurs confidently striking out on their own. But there is also a suspicion that, as profit margins in many areas of the economy have shrunk, companies have been offloading more of the business costs onto employees by effectively pretending that they are not employees. Jobs that would at one time have had regular pay and hours, entitling workers to the minimum wage, holiday pay and perhaps even a contract of employment, were increasingly done by people classified as 'independent contractors' who enjoyed none of those benefits.

Behind the algorithms through which you got your jobs were usually tech entrepreneurs, often based in California's so-called Silicon Valley. Thus while Dickens's proletariat had gone from the streets of London, so too had many of the capitalist overlords he depicted so brilliantly. The new masters were no longer fat wicked men in top hats who slipped into reveries about empire. Nowadays they were more likely to unbutton their shirt collars, roll up their sleeves and wax lyrical about diversity rather than chomp on a bulbous cigar or kick a tramp on their way home from a club. Yet as I was to learn soon enough, these people's capitalists – anti-establishment 'disrupters', as they liked to portray themselves – were, much like their predecessors, incredibly good at squeezing profit out of those at the bottom of the pile. More importantly, they were better at persuading you that the whole thing was for your own good. You were 'your own boss', as the PR departments of the 'gig' economy firms never tired of telling you. And who could argue with that?

17

My own attempt to join London's growing army of casual workers truly began when I posted an application to Transport for London (TFL) for a private hire driving licence. I had hoped to find work as a bicycle courier, but by this time I was awaiting an operation on a hernia; thus driving a car seemed like a more suitable occupation than careering around the city on a bike.

The process of getting a licence from TFL to drive with Uber was straightforward. In all it took around three months from filling out the initial application forms to getting on the road. The ease with which one can get out there is itself a source of worry for many existing taxi drivers, who are increasingly having to scrap for fares in a market saturated with drivers using an app that is massively reducing the costs of the average journey. A similar thing is happening in the world of couriering: bicycle couriers have to compete for jobs with more fellow riders than ever. If you pop down to Jamestown Road in Camden in the evening and stand outside the restaurants, you can see at least half a dozen bicycle couriers hanging around, one foot on the floor and another up on the pedal, waiting expectantly for algorithms and controllers to send a ping to their devices.

There is currently no cap on the number of drivers who can work with Uber, and that number has been dramatically increasing in recent years. Indeed, the number of private hire vehicle drivers in London has doubled in the past seven years, according to TFL, to more than 117,000.[11] Not all of those drivers will be using the Uber app, but the unprecedented increase roughly coincides with widespread customer take-up of Uber. The number of private hire drivers in London increased by 13,000 – 25 per cent – in the two years following the launch of UberX. While in 2012 there were 5,000 'riders' (passengers) using the Uber app in London, by 2016 there were 1.7 million. Every time I opened up my drivers' app, Uber would encourage me to 'invite a friend'.

Some fluctuation between the good and the bad days is inherent to most business models. Thus it is in the interests of companies like Uber to have a fleet of drivers on call at every hour of the day: one of Uber's unique selling points is that you can 'hail' a cab even when you cannot physically see one. No more standing shivering on a street corner only to fling your arm out like a maniac the moment a black cab swerves around the corner. This has resulted in a seemingly never-ending push to recruit more drivers. There were, after all, few sunk costs for the companies in doing so. They didn't have to deal with taxes. The contractor was on a piece rate so they didn't have to pay them if there was no work. Minimum wage legislation did not apply. Nor did the workers – because they were not, according to the companies, *workers* – accrue a set of employment rights. I witnessed for myself the clamour among people to join the 'flexible' economy during my topographical examination – a basic map-reading test that TFL makes you sit before granting your licence. Around forty people sat the test at the same time as me (all men apart from one woman), at one of

Uber's offices, a ten-minute walk from Charing Cross station. To give a sense of scale, aspiring drivers were sitting the exam on most days of the week at several accredited centres across London, and there was a thirty-day wait before Uber could fit me in to take the exam. It should therefore be no surprise that by 2015 the number of Uber drivers had overtaken the number of black-cab drivers in the city.

Most of those present when I sat the test appeared to be first- or second-generation migrants. When I asked some of the men lingering furtively outside the building (like me they had arrived half an hour early to be sure) why they wanted to drive with Uber, they spoke enthusiastically about the much-exalted flexibility. 'I can just work as I like,' said one man from the Indian subcontinent in broken English. 'It's like I'm in charge of when and how I do it,' said another, trotting out one of the clichés I had imbibed from Uber's online marketing.

And, in truth, the flexibility of the job appealed to me, too: I had a book to finish after all, and unlike the other jobs I had been doing, with Uber I could at least reduce my workload when I needed to catch up on my writing. To be your own boss – to be free of the enforced servility that comes with having a tyrannical line manager constantly in your ear – was no small thing. You could breathe more freely right away – never again would you be admonished or humiliated by some robotic orderly for a minor infringement of company policy. *I am free, no matter what rules surround me. If I find them tolerable, I tolerate them; if I find them too obnoxious, I break them.*

It was only later that I came fully to appreciate the dark

cloud that could sometimes form with the uncertainty that self-employment brought with it.

I scored an adequate 85 per cent in the exam – the minimum score required was 60 per cent. I had not revised at all, and I really needn't have done: the test involved no more than some basic map reading and naming the points on a compass as well as the motorways and counties surrounding London. Several companies were offering the topographical test, but you could sit it with Uber for free. This was welcome after I had already shelled out £432 to submit the initial licence application (this included £250 for the licence itself, £56.85 on another DBS check – which to my surprise only took a week this time – and £125 for a private medical at my GP surgery).

Once the entire process was complete I was issued with a PCO (Public Carriage Office) licence by TFL. With that in my possession I just had to find a suitable car. You have to choose a vehicle not more than eight years old to drive with Uber. You can either rent or buy outright, though the cost of buying a suitable model will probably set you back at least £5,000. I eventually found a car to rent at £201.77 a week from the company Enterprise Rent-A-Car – a price that covered the cost of insurance and required a minimum four-week rental period.

In truth it had seemed unusual that Uber should dictate to me which car I could use for what was supposedly my own business. Uber was granting me permission to use its app, and I was classified by them as a *self-employed contractor* – a *partner* rather than a *worker* or *employee*. 'Uber is a technology app, it's not a private hire company,' we were told later on by a member of Uber's team.

A similar business model is used at courier companies such as Deliveroo. Few of those being paid to cycle around London worked *for* the companies that paid them a wage. Instead, an army of 'independent suppliers' worked *with* them. You would often see a green-uniformed throng of Deliveroo riders careering around the city. Yet in order to maintain the notion that they were all free-spirited business people going about their daily work, in its so-called 'rider vocabulary guidelines' Deliveroo referred to the branded clothing each rider wore as an 'equipment pack' which was purchased from the company's 'supply centre'. Similarly, money earned at Deliveroo was a 'fee' rather than a wage, and a payslip was referred to as an 'invoice'.[12]

This is platform capitalism. We, as partners, are simply using a 'tool to connect Customers seeking Driving Services to Drivers who can provide the Driving Service',[13] as Uber liked to put it. Uber was a tech company that happened to hold a cab operator's licence.

And in some respects it would be a mistake not to admire the initiative and sheer bloody-mindedness that transformed Uber from something that began life, in former CEO and founder Travis Kalanick's words, as 'a black cab service for 100 friends in San Francisco' into 'a transportation network spanning 400 cities in 68 countries'. The extent to which disrupters like Uber were upending London's private hire market is plain to see out on the streets. Sat waiting patiently at a set of red traffic lights, as one of Uber's fleet of drivers you sometimes got the sensation that you were being watched. And then you turned swiftly around and there they were: two bloodshot eyes boring down on you under a hangdog frown: an angry cabbie. Occasionally an open mouth would bellow some garbled mess of trash-talk and these disgruntled traditionalists would drive off, their faces twisted into a grimace as they unleashed a volley of single-syllable abuse. 'Cunt.' 'Prick.' They called you scabs as well sometimes.

You grew accustomed to the hostility after a while; or at least you developed a skin thick enough for it to roll off you like the slights of a child having a tantrum. But it did, at least momentarily, give you a sense that you might be part of something worthwhile. Black cabs *were* too expensive. All the quaint nostalgia about the famous beetle-like structures being a part of the backdrop of London – like rosy-red telephone boxes and double-decker buses – could go to hell when set against the need for a cheap taxi home at two o'clock in the morning when the only bit of life left on the streets were the foxes tearing at the stinking refuse sacks. As a driver, it also felt far safer on London's roads with a sophisticated mobile app that could handle customer payments. Better that than a pouch stuffed with banknotes. A passenger was unlikely to pull a gun and put it to your head to demand the password to your PayPal account. And even if they did, Uber would have their details on file, which you assumed they would hand straight over to the police.

Much of the initial opposition to Uber seemed, then, a bit like the predictable opposition to most forms of innovation: there were vested interests who had done well enough out of the old way of doing things to want to assiduously resist anything that threatened their cushy status quo. The ability to overcome such technological traditionalism is very often a hallmark of progress. Few today lament the disappearance of Thames watermen or the horse and carriage. Although countries like Italy have completely blocked the use of smartphone apps like Uber due to the purported unfair competition the app posed to traditional taxi drivers, this is unlikely to be either workable or desirable in the long term; and certainly not in countries where consumers have a far stronger political voice.

And besides, for the customer the rise of the 'gig' economy has been a terrific boon. You can quickly download an app from a website and, *voila!*, you are connected with individuals willing to provide access to their car or home. Increasingly, there are apps for nearly every task and errand. There is an app that can summon someone to pick up your clothes, wash them and iron them, and drop them back again smelling sweetly. One of the UK's 15,000 Deliveroo riders can bike food over to you from a local restaurant. An app called Dropit can send someone to collect the heavy bags you don't want to carry home from the shops and deliver them straight to your door. With the Airbnb app, you can lease your property out to short-term lodgers. Meanwhile, DriveNow lets you borrow a BMW from a street near to your home and you drop it off in any legal parking space when you have finished with it. The possibilities are potentially endless. Together with the convenience, such services are almost always much cheaper than the traditional service, whatever that is. A black cab from Westminster Abbey to the Barbican Centre would cost you around £15. I could get you there in my Uber for about £8.

What is sometimes forgotten in the binary debate is that the 'gig' economy can (at least in theory) be an attractive proposition for workers, too. Or at least it could be if workers had some form of democratic control over the algorithm which dictates so much of their lives. I approached working with the Uber app with a great deal less fear and trepidation than I had had going into some of my previous jobs. Together with the purported flexibility of the hours, there was, at least in the case of Uber, the potential to earn reasonable money. This must have been the case for many of those who had downloaded the app and become drivers. A third of drivers had arrived in the job from neighbourhoods with an unemployment rate of more than 10 per cent, according to Uber.[14] Meanwhile, Uber claimed its drivers were earning an average wage of £16 an hour – more than twice the amount I was paid in my other jobs.[15] London may be the most expensive place to live in Britain, but it isn't quite *twice as expensive*. Not yet, at any rate. Before I started, I heard stories of some drivers taking home £400 to £500 over a single weekend – never, interestingly, from the drivers themselves – which was the equivalent of nearly two weeks' salary in some places. Set against the recent past, driving for Uber did not seem like such a bad life.

And so three months after filling out the initial forms for my licence application I went out on the road. Whereas I had clocked-in at previous jobs using a time card or a pen and paper timesheet, signalling my readiness to work with Uber required no more than a rightward swipe on my Samsung smartphone from the warmth and solitude of my car. On doing this, a map of the city with all its inbuilt potential flashed up on the screen. Sooner or later, my first passenger would be digitally waving me down for a ride. I stared intently at the glowing blue orb which pulsated on the map, and I waited.

18

I got my first pick-up on Ladbroke Road in Notting Hill, W11. This is an area of London which epitomises the phenomenon known as 'gentrification', whereby run-down urban areas are transformed by the arrival of affluent residents en masse. Nearby Portland Road has gone from being a slum where as recently as the sixties properties were sold for £10,000, to one of the most desirable places in London where properties sell for millions. I was already familiar with the area, having been drinking several times at the Earl of Lonsdale pub nearby, a peculiarly old-fashioned place which might have appeared in one of Patrick Hamilton's pub novels of the 1930s. I drove down towards here in my car because W11 – and the areas around Paddington, Bayswater and Kensington – had always felt like a landing strip for those first arriving in London. The area buzzes with tourists and tourists usually want to go somewhere. Hopefully they would want to go there in my car.

I felt nervous as I rolled up to collect the passenger to the point where I could feel myself perspiring. Fortunately, the woman who subsequently climbed into my car did not have a particularly acute sense of smell. Either that or she was far too polite to say anything, which is certainly possible.

Once you have done your first journey with Uber the whole process becomes much clearer. For the most part you simply follow a set of instructions on your phone. As soon as it begins to bleep, you have around fifteen seconds in which to decide whether to take a job or leave it for someone else. You follow the map to locate your passenger, you pick them up, and then you follow the map again until you arrive at wherever it is they want to go. If the rider fails to show up after five minutes you can claim a £5 no-show fee.

I drove black people, white people, and everyone in between; I collected polite people and rude people, blind-drunk party-goers and uptight chief executives. The best part of the job was arguably the fantastic array of people I encountered. There was a surprise element to the whole thing too, which could get addictive at times. You would, for instance, never find out where a passenger wanted to go until you had accepted the journey, made your way over to collect them and they were safely ensconced in your car. Nor did Uber disclose to you the passenger's full name or any other details about them. This, from one perspective, was the great beauty of the service. Uber ran the app like this, it said, to ensure that the company could 'provide a reliable service to everyone at all times'. That meant safeguarding against rider favouritism and controller nepotism, as well as protecting passengers from drivers who might purloin credit card details or turn up unexpectedly and unwelcomely at a female passenger's home at three o'clock in the morning.

But the three-way relationship in which you, the driver, were separated from your passenger by an intermediary could also lead to drivers accepting jobs which, in normal circumstances, they would have flatly rejected. In order to see what I mean, picture the scenario. You are coming to the end of a gruelling twelve-hour shift and decide to do one last job before heading home. You look at your watch and it is approaching four o'clock in the morning. It is so late, in fact, that the dawn chorus is faintly audible above the whirr of the exhaust when you wind down the car window. Getting home before the orange halo of light on the horizon washes over the city is a matter of urgency. But then your phone starts to bleep. The customer requesting the ride is a twenty-minute drive away. You accept the job. On picking them up, they say they wish to travel a short distance for the minimum £5 fare (that's before Uber's cut – I had one fare which paid out just £3.94). By the time you have driven for twenty minutes back to your starting position you will have completed an hour's work for less than £5. Alternatively, the customer might ask to be driven for thirty minutes in the opposite direction. In which case, by the time you have driven all the way back again you will probably walk through the front door of your house at six o'clock in the morning. You will have been at the wheel for nearly fourteen hours and will have driven for an additional fifty minutes of 'dead' time (time in which you are not earning). Once you slink into bed most of your neighbours will be sitting down to breakfast.

No sensible person would willingly agree to undertake a job like this. Which is perhaps why Uber does not allow you to reject work for very long. Uber informs drivers that they should accept 80 per cent of all trip requests to retain their 'account status'. If a driver rejects three trip requests in a row they can be automatically bumped out of the app. Some drivers have been logged off the app for rejecting two consecutive requests. For all the rhetoric about being your own boss, the fact that you are not allowed to log back into the app for a further ten minutes after you have been logged out smacks of punishment rather than a (more understandable) precaution against drivers accidentally logging on when they are unavailable.*

The important thing to note about all of this is that as a driver you have no real say over which jobs you accept once you have switched on the app. This, for the most part, means that you have to go where the Uber algorithm sends you. If it says you have to drive for forty minutes to the other side of London and back again in the middle of the night, that's what you have to do – unless you want to end up on Uber's naughty step (logged out of the app, summoned into the office, perhaps even 'deactivated' permanently).

This level of control adds up to shorter waiting times for cabs, which equates to happier customers and more rides taken with Uber. Yet it is a strange way of carrying on when drivers are supposed to be self-employed. As I discovered, there are several aspects of the job where 'self-employment' seems like a rhetorical illusion which bears little relationship to reality.

Being on the road could occasionally be addictive. Using behavioural science, Uber in the United States has employed psychological inducements to influence when drivers will work and for how long. As the *New York Times* revealed in 2017, in order to keep drivers out on the road, Uber has 'exploited some people's tendency to set earnings goals – alerting them that they are ever so close to hitting a precious target when they try to log off'.

---

* This could easily have been circumvented by simply logging drivers off but allowing them to log back in again as soon as they were ready.

'We show drivers areas of high demand or incentivise them to drive more,' said Michael Amodeo, an Uber spokesman. 'But any driver can stop work literally at the tap of a button – the decision whether or not to drive is 100 percent theirs.'[16]

A driver might head out in the evening with an idea in mind to go home when he has earned a certain amount of money – say £100. This of course is an incredibly inefficient way to work – if there is no work it is better simply to pack it in and come back out again when it is busier. Yet nearly everyone does it, at least when they first begin driving. I did. I set a rough income goal for the week, and I small-chunked that into amounts I would bank each day. The algorithm would sometimes send my phone the next fare opportunity before the job I was doing was even over, similar to the way a show playing on Netflix automatically loads the next programme in a series while the credits for the current episode are still rolling, encouraging binge viewing.[17]

By nudging drivers to stay on the road for longer – *You're £10 away from making £330 in net earnings. Are you sure you want to go offline?* – Uber tapped into the same psychological targeting techniques that keep a person playing a videogame: a feeling of incremental progression towards a set goal.

The courier firm Deliveroo nudges its fleet of bicycle couriers in a similar way, sending them weekly rider data and telling them what time is best to work and where, based on statistics from the previous week. Uber had also admitted experimenting with female personas in the United States to encourage the overwhelmingly male driver-base to work in certain places and at particular times.

Uber was able to do all this because of the company's capacity to track both our activity and general whereabouts. The upside of this was the way in which an app was able to harness excess capacity: the time in which a person or vehicle lay idle was in theory reduced and therefore productivity increased. A good example of this was the way in which, using the Uber app, if I was travelling home in one direction I was able to alert the app to find riders who wanted to travel in that direction too, therefore minimising what would otherwise be wasted miles. Phone apps have made it extraordinarily easy to connect to others and share this excess capacity.

Prior to getting out on the road I had to take an Uber 'Onboarding' class. Onboarding is a two-hour-long classroom session that every prospective driver is called in for by Uber once they are ready to start work. There was a registration process, we had photos taken for IDs, and an Uber representative talked us through the basics of using the app and picking up riders. In terms of the level of control Uber would exercise over us going forward, I found the session quite instructive. At Admiral we had been jokingly warned by a team leader about the 'very Big Brother eye' watching us. That was not strictly true, of course. With Uber, however, it really did feel as if we were under the constant observation of an all-seeing and inscrutable eye. At the more benign end of things, we received detailed instructions on 'respecting the rider': we were told to 'communicate calmly and professionally at all times. Keep the rider informed of the progress of the journey.' Then we were told to avoid certain conversational topics during journeys – things like religion, politics and sport, lest it offend the person riding in the back.

We were ultimately there to serve and to answer, not to offer our thoughts on the state of the world.

But an element of control was exercised over many aspects of the job. Once out on the road, the number of jobs you accepted, the types of jobs you accepted, and whether or not you cancelled trips was closely monitored by an organisation that liked to refer to itself only as our 'partner'.

'So how it works with Uber is you have your overall rating, your acceptance rating and your cancellation rating,' one of Uber's instructors told us during the classroom lesson.[18]

'So we know, for example, how many trips you're accepting and how many you are not, how many you are cancelling and how many you are not. So if we see one platform [i.e. UberPOOL or UberX] that you're cancelling more often than not, then there is an issue involved.'

An 'issue' invariably meant a 'problem'; though of course nothing was stated clearly in this world when a euphemism would do. It was during Onboarding that my expectations as to the freedom I might enjoy out on the road really began to diminish. 'The reason you're online is to accept any job that's given to you,' the instructor told us. 'How Uber works is you can't pick and choose. You can't pick and choose what jobs you want.'

Another side to the control exercised by Uber was through its rating system whereby partners and riders could award each other between one and five stars at the end of every journey. The company closely monitored the average number of stars awarded to each driver. You started out automatically with a five-star rating, and provided you did things properly, it seemed relatively easy to hang on to it in the short term. As well as the star rating system, inane e-badges were awarded to drivers by passengers based on the latter's assessment of the journey. 'Nice Car' or 'Well-stocked trip' were two examples. But the longer you worked – and the more unsociable the hours you worked – for that was when the real money was made – the easier it became to accumulate low scores. Sometimes the traffic was bad and you were late to pick someone up. They got angry about that. Sometimes the customer typed the wrong location into the app and were not where they said they were going to be when you arrived to pick them up. They blamed you for that as well. Occasionally a customer took umbrage because they were the sort of person who gets off on taking umbrage with those lower down the economic ladder. The Queen was still on the throne, the London Stock Exchange would still open in the morning, and you could still be an arsehole to cab drivers.

Sometimes riders barked commands at you as soon as they opened the door of the car. They wanted to talk *at you* rather than *with you*, and expected you to assume a markedly lesser role. Their voice raised itself a few decibels in the car and it was communicated to you that yours ought to become a little more hushed. It wasn't simply that you were not supposed to be their equal, which would have been par for the course in a job like this; it was the extent to which people expected *utter* subservience, which went beyond anything I had previously experienced at work. As much as Uber liked to say that the passenger was *your* customer, it felt much more like they were Uber's.

All of these things affected your rating. Retaining an exemplary rating was really a question of averages: a test match cricketer with a long and distinguished career may get bowled out for a duck occasionally. Yet a few ducks early in a career can very quickly become catastrophic. The company looked at your last fifty ratings, meaning that a few difficult customers who brought down your average could see you summarily hauled into one of Uber's central London offices for 'training'. If you continued to score below 4.5, you could be blocked from using the Uber app altogether.

'If you constantly get low ratings, then there is a chance that there could be a ban in place ... If it goes below 4.4, we do help our partners,' said the instructor. 'We do provide necessary training for them. If they're constantly getting low, after their training, then there have been temporary bans for six months and permanent bans as well.'[19]

Once you swiped right you were online, and it felt like you had to accept whatever the algorithm sent your way.

'If you do not accept trips, and if you constantly let the timer expire, we will put your account on hold for two minutes,' the instructor warned the assembled crew of budding drivers. 'And then if you continue to do that the time gets longer and longer and longer.'

All in all, it was a peculiar sort of freedom.

19

I found out during my first week on the road that the favourite book of Uber's former CEO and co-founder Travis Kalanick is *The Fountainhead*, by Ayn Rand. For those unfamiliar with her work, Rand was a Russian–American novelist and philosopher whose system of thought – known as 'objectivism' – found expression in her two best-selling novels (the other being *Atlas Shrugged*). Objectivism stood opposed to all forms of collectivism – the welfare state, trade unions, public hospitals.

Like communism, Rand's philosophy embodied a simplistic and 'total' view of the world that was perennially attractive to those whose main motivation was primarily to stop thinking. As Arthur Koestler phrased it in *The God that Failed*, the discovery of a complete ideology gave reassurance precisely because it supplied 'an answer to every question'.

Randian thought, extolling the supposed 'virtue of selfishness', is also attractive to the modern entrepreneur who wishes to believe his or her own hype. 'I swear – by my life and my love of it,' Rand once wrote, 'that I will never live for the sake of another man, nor ask another man to live for mine.' There were those who moved the world (entrepreneurs, captains of industry), and then there were those who sought to stifle greatness (bureaucrats, trade unions). Beyond the God-like heroes of her novels, and the 'looters' who constantly attempted to thwart man's highest ideals, there was a much larger class of people who were expendable. Only a few individuals 'move the world and give life its meaning', wrote Rand in a 1968 preface to *The Fountainhead*. 'The rest are no concern of mine.'

The toiling masses appear to be of little concern to Uber, either. At the time of writing, in 2017, Uber pays no VAT on booking fees by treating every driver as a separate business.[20] By legally operating its app via a sister Dutch company, Uber also pays most of its corporation tax in the Netherlands rather than in the UK.[21] The attitude towards drivers was something else again. Kalanick was to land himself in trouble in 2017 for engaging in a heated argument with an Uber driver who had complained from the front seat about drivers' pay. The argument culminated in Kalanick informing the driver dismissively that, 'Some people don't like to take responsibility for their own shit. They blame everything in their life on somebody else.'

It's your fault if you are poor – because you refuse to *take responsibility for your own shit*.

Uber's Randian attitude thus extended unsurprisingly to its employment practices. It classifies its drivers not as its employees but as its customers, who are essentially paying a small commission on each fare in exchange for permission to use the company's driving app. Disagreements over whether or not Uber drivers are really self-employed led to a landmark case being brought to an employment tribunal against Uber by two of its drivers. In October 2016, the High Court ruled in favour of James Farrar and Yaseen Aslam's claim that they were entitled to holiday pay and other entitlements deriving from 'worker' status. The judges gave short shrift to the idea that Uber drivers were self-employed.

'The notion that Uber in London is a mosaic of 30,000 small businesses linked by a common "platform" is to our minds faintly ridiculous,' the tribunal judges said. They added: 'Drivers do not and cannot negotiate with passengers ... They are offered and accept trips strictly on Uber's terms.'[22]

On winning the case, James Farrar immediately submitted a holiday request to Uber for the following week. Uber declined it, however, because it had already lodged an appeal against the ruling. Uber lost this subsequent appeal in late 2017. Yet, at the time of writing, Uber has requested permission to appeal again to the Supreme Court – meaning the case could potentially drag on for several more years before a resolution is reached.[23]

I had wanted to find out more about the case and James had agreed to meet me at a workmen's cafe in Guildford. James lives in Hampshire but is originally from Ireland. He has been driving for Uber since December 2014. Since then he had co-founded an organisation called United Private Hire Drivers, a trade union for cab drivers, which has subsequently been amalgamated into the Independent Workers Union of Great Britain. Having been made redundant by a technology firm in January 2014, James told me he joined Uber because he wanted to pursue new technology projects during traditional business hours while driving on the evening and at weekends. He was attracted to Uber for what he calls 'a very traditional reason'.

'I wanted the flexibility from the work that Uber could give me, but I quickly began to see that it was a rigged system and, I mean, people were being pretty desperately exploited.'[24]

Men in high-vis jackets flitted perennially in and out through the front door of the cafe as we sat down to two coffees. The conversation soon turned to the benefits that Uber had brought to the taxi trade. (James had no desire to see Uber banned or driven out of the country – 'I don't think it's a case of banning Uber at all ... Our focus is to get a better deal for these workers.')

'Uber did bring a lot of good things to drivers ... and we've got to acknowledge that,' he told me.

It was James's theory – and one I heard repeated by several of the drivers I spoke to – that many traditional cab drivers had joined the Uber platform precisely because it put an end to the tyrannical power exercised by traditional taxi controllers. In coming to work for an algorithm, drivers believed they were circumventing the petty bundle of irrational likes and dislikes which came with human controllers and which could lead to a huge amount of stress.

'What technology brought, and what automation of dispatch brought, is taking these controllers out of the loop. I mean, these were people who decided whether you and your family were gonna eat next week. And there were drivers who were fed and drivers who were starved, and if they wanted you out of a job it was very easy – they just don't give you any work, mess you around ... I think some of them [the drivers] were prepared to accept less money to get away from some of the nasty firms they were working for. But it's [the algorithm] become a bit of a monster of its own.'

In the 'gig' economy, whoever controls the algorithm controls what is inputted into it. This seems obvious when put like this. But tech utopians were essentially asking those of us who were managed by algorithms to accept them as neutral entities, when in reality they were the creations of those with their own distinct interests – interests very often antagonistic to the interests of those who requested work from the apps. To cite one admittedly anecdotal example, some of the drivers I spoke to did not believe the algorithm always gave the available job to the closest driver. James was not convinced either. However, the important point to note is that there is no way of knowing whether the algorithm is discriminating based on ratings, revenue earned or how long a driver has been online. As a worker, you had no more control over what is fed into the algorithm than you did over which side of the bed an old-school controller got out of. 'Trust us,' Silicon Valley capitalists essentially said to the army of contractors on whose backs much of their success was built.

Ideally, Uber wanted to see a fleet of its drivers on the streets of London at all hours of the day. But it wasn't always beneficial for drivers to be out on the road. To use another example from experience: one Tuesday evening I drove all the way from Mitcham in Surrey to Westminster Abbey without hearing a single hopeful ping on the app. Even the limited flexibility that did exist in the job – the ability to decide when to switch the app on or off – came stacked with weighty caveats. Making money depended very much upon when you went out.

'If you're not working those early shifts, if you're not working those late hours on the weekends, then you won't do well,' James told me.

But it was Uber's ultimate aim, in the words of Kalanick, to 'make transportation as reliable as running water, everywhere and for everyone'. Instant response time was key. A fleet of drivers constantly circling London meant that, as a rider, you could pull the phone out of your pocket, fire up the app and summon a driver whose car would roll up within seconds. This explained the seemingly never-ending treadmill of more and more drivers being pumped out by Uber via Transport for London and sent onto the streets. Uber's business model was built on the idea that the market could continuously expand – that by dropping the price of a ride far below that of traditional cab companies, Uber could tap into pent-up demand – or 'liquidity', as the jargon called it. But by not putting a cap on the number of drivers, Uber seemed to believe it could do this in perpetuity. The company could keep on expanding the market, meaning more drivers would compete for cheaper fares while simultaneously making more money. It was win-win for everyone. Or at least that was the huge claim Uber made for itself.

In 2015, Uber backed this up with data from New York that appeared to show drivers earning 6.3 per cent more per hour than in the previous year – even though there were more drivers on the streets. James was sceptical, however, and believed that over the long term it 'defies all economics that you can keep flooding the circuit'.

'If you flood the market at any price point the work dries up because there's too many people. And so yes, if you drop the price and expand the market there's the pent-up supply and demand, it gets cleared and resolved, and in the short term everybody thinks that's great, but the downward trend is to hell, right?'

Once the supply of drivers had risen beyond a certain level, a system built on a level of liquidity that Uber could only ever estimate (how was it possible to calculate the number of untapped future taxi passengers there would be?) was liable to produce a great deal of waste. The important question then was: who bore the cost of the waste? For James, it was the driver who picked up the tab. At some point the number of drivers on the road would outstrip demand, especially in a city as congested as London. And notably, Uber had not published data on hourly earnings amongst its *London-based* drivers.

'So what is a network effect? I pick up the phone and there is a dial tone, right? There is *always* a dial tone. And you will not be happy with your phone service if you pick up and there's no dial tone because it's busy ... I'll have to wait twenty minutes, you know. That's not what you want. It's the same with Uber ... in order for that peak to be met, there has to be many more drivers on the road than is necessary.'

You were serving the platform when you logged on, even when no one was sat in the back of your car. The authors of the 2016 tribunal judgment summed up this point by quoting from Milton: *They also serve who only stand and wait.* The success of the service was built on the army of surplus labour that drove around London awaiting a ping on their phones. But the individual driver was effectively making a loss as he or she meandered around the city. Uber wasn't losing anything. It had passed that risk on to us, its growing band of self-employed contractors.

In order to accept Uber's upending of the traditional laws of economics – 'It is super-counterintuitive until you have dug into the data and seen it for yourself,' Uber's UK general manager, at the time, Jo Bertram told the *Guardian* in 2016 – you have to believe several things. First of all, you have to accept that Uber will stop sending new drivers out into the market once a tipping point has been reached and driver idle time had started to move upward (which might have already happened, for all we know). And in a city with a relatively cheap public transport system and a finite amount of road space, there must be a tipping point.

The other thing you have to accept is that a company founded by an admirer of Ayn Rand has the interests of its drivers at heart. The desperation with which Uber tried to wriggle out of any obligation to pay its partners worker entitlements such as holiday pay and the minimum wage tells another story.

Historically, it is typically the poor who grease the axles that keep the wheels of progress turning, while those sitting in the comfortable carriages above look on indifferently. Yet if things are so bad, why do Uber drivers not simply exit the market and do something else? Why do they not 'get a handle on their shit'? as any Randian was well within their rights to ask.

Indeed, some of the drivers I chatted to at Heathrow's Authorised Vehicle Area (AVA) told me they were happy enough driving with Uber. For others it was a question of choice. Genuine freedom requires an income, savings or a stipend, and the extent to which you are free usually depends on how much you have in your pocket. In Joseph Heller's *Catch-22*, a war profiteer by the name of Milo Minderbinder captured the delusional air of the dogmatic free-market utopian when, caught swindling his fellow countrymen, he evokes the 'historic right of free men to pay as much as they have to for the things they need in order to survive'.

Minderbinder may have been a parody, but there are times in life when his 'type' is instantly recognisable. Similar theories are today propounded with respect to the growing numbers of people who toil away in the 'gig' economy. What the Uber driver, the courier or the van driver really require is for the state to get off their back – or so some talking head from the Adam Smith Institute, fresh out of university, might grandly proclaim on BBC News. Any attempt to rein in the power of the Randians of the world puts humanity on the slippery slope to rubber truncheons and labour camps.

'What we don't know is how desperate people are for money, what their options are,' James told me as we drank coffee in the Guildford cafe. 'We have a minimum wage for a reason, you know.'

I put the question of worker choice to Aman, a forty-two-year-old Eritrean cab driver who came to live in the UK as a teenager and had, when I spoke to him, been working for Uber for two years. If it was so bad, why didn't drivers just stop using the platform?

'It's like they've accepted it because they're immigrants, you know. I mean, they don't really have any options ... People who used to work in kitchens and, like, waitering jobs, and now they're given the opportunity to drive people around. It's better than what they were doing before so they're happy, you know ... They were exploited before as well in their other jobs. And now they can put in more hours into [their] work and earn better than what they were doing before. Some of them do, like, ninety hours a week, a hundred hours a week.'

I met Aman in the Shepherdess Cafe, just off City Road in Old Street. Many of the drivers he knew personally 'don't really have options', he told me. In the early days, there were the same stories going around that I had encountered myself: reports of drivers taking home as much as £400 or £500 a night.

'I mean, I used to tell them [my friends] how things were going to be. You know, I used to tell them Uber is a good thing, we are independent; even though it's cheap we can still make more money than other companies. But slowly they start realising how things were going. The guys that used to do minicabbing before, obviously they're not happy but I've got friends that used to work in restaurants and stuff, those guys they're still, I wouldn't say happy, but they're OK with it.'

Surge pricing was one way that drivers could make more money if they anticipated it correctly and were in the right part of town when the bars and clubs started kicking out. When customer demand for cabs outstripped drivers in a particular area, drivers could earn up to three times as much from a fare. This was to encourage drivers to migrate to areas with high demand, meaning happy customers were able to find a cab. A surge was effectively an inducement to drivers to right a distributional imbalance of cabs across the city. Yet you could never fully escape the mentality that ultra-cheap fares seemed to engender amongst the public.

'Uber, what they've done is they've got the customer [so] used to this cheap, cheap service that when it's surging, they think they're being extortion [sic],' said Aman. And for that, he said, they 'blame the drivers'.

'Even if they know it's nothing to do with the driver, they would give the driver low rating.'

'We all know when the surge comes on your ratings go down,' James had told me. 'Is that my fault? I mean, it just proves I'm rated for factors beyond my control. If you're going to performance manage me, manage my performance ... It forces you to do things you see drivers doing when their ratings start to slip. You know, they start desperately providing mints and water.'

'Some partners do provide water,' we were told suggestively by an Uber employee during Onboarding. 'Some partners provide sweets. It's entirely up to you if you wanna do that.'

Another thing that cropped up in conversations with drivers was a sense that falling fares were fostering disrespectful attitudes. Drivers felt they were viewed almost as a servant class who existed for entitled Londoners to order around.

'You see because it's a low-paid job, when you do low-paid jobs, unfortunately people look down on you, you know. People don't respect you,' said Aman.

Everyone had their own methods of dealing with difficult customers. If the level of snobbishness was dialled up to a particularly high level, I used to disconcert riders by telling them the story of my great-great-grandmother, who was born in Buckingham Palace. This usually created a state of confusion with those who were trying to assert some degree of pedigree. Some drivers seemed to have a much rougher time, and it was hard to escape the view that this had something to do with the fact that they weren't English. Driving around the West End late on a Saturday night, you would occasionally see one of the young Somali or Pakistani drivers trying hopelessly to deal with an inebriated passenger who either refused to get into the car, was opening and closing the doors wildly while the car was in motion, or else insisted on smoking or doing something else undesirable in the vehicle. You were there to cater to the whims of the upper layer of London life with a mute obedience, much like a dog might be ordered around a field by a farmer. You were expected to remain in the background, one of the props for the stories people told themselves about where they slotted into the city's invisible hierarchy. From the drivers' point of view, the ratings system didn't necessarily help a great deal either: it was implied at our Onboarding session that riders could see how many stars we had left them before they chose whether or not to rate us. And so you were reluctant to leave anything below three stars lest the recipient turn the tables on you. On one occasion I obsequiously left four stars for a woman who had talked to me in the manner of a mother berating a small child. 'That's the worst part,' said Aman. 'When passengers get into your car and start giving you orders. I mean, before I used to take it, but now I tell them, if you don't have respect with me I'm just gonna end the trip and you're gonna have to leave my car ... On one occasion, I was in Soho, and in certain busy places you have twenty people like looking for an Uber at the same time, at the same spot. They just come out from a club, so what you do is you lock the doors, because people are intoxicated they just like to open your door and say, "Oh, are you my cab?" One time I've locked the doors, and this guy he came and he tried to open the door. And I asked him, you know, can you confirm your name. And he said, "Just fucking open the door." And I turned on the app, cancel: "I'm not taking you, I've cancelled it." And he starts taking pictures and, "I'm gonna report you."'

Aman believed the lack of respect for drivers has something to do with the dwindling amount that customers expected to pay when they hailed an Uber.

'It's to do with the rates, James, you know ... For any service you pay, if you pay a high price you tend to have respect for that person. I mean, even though it's the same job, or it's the same service you are receiving, you're gonna respect whoever is helping you more, unfortunately.'

If someone kicked off in the back of your cab, beyond cancelling the job – which might get you into trouble with Uber if you did it too often – or calling the police, there wasn't a great deal you could do.

'How can we have 30,000 vehicles on the streets of London and have no twenty-four-hour cover?' James had asked back in Guildford. 'Nobody to phone. Nobody to help you.'

Once you had completed ten trips with Uber you were congratulated and informed excitedly that you had, 'Now unlocked UberPOOL!' This was another of the rider options customers were presented with when they opened the app. They could choose UberX, and ride solo at the standard rate, or opt for UberPOOL, and potentially save money on the journey by sharing it with another rider travelling in the same direction. Many drivers didn't like POOL (every driver I spoke to hated it) because of the potential it generated for antagonisms erupting in the back of your car when total strangers were brought together, often in a drunken state. But also because the fare was potentially lower for drivers than an average fare with UberX.

Our Onboarding instructor had told us confidently that accepting UberPOOL jobs worked out better for drivers.

'Most definitely, it does. We try and match you with as many trips as we possibly can, because it's beneficial for our partners, it means they're making more money.'

Aman laughed when I relayed this conversation to him.

'UberPOOL, *Uber-poor* they [the drivers] say. That's what they call it. It's just enough to cover your expenses. And also the price they give to the customer is a fixed price, so say you get stuck in traffic or if it takes longer it's not gonna make any difference. And on top of it the commission that Uber takes. They're giving the customer 10 per cent off the price [and] on top of it Uber takes 35 per cent ...'

James had learned first-hand about the potential for conflict among passengers on an UberPOOL job in the summer of 2016. He had picked up two passengers in Kensington, who were apparently unaware that they had ordered an UberPOOL service. The two men then attacked the female passenger who was already in the car. The episode was reported in the *Evening Standard*.

'They were probably high or something, and I had a girl in the car already, and a row broke out. They didn't want to share the car ... And it got pretty nasty. These guys attacked her, dragged her out of the car [and] pinned her up against the wall.'

James tried to defend the woman and they set on him as well.

Uber said in response that it was always 'very clear to passengers' that they were opting to share their journey when they select

UberPOOL.[25] But James wasn't convinced, and wanted to see the service banned – or at least a panic button installed in the app.

'In the old days, what guys would tell me is that if you worked for the local minicab firm, if there was a problem like that, you just called on the radio. Your controller knows where you are, they'll send any of the other guys ... and the overwhelming force of people around, from the firm, watching what's going on ... certainly more people there really helps.'

That was the other thing about Uber and the rest of the 'gig' economy: the grim atomisation of it all. It hardly resembled a 'gig' at all: you certainly had no fellow band members. It was just you, strapped inside a metal shell and directed around town by an algorithm. It was not so much autonomy as isolation. There were more of you, but you felt, as Aman had put it to me, like 'just a number'.

'I'm not a person to them,' Aman said as we left the cafe and strolled back in the direction of our respective cars. We had spoken for about an hour and it was time to get back on the road. After all, *if your wheels aren't turning, you're not earning* – as another of the sickly corporate aphorisms went.

20

Many riders who got into my cab did not want to make conversation. You did not want to force conversation onto them either. Behaving like the over-enthusiastic waiter who keeps on enquiring as to the quality of a meal could leave you with a disastrously low rating.

That said, occasionally a rider would ask your opinion of Uber from the back seat. They had usually gleaned enough information from the news to know that there was some sort of stand-off taking place in the background over whether or not we were really self-employed. 'So don't you get any holidays, then?' a middle-aged lady asked me one evening as I dropped her home. 'We do, madam,' I replied, 'but we don't get paid for them.' 'That's a bit rough, isn't it?' she replied incredulously.

And I suspect that most reasonable people would agree if presented with the facts. Striking out on your own to become self-employed, you forfeit certain benefits derived from being a worker or an employee. But set against this, you are supposedly retaining your freedom.

Yet working for Uber I had very little freedom beyond choosing the time at which I decided to leave the house and switch on the app. Several employment tribunals were ongoing over the status of workers in the 'gig' economy, but Citizens Advice believed that as many as 460,000 people could have been falsely classified as self-employed.[26] This was potentially costing the taxpayer up to £314 million a year in lost tax and employer national insurance contributions – as well as denying workers the entitlements that previous generations had fought hard for. Some of the big London courier firms were also offloading a large portion of business risk onto their contractors. One way in which they effectively did this was by 'flooding the circuits' to ensure a cyclist was in the right place when a customer placed an order.

'The courier firm gets slapped with loads and loads and loads of work and hasn't got anybody to do it, so they try and have as much man power as possible,' I was told by Scott Cadman, a London-based bicycle courier. When it was busy this didn't necessarily matter.

'But on those slow days it becomes ridiculous for us to even be there at times,' Scott went on.

When I met him Scott worked as a cycle courier for a small, West End firm that he described to me as 'the better of a bad bunch'. There could be something attractive to many couriers like Scott about the exhilarating highs and restless lows of the job. As I was starting to discover with Uber, knocking out a hundred pounds on a good day seemed to make up for the times when you feared that you were not going to take home enough money to pay the rent. In this sense, the incentives inherent to the 'gig' economy resemble those that draw people into casinos or bingo halls, where unpredictable rewards stimulate you just enough to reel you back in – you carry on dipping your hand in your pocket in the hope of beating the odds. Like a slot machine, there is something almost thrilling about playing a game that you are not sure will give you something worthwhile in return.

'It's quite exciting – you're racking up jobs almost like a score,' Scott confessed to me.

'That's exciting when you know you've earned more than £200 a day, just you, your bike, your legs, your bag, smashing it out, it's a fantastic feeling.'

When work was plentiful Scott might cycle as much as sixty miles a day. Sometimes a job would take him just a few blocks away and be done in five minutes, whereas on other occasions he could be sent from one end of town to the other. Lots of courier firms pay a flat rate of £2 to £3 per job, meaning that the mileage you are putting on the bike can bear little relation to the amount of money you are bringing home. As a self-employed contractor, a courier was not covered by minimum-wage legislation, just as I did not fall under its umbrella driving for Uber. Freedom sometimes translated into the freedom to open your wallet and see nothing bar a few lonely clumps of lint. Scott explained to me how he was sometimes left with barely enough money to buy a coffee after an entire morning's work.

'I have come into work [before], ridden all the way [there] for half an hour … from wherever I was living at the time, sat around waiting for work for forty-five minutes; the job that I'm [then] given … it's going all the way down to the other side of town … quarter to ten your controller makes you wait around [again] for more work, which doesn't appear, you leave [for the next job] at quarter past ten, arrive down there, again have some trouble delivering it, finding the address perhaps, you lock up your bike, you get sent round [to see] the security guard round the back, and, you know, it could be quarter to eleven and you've got £2.25 under your belt.'

In a refreshing bit of honesty, Patrick Gallagher, the chief executive of the courier firm CitySprint, told *Fleet News* in November 2012 that, 'If you're paying somebody per job as opposed to paying them per hour, they're going to work harder.'[27] A CitySprint courier earns a piece rate of around £3.50 per delivery. Even with a higher rate like this you would have to do three jobs in an hour to earn a living wage before your expenses were deducted. This could mean cycling across London several times for the price of a portion of fish and chips in a London pub.

'Massively so,' Scott responded when I asked about the fluctuation in a courier's weekly income due to piece rates.

'Some people put up with dire, dire guarantees. I met a guy yesterday who was very, very happy at his new job, which pays him, as a self-employed person, he's covering all his costs, all his taxes, £60 pounds a day.' Scott repeated the figure to drum the point home – '*60 quid a day!*'

The costs a contractor had to deduct from the headline figure on their payslip could sometimes wipe out most of their earnings. This was also true with Uber, where the minimum price at which you could rent a car was almost £200 a week. Then you had the cost of petrol, cleaning the vehicle, plus any parking fines you picked up. This led to some drivers working eye-wateringly long hours to make ends meet. Uber seemed initially to welcome this, encouraging drivers on its website to work sixty-five-hour weeks.[28]

Many couriers seem to get by as a result of the camaraderie that is almost unique to the job. They work alone, but they often drink together, organise uproarious races against each other, and generally look out for one another. They sometimes live together, too. I met Scott in a block of cooperatively owned flats where several other couriers were staying.

'I'd say it all springs out from our hardship ... And possibly drinking culture as well,' Scott told me. 'It used to be pubs and couriers but now couriers can't really afford pubs, so our last spot was outside a bike shop and an off-licence ... cans of Tyskie on street corners.'

This sense of shared resistance to adversity was familiar to me from South Wales. 'We are going to "Tredegar-ise" you,' Aneurin Bevan had told the country back when he created the NHS in the 1940s. What Bevan meant was that he was going to expand the principles embodied in the Tredegar Workmen's Medical Aid Society to the country as a whole. The society was organised based on universal donation during wellness for universal provision during sickness. The London Courier Emergency Fund (LCEF) was a DIY pay-out system set up along similar lines. It was run by couriers, for couriers and a minimum payment of £150 was available to anyone who was kept off the road for more than two weeks through injury, with larger sums available in special cases. It was paid for by the sale of merchandise and by races and events organised throughout the year.

'You ride around for a week in the pissing rain, or you slip on a manhole, and *bang*, that's you out of work with no access to any money,' Scott said with a cynicism that felt odd for a twenty-two-year-old.

But Scott's words rang true as I moved around this world of casualised labour – a world repackaged as something glamorous and chic. Dan, another bicycle courier I spoke to, had been forced to take time off after damaging ligaments in his arm. In order to afford to live while he was *hors de combat*, Dan had to sign on and claim Employment and Support Allowance (ESA) together with housing benefit until he was fit enough to ride again.

It has been estimated by industry insiders in the US that relying on independent contractors rather than employees can lower direct business costs for companies by as much as 25 per cent.[29] At least some of those costs are being offloaded onto the state, and by extension onto taxpayers and other workers. Due to the paucity of many people's earnings in the 'gig' economy, signing on for social security when you fall ill is sometimes the only option. Thus the taxpayer is essentially out of pocket twice over – first as employer national insurance contributions fall, and secondly as this casual workforce turn to the state to survive.

On an individual level, the pay-off for the lack of basic worker entitlements is supposed to be the much-vaunted flexibility of the work. It ought, then, to have been possible for someone like Scott to work for more than one courier firm at a time. Yet he laughed when I raised this point with him.

'You have to be on call for all of those companies, really ... It would get awkward, you know. Picture the situation: you get one job from the Uber app, and you get a job from CitySprint at the same time going in two different directions. What you gonna do? Which one you gonna turn down? What kind of situation would that leave you in? You turn down the CitySprint job you get put on the naughty step by your controller for the next week or something. You deny the Uber job, that's another step towards you being barred, you know. So it's not really realistic.'

'Nah,' Dan said straight away when I asked him if he felt like he had the 'freedom' and 'autonomy' to turn down work from the courier companies, however brilliant the algorithms supposedly were.

'There's so many times I've heard that people have been threatened with [being] sacked for turning down work or actually getting sacked for turning down work ... The whole thing seems weird to me because the very idea of getting sacked ... I mean, I'm self-employed!'

Ultimately, it is judges who will decide whether or not the 'gig' economy workforce is genuinely self-employed. But it did feel as if there was an overwhelming wave of misinformation being unleashed on both those who used the apps for work and the wider public about the nature of the 'gig' economy. In his book on Dickens, the biographer Peter Ackroyd wrote that if a person living today were to somehow find themselves in a tavern or house of the period in which Dickens was writing, he or she would 'be literally sick – sick with the smells, sick with the food, sick with the atmosphere around him'. I suspect that if some of those who today make a comfortable living writing newspaper columns extolling the virtues of the 'gig' economy were to find themselves doing some of the lowly jobs that keep London afloat, they too would eventually sink to their knees prostrate with illness. As the grievances of the 'gig' economy contractors have become louder, so it feels as if journalists and commentators have become more willing to acquiesce in the fiction that workers' rights are the sworn enemy of autonomy and flexibility. As I sat behind the wheel of my car after a drop-off on one occasion, I listened to a commentator on the radio saying precisely that: a talking head waxing dispassionately about how we drivers could not possibly want, say, paid time off or a minimum wage because we valued our flexibility too much. This cast those campaigning for the rights of couriers, drivers and riders as busybodies who wanted to snatch away freedom from workers. The false binary of workers' rights versus flexibility is a message that has been transmitted directly from some of the companies themselves. William Shu, the founder of takeaway delivery app Deliveroo, blamed confusion inherent in British law for the fact that Deliveroo riders were denied worker and employee protections. In early 2017, Shu told BuzzFeed News that Deliveroo 'would like to offer more entitlements and security', but that if they offered those things then the flexibility that allowed riders to decide their own hours would be lost. 'It's as simple as that,' he added confidently.[30]

It was bad enough that this line was being used at all; worse was the fact that the purported flexibility of the work was itself questionable. When the court hearing James Farrar and Yaseen Aslam's case against Uber ruled in October 2016 that the company could no longer classify the drivers involved in the case as self-employed, Uber's then regional manager in the UK, Jo Bertram, responded by claiming that most Uber drivers did not want to be classified as workers and instead wanted to remain 'self-employed and their own boss'.

'The overwhelming majority of drivers who use the Uber app want to keep the freedom and flexibility of being able to drive when and where they want,' Bertram added. In other words, we were being told that granting drivers worker status would result in the very thing that had attracted many to Uber in the first place evaporating. You either kept quiet and accepted that you were individual business people – working alongside thousands of other lone, isolated business people – or you became a salaried employee with a set number of hours, clocking in at the same time each day and doing whatever the company told you (which you sort of did already).

Yet this was a bit like saying that a person who enjoyed eating bananas did not need the right to own property. The claim was a non sequitur: one thing did not derive from the other. Not to delve too deeply into the murky and turgid world of employment law, there are many casual, freelance and self-employed people with worker status – workers receiving entitlements like holiday pay. There is little contradiction between the autonomy many casual workers enjoy and certain statutory rights. In a landmark 2002 case, a self-employed joiner who worked exclusively for one firm of building contractors was found to be a *worker*, despite supplying his own tools and paying his own tax and national insurance.[31] A 'worker' was defined as someone who worked under a contract of employment (or an implied contract of employment) and who could not send someone else to carry out his or her job. They also could not be a client or customer of the individual's profession or business. In three recent cases involving Uber, CitySprint and Pimlico Plumbers, supposed 'independent contractors' were declared workers by tribunals. The law itself is not as clear as it might be, but only in the sense that it currently allows employers to obfuscate and shirk their responsibilities. *Some people don't like to take responsibility for their own shit*, as someone once said. Employment law also requires that individual workers come forward with their own cases, rather than any rulings being automatically rolled out to others in the sector.

I am sure that workers in the 'gig' economy often do enjoy their flexibility and the freedom this grants them to work as and when they choose – when it is meaningful. For the most part I found this to be true for myself: the fact that I could go out and earn some money when I was at a loose end was incredibly useful. Similarly, the ability to turn off the app at will was like a breath of fresh air after the authoritarian strictures laid down in some of the other places I had been.

But a person genuinely running their own business would surely be entitled to decide which jobs they took on and which jobs strayed into the realm of diminishing returns. You suspect they would also possess the ability to set their own fares to ensure that, if they were going to undertake a difficult task, it would be financially worth doing. If not, then they ought to have been granted the rights which, in law, those under the control, direction and supervision of a company were entitled to.

So how much did an Uber driver typically make?

It would obviously be a truism if I said 'it depends'. It was I think possible, however, to identify certain trends and to substantiate some of the driver complaints about pay, even if it did vary depending on how much time you spent out on the road. Uber claimed its drivers made an average of £16 per hour. Realistically, after my expenses had been deducted, I was earning quite a bit less than that.

There were all sorts of factors that impacted on what you were able to earn: whether you hired your car or owned it; the model of the car; what times you went out; where you lived; whether you got lucky with the surge; how many UberPOOL trips were sent your way, etc.

To break it down, *before* my expenses (but after Uber had deducted its 25 per cent rate of commission on every fare) I was earning £16.76 per hour. This was about the sum Uber said I could earn. This would add up to around £670 for a forty-hour week. There would always be some variation here, but I do not feel like I was a particularly exceptional *or* clueless driver. I had a fairly good idea where to go to find people in London looking for rides and at what times.

That £670 translated into £2,905 a month and £34,860 a year. However, that figure would tell you almost nothing because it is the figure before I have deducted my expenses.

Firstly, there was the cost of the fuel. At a conservative estimate, this came in at around £70 a week – or £290 a month. The cost of cleaning the car – because riders started to leave poor ratings if the car was dirty – came in at £16 a week. It might seem a lot but it really isn't when you are using the vehicle for forty hours a week. That works out at two hand washes and twice-over with the vacuum (I paid to have this done because it was quicker).

You will also pick up at least one parking ticket a month. I got one on my very first day. Riders were requesting Ubers from all over the place – bus lanes, roundabouts, by the side of A-roads – while Transport for London were investing heavily in parking and traffic enforcement. James Farrar summed up the situation well when he told me that TFL were 'licensing like confetti from nine till five, and then from five till nine they're sending out their enforcement officers to harangue you for what amounts to symptoms of overcrowding'. You could deduct another £100 a month for the fines, and that was if you were careful. Both TFL and Uber were also pushing for drivers to shoulder the cost of the London Congestion Charge at some point in the future. The extra data you used on your phone added another £5 a week and the respective annual TFL inspection and biannual MOT cost a further £200 altogether over the year. The biggest lump sum of cash disappeared on renting a car. The Ford Focus I was driving cost me £201.77 a week, or £10,492 a year. This was the cheapest car available from the rental garage at the time. There was also the £200 deposit, which I did get back but only because I was conscientious enough to take photos of some pre-existing scratches the rental firm subsequently attempted to charge me for. Obviously it would have made more sense to buy a car, but many drivers are not in a position to make such an investment (remember the statistic about many of Uber's drivers coming from some of London's most economically deprived boroughs?). A second-hand Toyota Prius – the cheapest and most fuel-efficient car to use with Uber – costs around £5,000, provided you want something you can use for more than a year. Insurance on your own vehicle, which was covered by the hire company when you rented, could cost as much as £3,000 a year.

Before tax, then, I was left with an annual salary of £18,115, which broke down into a monthly salary of £1,509.58 and a weekly wage of £348.36 – for forty hours of work. My hourly wage was about £8.69 an hour. After tax I would have been left with £15,597, which did not seem like a great deal of money – especially not in London – considering I would have to dip my hand in my own pocket to cover things like vehicle repairs, illness and holiday. Aman had told me of the times he would stay at home when, say, his two children were on half-term.

'So certain weeks I don't have no earnings,' he said.

Fortunately, Aman's wife also worked, but the point was that he – and the rest of us – had to put money aside on top of the usual expenses to cover these contingencies.

All of my calculations were based on standard jobs with UberX. These rates broke down as: base fare: £2.50 + £1.25 per mile + £0.15 per minute minus Uber's 25 per cent commission.

You could make less money if you were sent a lot of UberPOOL trips, when Uber took a 35 per cent cut. You also had no real say over whether you accepted these journeys. During my Onboarding session, I was told explicitly by an Uber employee that I had to accept them.

'I understand some partners don't want to use POOL. But POOL is a *formality*, it is part of your terms and conditions as a partner. If you constantly refuse POOL, it will come up on our system ... then we will need to find out a reason why you haven't been accepting them. The whole purpose of going online means that you are ready to work, ready to make money.'

James had told me that all drivers were 'dead against it ...

because all POOL does … it increases market size for Uber, it increases yield for Uber, it increases capacity for Uber, and it does all the opposite for drivers …'

As I neared the end of writing this book Uber was clashing with TFL as well as with its drivers. On 22 September 2017, the regulator rescinded Uber's operating licence – suspending the company from operating legally in the city subject to appeal. In a statement, TFL said that Uber demonstrated 'a lack of corporate responsibility in relation to a number of issues which have potential public safety and security implications'.[32] These included the company's approach to reporting serious criminal offences; its use of Greyball technology, which could, in theory, prevent regulators from gaining access to the Uber app; and the company's method of acquiring drivers' medical papers and criminal record checks.

Uber appealed against the decision a few days later – meaning its drivers were not immediately thrown out of work – and it seems likely the company will clean up its act in relation to TFL's specific concerns. Not to do so would see the company locked out of one of its most lucrative markets. In the weeks after the initial ruling, the Mayor of London Sadiq Khan said the 'humility' shown by Uber in light of the decision 'bodes well' in terms of the company getting its licence back.[33]

Some of the grievances of other 'gig' workers became more voluble in 2017, too. In July, around 200 delivery drivers, many of them working with companies such as UberEATS and Deliveroo, staged a noisy protest outside the Houses of Parliament after a spate of acid attacks on moped users. 'No more acid attacks,' the protesters chanted. 'Stop acid attacks, bike theft, motorcycle crime.'[34] There has been a huge rise in acid attacks in London over recent years,[35] with some of those falling victim delivery drivers whose mopeds have been targeted by vicious thieves.

Some of the most important work in the 'gig' economy is being done by the Independent Workers Union of Great Britain and – for drivers – by United Private Hire Drivers, a branch of the IWGB. The IWGB was, at the time of writing, fighting, inter alia, for Deliveroo to recognise the first collective bargaining agreement in the 'gig' economy. It was the General Secretary of the IWGB, Jason Moyer-Lee, who said something that would stick with me when I asked him why customers ought to worry about the terms and conditions of Uber drivers and the people who delivered their takeaway meals.

'The point is if we don't nip this type of stuff in the bud, because this type of work is spreading ... tomorrow we're all going to wake up and we're not going to have any employment rights.'

That person ordering the food, getting a cab home from the club or pinging an order through on their internet browser as they put the tea on – *they could be next.*

EPILOGUE

I have no intention of rounding off this experiment with a long manifesto, or a list of wonkish policy proposals dictating *what must be done* or mawkishly setting out *why we must act now.* From the very start, my purpose in writing this book has not been to offer a solution as such, but to draw attention to certain issues and perhaps alter the common perception of them. I am not a politician, nor the sort of person who is good at formulating policy, but as a writer I do think I can add value by going out and describing things as accurately as possible.

Above all, I wanted to illustrate the contrast between the prosperity of 'Middle England' on the one hand and that dark, insecure world where low pay is synonymous with tyrannical landlords, bad bosses and an overwhelming sense of hopelessness on the other.

At times on my travels I was treated almost as an interloper, a strange being from a distant and alien social class. 'Why are you here? You don't have a picker's face?' one young Romanian woman said to me when I was working at Amazon. What she really meant, of course, was that I looked too healthy, too young for my age, *too English and too middle class* to be doing a job like that. Friends would similarly ask, with a touch of incredulity, how I could move unrecognised through this world. They did not mean that as a writer intent on gathering material for a book about low-paid work, I might be recognised in the sense that a public person might be recognised; it was more an allusion to my social status. *Would people not find it peculiar that a person such as yourself was doing a job like that?*

It was, in other words, normal for one type of person to be treated in this way, but a minor scandal if it fell upon the head of someone else. In reality I had some experience of skirting between these two worlds already, for my own background was in what Orwell, with his acute eye for detail, might have described as the *upper-lower-middle-class*. I did not grow up as far away from a dreary future of running up and down warehouses as I might have liked. I too could have ended up with a precarious job as my only source of income, and I understood even before sitting down to write this book not only how easy it would have been to become trapped in that world, but also how the superiority of those who stood a few rungs above was often illusory. The 'talent' upon which one's social superiority rests is often little more than the confidence to say, 'I think I'd be rather good at it', to paraphrase the former Prime Minister David Cameron.

Unsurprisingly, immigration reared its head in many of the conversations I had on my travels. I had expected this to happen, though I had not anticipated the grumbles necessarily taking on the shape that they did. On the whole I am fairly relaxed about immigration. In an increasingly interconnected world, the border-obsessed nation state probably has a sell-by date. As each day passes, there are fewer reasons to cling to the idea that it is the job of the British labour movement to look out simply for British workers.

It is not a satisfactory response when private companies are fighting their own battles globally, and it is probably a dereliction of a genuinely principled internationalism. Above all, the challenges posed by some of the things that appear in this book require a coming together of workers of many nationalities, and a putting to one side of the superficial differences that others seek to amplify to suit their own ends.

But that does not mean that some of the grumbles are never worth listening to. It is worth remembering that setting oneself firmly against change is sometimes an attempt to assert control in a world where the ground is constantly shifting. Like many people, I had for a while carried around with me the vague feeling that disquiet over immigration was a class issue; typically, that of an ill-educated working class that was set against moving with the times. This is a very middle-class sort of prejudice – and one of the few prejudices that it is still more or less acceptable to hold in liberal circles. It is everywhere nowadays – a vaguely left, half-baked retelling of the 'End of History' in which the working class has been consigned to the dustbin of history and replaced by more deserving categories of people.

It would be far better if, instead of doing this, the left was simply honest with people as to the challenges that immigration can sometimes bring with it. It is perfectly possible to do that *and* make the argument that there are better ways of dealing with it than border controls. Instead, it has become fashionable to treat people as fools, and pretend that it makes no difference if ten people are chasing every job and if nine of them are from some poor Eastern European country. Yet this goes against what we theoretically know to be true about the price and power of labour if it can be turned on like a tap. A different approach is also sometimes required to unionise people who only intend to stay in the country a few months at a time.

Many of the things that appear in this book exist because of the widely accepted creed of meritocracy. In this view of the world, it is primarily the job of politicians to sort the sheep from the goats. It is perfectly acceptable for *someone* to toil away hopelessly in a rotten job, as long as that person has been judged to lack the requisite merit to do anything better. Our entire political vocabulary – *social mobility, bright but poor kids, grammar schools* – is geared towards pulling a few people out of the soup without changing its basic ingredients. The debate in 2017 around grammar schools is instructive in this regard: it is not seen as wrong that a child who fails the 11-Plus exam should have to spend a lifetime doing soul-destroying work; rather, the tragedy is that it should happen to the *wrong* child. Woe betide if a 'bright but poor child' should slip through the net, so to speak. One can do what one likes with the other lot.

This is perfectly understandable from one perspective – it is logical for a ruling class to want to acquire the most talented people rather than those whose fathers were endowed with the largest share of dividends or a Norman Conquest surname. It is also understandable that a certain type of conservative, with his desire to apply a façade of science to the process of exploitation, should believe in an unalterable hierarchy of human worth – an elite at the top and a cognitive *lumpenproletariat* at the bottom. But the left increasingly accepts this view of the world too, even if unconsciously, and once it does, politics turns into little more than a way to grease the levers of social ascent.

One of the great difficulties in challenging this ideology is the gap between so-called 'progressive' thought and, more broadly, the traditional left. Both have very different priorities as to where the real problem in contemporary society lies. Projecting into the future, the progressive would be more or less happy with a Britain that retained the same economic structure if it was a little more 'representative' at the top. Of course, representation is no bad thing in itself – it is profoundly unjust that opportunities should be denied to a person based on who they are – but for some people that appears to mean the 'equal opportunity' to lord it over somebody else. Equality is a multinational with a few ethnic minorities in the boardroom and a female CEO. In practice, making the FTSE 100 *representative* – let's say by appointing chief execs who come from council estates – would do very little for the people on minimum wage labouring away in the post-room or cleaning the floors. Tuning up elites is a quite different thing to abolishing them altogether, even if it is an improvement on what went before.

The labour movement has itself sowed some of the seeds of this problem by traditionally sidelining groups beyond the stereotypical working man. But nowadays more of us are middle class, and middle-class self-interest has also found its way into progressive politics. There was always a section of the left that viewed the working class in purely instrumental terms. They were a weapon to be wielded against the bourgeoisie rather than human beings who required liberation. These types of activists were motivated more by a detestation of others than by any real sympathy with the poor. Nowadays, they are less likely to be seen on a picket line than at a demonstration outside the Israeli Embassy. The deserving poor are *over there* – in Cuba, in Palestine, or in another exotic-seeming land. Thus there is much less interest in class politics, and this left sits amicably alongside a middle-class liberalism that does as liberalism does – trembles with a slight terror at the prospect of genuine equality between the classes.

We live in harsh and uncaring times partly as a consequence of a tide that has swept across the globe in recent decades. One of the paradoxes of the fall of the Berlin Wall is that, while it represented a revolutionary liberation of human beings from under the yoke of totalitarianism, it also resulted in the unshackling of a particularly virulent strain of capitalism. A pessimist might even argue that the social democratic gains of the twentieth century depended to some extent on the existence of a class of semi-slaves toiling away behind an 'iron curtain'. Once people had liberated themselves from the power of the commissars, capitalist countries could once again risk antagonising the working poor with little fear of communist subversion.

But we also live in the world we do today because of conscious choices made by our own politicians. There exists a discernible thread running right the way from the Welsh Valleys and the men and women I met there to the dingy warehouses, private care homes, call centres and the fleet of Uber drivers who, as I write this, swarm around the West End of London searching desperately for riders. As Selwyn in Merthyr Tydfil put it to me, 'When Maggie Thatcher beat the miners' union, a lot of people in this country didn't give a damn about it, but it affected everybody that's working, even up to this day.'

Strangely enough, events that took place during the year I set out on my travels have ignited a renewed political interest in the working class – often referred to collectively as the 'left behind'. The political eruptions of 2016 perhaps offer a useful reminder that a society cannot simply write people out of its story because it assumes they have exhausted their historical role. A burgeoning consumer class may believe it is entitled to permanently draw upon a reserve army of drudges. However, there is no guarantee that the servitors will themselves be forever willing to play their allotted role.

Britain is not a bad country to live in on the whole. Should you misspeak you will not receive a knock at the door in the middle of the night. If you post a letter it will usually reach its destination. Your vote still means something, and if you are sick someone will invariably be on hand to care for you. Britain is one of the best places in the world to be born if your parents have a bit of money put away. But life can still be hard if you wind up in the wrong town or with a certain set of choices laid out before you. The market does not guarantee the good life, and working hard does not always bring that life any nearer. By destroying traditional safety nets and undermining old coping mechanisms, the atomisation modern life carries with it can sometimes make the struggle feel even more arduous. Freedom, if it is to mean anything at all, must mean the freedom for everyone to live decently rather than the freedom of a growing consumer class to order another class around, even if extra ladders are occasionally sent down to raise up a fortunate few and turn them into *Eloi*.

The rest of us will have to pick a side at any rate, for life is not a series of independent moments, nor the blind adherence of sixty-five million people to a set of infallible economic 'laws'. Rather, it is a struggle between competing forces in which one side must inevitably come out on top.

NOTES

Part I

1   Remarks overheard by author, 24 March 2016.
2   Remarks made by colleague, 23 March 2016.
3   Remarks made by colleague, 3 April 2016.
4   Remarks made by colleague, 24 March 2016.
5   https://archive.org/stream/principlesofscie00taylrich#page/40/mode/2up
6   http://www.bus.lsu.edu/bedeian/articles/MostInfluentialBooks-OD2001.pdf
7   Remarks made by supervisor, 24 March 2016.
8   http://www.hemeltoday.co.uk/news/worker-suspended-over-suckers-slur-1-5382838
9   Remarks made on first day, 15 March 2016.
10 Author interview with Chris, 16 April 2016.
11 http://amazon-operations.co.uk/the-complete-package/about-our-fulfilment-centres
12 https://www.ft.com/content/90fb85a8-ff5d-11e6-8d8e-a5e3738f9ae4
13 http://www.ft.com/cms/s/0/0d4434d6-fbe3-11e5-b3f6-11d5706b613b.
    html#axzz4AJgkDRug
14 http://www.thisismoney.co.uk/money/mortgageshome/article-3464221/Property-
    earns-two-five-workers-Average-house-price-rise-exceeds-38-salaries.html
15 http://www.insse.ro/cms/en/content/earnings-1991-monthly-series
16 http://www.ilivehere.co.uk/statistics-rugeley-staffordshire-33040.html
17 https://campaign.goingtowork.org.uk/petitions/amazon-co-uk-work-with-gmb-to-
    give-temp-workers-a-decent-job
18 Author interview with Claire, 22 April 2016.
19 https://www.theguardian.com/money/2017/jan/31/employment-tribunal-cases-
    down-70-since-fees-introduced
20 Remarks made by supervisor, 23 March 2016.
21 Remarks made by Transline rep, 8 April 2016.
22 Author witnessed incident on 25 March 2016.
23 Remarks overheard by author, 31 March 2016.
24 http://www.expressandstar.com/editors-picks/2015/03/04/in-pictures-pit-sites-after-
    the-mining-years/
25 https://www.thesun.co.uk/news/1246497/sports-direct-founder-mike-ashley-
    accused-of-running-a-gulag-after-mp-grilling/
26 Author interview with Alex, 7 April 2016.
27 Author interview with Alex, 7 April 2016.
28 Ruth Cherrington, *Not Just Beer and Bingo! A History of Working Men's Clubs*,
    AuthorHouse, 2012.
29 http://www.bbc.co.uk/history/domesday/dblock/GB-404000-318000/page/5
30 Remarks made by Jeff, 7 April 2016.
31 http://www.mirror.co.uk/money/youll-work-81-same-retirement-7472990

32 http://www.theguardian.com/money/2012/jun/13/number-working-pensioners-up-ons

33 https://www.theguardian.com/business/2014/oct/18/economy-bleak-british-workers-technology

34 http://www.expressandstar.com/news/2011/09/17/rugeley-amazon-swamped-with-job-applicants/

35 http://www.centreforcities.org/wp-content/uploads/2015/03/15-03-04-A-Century-of-Cities.pdf

36 Remarks made by Transline rep, 1 April 2016.

37 Remarks made by Amazon rep, 1 April 2016.

38 http://www.dailymail.co.uk/news/article-2304042/Iain-Duncan-Smith-right-You-CAN-live-just-53-week-says-cash-strapped-teacher-Kath-Kelly-survived-year-1-day.html

39 https://www.jrf.org.uk/report/minimum-income-standard-uk-2015

40 Author interview with Norbert, 20 April 2016.

Part II

1 Remarks made by colleague, 25 August 2016.

2 Author interview with Rochelle, 29 September 2016.

3 http://www.skillsforcare.org.uk/Document-library/NMDS-SC,-workforce-intelligence-and-innovation/NMDS-SC/State-of-2014-ENGLAND-WEB-FINAL.pdf

4 Remarks made by Vicky on the first day of training, 25 July 2016.

5 http://www.skillsforcare.org.uk/Document-library/NMDS-SC,-workforce-intelligence-and-innovation/NMDS-SC/State-of-2014-ENGLAND-WEB-FINAL.pdf

6 Author interview with Hazel, 19 September 2016.

7 http://www.blackpoolgazette.co.uk/news/homelessness-worse-than-in-parts-of-london-1-7864998

8 https://www.theguardian.com/society/2016/sep/28/eviction-by-private-landlord-making-record-numbers-homeless-in-uk

9 http://www.lythamstannesexpress.co.uk/news/suicide-rate-in-resort-is-uk-s-fourth-worst-1-7732342

10 https://www.theguardian.com/money/2016/aug/09/england-one-in-three-families-one-months-pay-losing-homes-shelter-study

11 https://www.housing.org.uk/blog/the-fall-and-rise-of-homelessness-in-the-uk/

12 http://www.skillsforcare.org.uk/Document-library/NMDS-SC,-workforce-intelligence-and-innovation/NMDS-SC/State-of-2014-ENGLAND-WEB-FINAL.pdf

13 https://www.kingsfund.org.uk/projects/time-think-differently/trends-workforce-social-care

14 https://www.kingsfund.org.uk/projects/time-think-differently/trends-workforce-overview

15 http://www.parliament.uk/business/committees/committees-a-z/commons-select/public-accounts-committee/news/adult-social-care-substantive/

16 https://www.theguardian.com/society/2016/dec/12/social-care-spending-falling-

postcode-lottery

17 http://www.mbs.ac.uk/news/research/people-management-organisations/where-does-the-money-go-when-your-local-authority-pays-more-than-5001-per-week-for-a-care-home-bed/

18 http://www.communitycare.co.uk/2015/09/23/home-care-visits-last-least-30-minutes-says-official-guidance/

19 https://www.unison.org.uk/news/article/2014/12/15-minute-home-care-visits-in-england-on-the-rise/

20 http://www.telegraph.co.uk/news/health/news/11302534/Revealed-more-than-500000-home-care-visits-last-less-than-five-minutes.html

21 http://www.fabians.org.uk/labour-will-never-return-to-power-unless-it-wins-over-older-voters/

22 Author interview with Hazel, 19 September 2016.

23 Author interview with colleague, 25 August 2016.

24 Author interview with colleague, 25 August 2016.

25 http://www.ageuk.org.uk/latest-press/age-uk-pilot-programme-shows-great-promise-in-reducing-loneliness/

26 http://www.telegraph.co.uk/news/health/elder/9011050/Half-of-care-home-residents-exposed-to-medication-errors.html

27 http://dera.ioe.ac.uk/28575/1/CBP-7905_Redacted.pdf

28 Author interview with Rochelle, 29 September 2016.

29 https://www.blackpool.gov.uk/Your-Council/The-Council/Documents/Child-Poverty-Framework.pdf

30 Alan Wade, 29 July 2016.

31 Author interview with Gaz, 15 August 2016.

32 https://www.gov.uk/government/uploads/system/uploads/attachment_data/file/347915/Elitist_Britain_-_Final.pdf

33 http://www.bmstores.co.uk/news/bandm-celebrates-opening-of-500th-store

34 https://issuu.com/abpl/docs/globalrichlist2016

35 http://www.express.co.uk/news/uk/362916/How-one-family-has-transformed-the-high-street-and-plans-to-conquer-Britain

36 http://www.liverpoolecho.co.uk/news/business/sunday-times-rich-list-shows-11221011

37 http://www.mirror.co.uk/money/discount-supermarkets-booming-figures-reveal-8132530

38 http://www.telegraph.co.uk/finance/newsbysector/retailandconsumer/6570626/Woolworths-the-failed-struggle-to-save-a-retail-giant.html

39 Author interview with Steven, 15 August 2016.

40 https://www.streetcheck.co.uk/postcode/fy15ee

41 https://www.blackpool.gov.uk/Your-Council/The-Council/Documents/Child-Poverty-Framework.pdf

42 William Hutton, *A Description of Blackpool in Lancashire Frequented for Sea Bathing*, Pearson and Rollason, 1789.

43 Author interview with Aiden, 17 August 2016.

44 http://news.bbc.co.uk/1/hi/uk/5260652.stm

45 http://www.citymetric.com/business/britains-fastest-growing-cities-are-all-south-and-its-shrinking-ones-all-north-1323

46 http://www.chroniclelive.co.uk/news/north-east-news/north-east-unemployment-still-worst-11640943

47 http://www.djo.org.uk/household-words/volume-viii/page-553.html

48 http://www.lancashire.gov.uk/lancashire-insight/economy/employment-surveys/sector-c-manufacturing-plus-focus-on-arospace.aspx

49 http://www.parliament.uk/business/committees/committees-a-z/commons-select/communities-and-local-government-committee/news-parliament-2015/adult-social-care-full-report-published-16-17/

Part III

1 https://www.theyworkforyou.com/debates/?id=2013-06-27a.566.0

2 https://www.oecd.org/g20/topics/employment-and-social-policy/The-Labour-Share-in-G20-Economies.pdf

3 https://www.ifs.org.uk/uploads/publications/wps/WP201431.pdf

4 http://www.nuffieldfoundation.org/news/students-poorer-backgrounds-do-less-well-university

5 http://www.bbc.co.uk/news/education-33983048

6 https://www.ft.com/content/6a8544ae-9d9e-11e4-8ea3-00144feabdc0

7 https://www.unison.org.uk/at-work/energy/key-issues/call-centres/

8 Remarks made to author, 8 November 2016.

9 https://www.theguardian.com/money/2013/sep/05/payday-lenders-hit-pay-dirt-analysis

10 http://www.bbc.co.uk/news/uk-36389824

11 Remarks made by trainer, 14 November 2016.

12 Author interview with 'Flash' Allan Price, 14 December 2016.

13 Francis Beckett and David Hencke, *Marching to the Fault Line: The Miners' Strike and the Battle for Industrial Britain*, Constable & Robinson, 2009.

14 http://www.nationalarchives.gov.uk/pathways/census/pandp/places/seng.htm

15 http://www.ehs.org.uk/dotAsset/74c65162-f125-4cb4-9d79-c148b2cc42d2.pdf

16 http://www.bbc.co.uk/wales/history/sites/themes/periods/wwll_coal_industry.shtml

17 http://www.channel4.com/media/c4-news/pdf/coalfields.pdf

18 Author interview with Aiden, 9 December 2016.

19 Author interview with Selwyn, 9 December 2016.

20 http://www.nytimes.com/1984/11/14/world/macmillan-at-90-rouses-the-lords.html?mcubz=0

21 https://beastrabban.wordpress.com/2016/06/04/the-miners-strike-and-times-editor-charles-moores-hatred-of-the-working-class/

22 http://www.walesonline.co.uk/news/wales-news/miners-strike-five-months-south-6841329

23 http://www.walesonline.co.uk/business/business-news/best-wales-contact-centre-industry-10987338

24 http://www.walesonline.co.uk/business/business-news/bbcs-call-centre-gives-distorted-4705677

25 http://citeseerx.ist.psu.edu/viewdoc/download?doi=10.1.1.502.9852&rep=rep1

&type=pdf

26 http://www.dailymail.co.uk/news/article-2351291/One-people-town-anti-depressants-Is-local-GPs-fear-benefits.html

27 http://www.southwalesargus.co.uk/news/11297957.BEHIND_THE_HEADLINES__Pit_closures_still_blighting_Gwent/

28 http://www.bbc.co.uk/news/uk-wales-35930158

29 http://www.poverty.ac.uk/editorial/over-4-million-working-families-state-benefits-0

30 https://fullfact.org/europe/is-uk-calling-for-lower-eu-duties-chinese-steel/

31 Author interview with Anne, 9 December 2016.

Part IV

1 https://files.datapress.com/london/dataset/housing-london/2017-01-26T18:50:00/Housing-in-London-2017-report.pdf

2 https://files.datapress.com/london/dataset/housing-london/2017-01-26T18:50:00/Housing-in-London-2017-report.pdf

3 https://www.theguardian.com/money/2017/jul/03/one-in-seven-private-tenants-pays-more-than-half-income-in-rent-study-finds

4 http://www.lgiu.org.uk/2016/11/14/is-affordable-housing-affordable/

5 http://www.bbc.co.uk/news/uk-england-london-40025487

6 https://files.datapress.com/london/dataset/housing-london/2017-01-26T18:50:00/Housing-in-London-2017-report.pdf

7 http://news.sky.com/story/welfare-reforms-fuel-rise-in-homelessness-says-national-audit-office-11033248

8 https://www.standard.co.uk/news/london/londons-3bn-ghost-mansions-foreign-investors-are-using-capital-s-finest-homes-as-real-life-monopoly-9128782.html

9 https://www.ons.gov.uk/employmentandlabourmarket/peopleinwork/employmentandemployeetypes/articles/trendsinselfemploymentintheuk/2001to2015

10 http://www.telegraph.co.uk/finance/jobs/12106318/The-self-employed-will-overtake-the-public-sector-with-the-gig-economy.html

11 https://tfl.gov.uk/info-for/taxis-and-private-hire/licensing/licensing-information#on-this-page-0

12 https://www.theguardian.com/business/2017/apr/05/deliveroo-couriers-employees-managers

13 https://www.judiciary.gov.uk/wp-content/uploads/2016/10/aslam-and-farrar-v-uber-employment-judgment-20161028-2.pdf

14 https://www.uber.com/sw-KZ/helping-cities/

15 https://www.theguardian.com/business/2017/feb/06/uber-driver-mps-select-committee-minimum-wage

16 https://www.nytimes.com/interactive/2017/04/02/technology/uber-drivers-psychological-tricks.html

17 https://www.nytimes.com/interactive/2017/04/02/technology/uber-drivers-psychological-tricks.html

18 Uber Onboarding session, 8 April 2017.

19 Uber Onboarding session, 8 April 2017.

20 https://www.ft.com/content/190f12c4-0d92-11e7-a88c-50ba212dce4d

21 https://www.ft.com/content/c63f9500-1965-11e4-9745-00144feabdc0

22 https://www.theguardian.com/technology/2016/oct/28/uber-uk-tribunal-self-employed-status

23 https://www.theguardian.com/technology/2017/nov/24/uber-to-take-appeal-over-ruling-on-drivers-status-to-uk-supreme-court

24 Author interview with James Farrar, 21 April 2017.

25 http://www.standard.co.uk/news/transport/call-for-uberpool-to-be-banned-after-woman-attacked-by-men-who-didnt-want-to-share-minicab-a3270581.html

26 https://www.citizensadvice.org.uk/about-us/how-citizens-advice-works/media/press-releases/bogus-self-employment-costing-millions-to-workers-and-government/

27 http://www.fleetnews.co.uk/fleet-management/fleets-in-focus-citysprint/45492/page/3

28 http://www.telegraph.co.uk/news/2016/04/30/fears-overexcessive-and-unsafe-65-hour-weeks-for-uber-cabdrivers/. As a point of comparison, the legal safety limit for a bus and lorry driver is fifty-six hours a week.

29 https://www.nytimes.com/2015/12/11/business/a-middle-ground-between-contract-worker-and-employee.html?_r=2

30 https://www.buzzfeed.com/saraspary/deliveroos-founder-says-he-cant-give-workers-more-rights?utm_term=.ncKlwpJWJ#.aaqepWx5x

31 http://lexisweb.co.uk/cases/2002/november/flynn-v-torith-ltd

32 https://tfl.gov.uk/info-for/media/press-releases/2017/september/licensing-decision-on-uber-london-limited

33 https://www.theguardian.com/technology/2017/oct/05/ubers-change-of-tone-future-london-mayor-sadiq-khan-apology-licence-tfl

34 https://www.theguardian.com/uk-news/2017/jul/18/acid-attacks-delivery-drivers-parliament-protest

35 https://www.theguardian.com/uk-news/2017/jul/07/surge-in-acid-attacks-in-england-leads-to-calls-to-restrict-sales

INDEX

* JB indicates James Bloodworth.

Aberfan disaster (1966) 170–1
ACAS 38
acid attacks, delivery drivers protest
    against, London (July, 2017) 256–7
Ackroyd, Peter 249
Admiral Insurance call centre, Swansea
    150, 153–64, 180–1, 183, 185–6,
    224
    commission used as incentive for
        employees at 162–3
    'fun' culture 155, 161–2, 163, 164, 181
    management 162–3, 224
    performance league tables 183
    politics, employee attitudes towards 164
    'Renewals Consultant' role 154
    share scheme and dividends 159
    staff turnover rate 159
    training 155, 160–1
    unions/collective action and 185, 186
    university graduates employed at 153–4

    wages/pay 155–6, 158–60, 164, 180
    working hours and conditions 155,
        160–4, 180–1, 185–6
Age UK 113
Aiden (building site worker) 135–6
Aiden (former miner) 175
Airbnb 217
Alex (former pit mechanic) 55, 57, 62–3
algorithmic management systems 16–17,
    209, 210, 211, 217–18, 222, 223,
    227, 231, 232, 242, 249

Aman (Uber driver) 236–8, 239–40, 241,
    242, 255
Amazon:
    accommodation, employee 20–2, 24–6
    algorithmic management system 16–17
    blue badges 20, 41
    breaks, employee 12–14, 36, 48, 49–50,
        52–3, 64–5
    British workers and 31, 33–4, 35–41,
        57, 65, 72–3
    diet/health of employees 51–2, 64–5,
        70–1
    disciplinary system 36, 39–41, 42–4
    employment agencies, use of 19, 20,
        37, 38, 39, 40, 41, 43, 65–6, 86
        see also Transline *and* PMP
        Recruitment
    employment contracts 19–20, 53, 58
    food served to employees 12–13, 14, 64
    fulfillment centres in former mining
        areas 54–5
    JB's weekly budget whilst employed at
        68–9
    migrant labour, use of 11, 12, 13, 15,
        20, 21, 22–7, 30, 32, 33, 34, 44, 45,
        46, 51, 53, 57, 61–2, 65, 71–5, 258,
        260–1
    picker role 14, 16, 18, 19, 49, 65, 119,
        258
    process guide role 22–3
    recruitment process 19–20
    Rugeley distribution centre,
        Staffordshire 11–76, 79, 86, 119,
        127, 128, 159, 258

security/security guards 11–13, 47, 48–9, 52
survey of employees, GMB 36
Swansea, warehouse in 145–6, 194
tax paid in UK by 146
tiredness/exhaustion of employees 44, 50–1, 65
transgender employees, treatment of 40–1
wages/salary 18, 19, 37–9, 42–3, 65–6, 68, 69, 70, 159
Amodeo, Michael 223
Anne (pensioner in Cwm) 197–8
anti-depressant medication 188
Armitage Shanks 57
Arora brothers 124–5
Aslam, Yaseen 229–30, 250
Assured Shorthold Tenancy 96
Attlee, Clement 173
'austerity' policies 1–2, 6, 108

B&M Bargains 124–5, 126–30
BBC 138, 157, 173, 236
Bentham, Jeremy 182, 194
Berlin Wall, fall of (1989) 263
Bertram, Jo 235, 250–1
Bevan, Aneurin 144, 149, 192–3, 247
Bezos, Jeff 18
Big Issue, The 122
Big Pit National Coal Museum, Blaenavon 167, 170
Blackpool, Lancashire 77–140, 169, 187
accommodation in 80, 124, 137–8
B&M Bargains warehouse in 124–5, 126–31
Bloomfield district 137
building site work in 135–6
Central Drive 81, 120, 132–3
Golden Mile 121–2
health of residents 137
home care work in 81–90, 106–20, 140
homelessness in 95–105

job centres in 133–5
suicide rates in 100
unemployment in 121–3, 138, 139–40
Blaenau Gwent, Wales 187, 188, 190 see also under individual area and place name
Booth, William 205
Brereton Colliery, Staffordshire 55
Brian (former miner) 196
Bryn Colliery, Wales 196
Brynmill, Swansea, Wales 150–1
building site work 121, 124, 135–6
buy-to-let housing market 24

Cadman, Scott 244, 245–6, 247–9
call centres 35, 61, 139, 150, 153–64, 180–6, 192, 199, 224 see also Admiral Insurance call centre, Swansea
Cameron, David 259
Cannock Chase 21, 28, 54
capitalism 83, 145, 181
co-opts rebellion against 149
consumerism and 146
debt, reliance on 62
English culture overwhelmed by 32–3, 198–9
fall of Berlin Wall (1989) and 263
'gig' economy and 210, 215, 232
platform capitalism 215
religious fatalism appropriated by 161
care sector:
Eastern European migrant labour and 114–15
length of home care visits and 108–9, 110
local authority budget cuts and 107–10
privatisation of social care and 106–8, 109
staff training in 85–6
staffing crisis within 84–5, 119
zero hours contracts and 87
see also home care worker

Carewatch UK 81–90, 109, 110, 118, 132, 135, 136, 150, 159
  Disclosure and Barring Service (DBS) process and 88–90, 109–10
  employee reviews of 83–4
  employment contracts/conditions 87–8, 118–19
  length of care visits and 110
  MAR (Medication Administration Record) sheets and 114, 115
  recruitment 81–2, 84–5
  'shadowing' process 88, 109–10
  training 85–6
  see also care sector *and* home care worker
Cefn Mawr No. 2, Afan Valley, Wales 171–2
Celcon 57
Centre for Cities 61
Chartered Institute of Personnel and Development 153
Chartists 144, 149
China 183, 196–7
Chris (Amazon employee) 20, 21, 22–6, 65
Citizens Advice 243–4
CitySprint 246, 248–9, 251–2
Claire (Amazon employee) 36, 37–41, 50, 53
class:
  death of 4
  erosion of class solidarity 193–4
  fall of Berlin Wall and 263
  liberalism and 263
  scientific theories of 4, 17
  see also middle-class *and* working-class
Claudiu (housemate of JB) 22
coalition government (2010–15) 109, 115–16
coal mining:
  decline of industry 54, 55–6, 58, 144–5, 172–9
  danger of/disasters 169–72

General Strike and 173
Miners' Strike (1984–5) 3, 174–7
South Wales Valleys and 143–4, 147–9, 165–79, 180, 188, 189, 190–1, 193, 195, 196
Thatcher and 174–5, 263–4
collectivism 228
communism 17, 173, 178, 228, 263
Compare the Market 155
Conservative Party 3, 7, 109, 175
consumerism 146
Coombes, B. L.: *These Poor Hands* 23, 149, 190
courier firms 211, 215, 217, 223, 236, 244–7, 250, 256, 257
Cwm, Wales 147, 148, 187, 190, 195, 196, 197
Cwmbran, Wales 143

Daily Express 124–5
Daily Mail 66, 134, 188
Dan (bicycle courier) 248, 249
Dangerfield, George 72
Davies, Idris 148–9
  Gwalia Deserta (Wasteland of Wales) 148
  'The Angry Summer' 174
debt 62, 69, 146, 151, 153
Deliveroo 215, 217, 223, 250, 256, 257
democratic socialists 192
Department for Work and Pensions 133
Dickens, Charles 29, 205, 210, 249; *Hard Times* 138–9
Disclosure and Barring Service (DBS) 88–90, 109–10, 214
Dorothy (housemate of JB) 203, 204–5
DriveNow 217
Dropit 217

Eastern Europe, migrant workers from 11, 13, 15, 21, 24, 26–7, 30, 32, 33, 34, 45, 57, 61–2, 75, 114–16, 128–9,

154, 203–4, 260–1 *see also under individual nation name*
Ebbw Vale, Wales 147, 149, 154; legacy of de-industrialisation in 187–200
Elborough, Travis 93
emergency housing 96
employment agencies 1, 16, 19, 20, 23, 37, 38, 39, 40, 41, 42, 43, 56, 65–6, 70, 72, 73, 82, 86, 127, 130, 158, 189, 194 *see also under individual agency name*
Employment and Support Allowance (ESA) 248
employment contracts/classification:
 Amazon 19–20, 53, 58
 care sector 87–8, 107–8, 116
 Uber 214–15, 222, 229–35, 243, 245, 250–2, 257
 zero-hours *see* zero-hours contracts
employment tribunals 38, 229–30, 243–4
English seaside, debauchery and 92–3
Enterprise Rent-A-Car 214
ESOL (English for Speakers of Other Languages) programmes 115–16
European Economic Community (EEC) 195
European Referendum (2016) 61, 195–6
Evening Standard 208, 241
Express & Star 59–60

Fabian Society 109
Farrar, James 229–31, 232, 233, 234, 236, 238, 240, 241–2, 250, 254, 255–6
Fellows of the Academies of Management 17
Fernie, Sue 182
financial crisis (2008) 1, 2, 45, 125, 195, 209
Flash (former miner) 165–8, 170, 171–2, 174, 175, 176–8, 179, 188, 196
Fleet News 246
Foot, Michael 149

football 56, 58, 92, 94, 97, 98, 126, 135, 169
fruit picking 61
FTSE 123, 262

Gag Mag 122
Gallagher, Patrick 246
Gary (homeless man, Blackpool) 96–104, 105
Gaz (*Gag Mag* seller, Blackpool) 122
GDP 146
General Election (2015) 109
General Strike (1926) 148, 149, 173
gentrification 219
Geoff (former miner) 189, 190, 191, 193
'gig' economy 2, 208–10, 217–18, 232, 236, 242, 243–4, 248, 249–50, 252, 257 *see also* Uber
Gissing, George: *New Grub Street* 64
GMB union 36
grammar schools 261
Guardian 5, 235

Hamstead Colliery, Great Barr 169
Hazel (home carer) 110–11, 114, 115, 116, 117, 119
Heller, Joseph: *Catch-22* 235–6
Hemel Hempstead 54, 70
Henley, William Ernest: 'England, My England' vii
Hoggart, Richard: *The Uses of Literacy* 45
home care worker (domiciliary care worker):
 Disclosure and Barring Service (DBS) checks 88–90, 109–10
 employment contracts 87–8, 107–8, 116, 118, 120
 length of home care visits 108–9, 110
 local authority budget cuts and 107–10
 MAR (Medication Administration Record) sheets 114, 115
 migrant workers as 114–16

negligent 86–7
privatisation of social care and 106–8, 109
recruitment 82–4
'shadowing' process 88, 109–10
societal view of 106
staffing crisis 85–6, 119
suicide rate among 100
typical day/workload 110–14, 118
unions and 88
view job as vocation 86–7
wages/pay 107–8, 117, 118–19, 159
Home Instead 119
homelessness 95–105, 138, 187, 208
hostels 95, 96, 101, 102
housing/accommodation:
  Amazon workers, Rugeley 20–2, 24–6
  Blackpool 80, 124, 137–8
  buy-to-let housing market 24
  emergency housing 96
  homelessness and 95, 96, 101, 102, 137–8
  hostels 95, 96, 101, 102
  inability to buy 62
  landlords and 12, 21, 24, 39, 67, 69, 95–6, 137–8, 164, 204, 206, 258
  London 203–8
  migrant workers and 20–2, 24–6, 197–8
  social housing 62, 206
  Swansea 124, 150
housing benefit 96, 137–8, 248

immigration 26–7, 61, 115–16, 128–9, 144, 193, 197–9, 236, 259–61 see also migrant workers
indeed.co.uk 83–4
independent contractors 209, 248, 251–2
Independent Workers Union of Gr eat Britain (IWGB) 230, 257
inequality 18, 73, 123, 125, 207–8, 226, 238, 262, 263

inflation 2, 122

job centres 19, 96, 133–6, 139–40, 156, 158
Joe (housemate of JB) 22
John Lewis 23, 83
Joseph Rowntree Foundation 70, 159
June (call centre employee) 181–2, 183, 184

Kalanick, Travis 215, 228, 229, 233, 235
Kelly, Kath 66
Khan, Sadiq 256
Koestler, Arthur: *The God that Failed* 228

Labour Party 7, 57, 59, 61, 109, 144, 149, 150, 173, 174
Ladbroke Road, Notting Hill, London 219
Lamb, Norman 109
Lancashire Evening Post 104–5
landlords, private 12, 21, 24, 39, 67, 69, 95–6, 137–8, 164, 204, 206, 258
Lea Hall Colliery, Staffordshire 31–2, 54, 55, 56, 57
Lea Hall Miners' Social Club, Staffordshire 55, 56, 74
Len (step-grandfather of JB) 143–4
Lili (London) 203–4
living wage 1, 85, 160, 246
Lloyd George, David 172
loan sharks 151, 156
local councils 104–5, 164
London 201–57
  accommodation/housing in 65, 203–8, 218
  gentrification in 219
  'gig' economy in 208–57, 263
  homelessness in 95
  migrant labour in 205–6, 213, 239
  wealth divide in 207–8, 238
London Congestion Charge 254

London Courier Emergency Fund (LCEF) 247
London Metropolitan Police 90
London, Jack 205
low-skilled jobs, UK economy creation of 153
Lydia (Amazon employee) 70

Macmillan, Harold 3
manufacturing jobs, disappearance of 59, 139
Marine Colliery, Cwm, Wales 190
Mayhew, Henry 4, 205
McDonald's 52, 68, 83
Merkel, Angela 196
Metcalf, David 182
middle-class 6, 39, 51, 67, 68, 69, 72–3, 74, 75, 149, 178, 205, 258, 259, 260, 262, 263
migrant labour:
    Amazon use of 11, 12, 13, 15, 20, 21, 22–7, 30, 32, 33, 34, 44, 45, 46, 51, 53, 57, 61–2, 65, 71–5, 258, 260–1
    care home workers 114–16
    'gig' economy and 203–6, 213, 239
    restaurant workers 154
    retail sector and 128–9
Miliband, Ed 109
mining see coal mining
Miners' Federation of Great Britain (MFGB) 173
Miners' Strike (1984–5) 3, 174–7
minimum wage 1, 7, 55, 62, 84, 107, 108, 118, 135, 155, 159, 173, 189–90, 209, 212, 235, 236, 245, 250, 262
Morecambe, Lancashire 137–8
Morgan family 156–8
Morgan, Huw: How Green Was My Valley 147
Moyer-Lee, Jason 257

National Coal Board (NCB) 54, 170, 171
National Institute for Health and Care Excellence (NICE) 108
National Union of Miners (NUM) 174, 176
New York Times 222
NHS (National Health Service) 106, 108, 247
Nirmal (Amazon employee) 45–6, 51
Norbert (Amazon employee) 71–5
nostalgia 3, 60, 93–4, 216
Nottingham 2, 151–2

objectivism 228
oil crisis (1973) 122–3
Oliver, Jamie 154
Orwell, George 56, 169

Palmer, William 29
pay see wages and under individual job title and employer name
payday loans 156
PayPal 216
Pimlico Plumbers 251–2
platform capitalism 215
PMP Recruitment 19, 189–90
Poland, migrant workers from 128–9, 130, 135, 197–8
'poor, the' 145
Port Talbot, Wales 166, 176, 190, 196
'post-truth' discourse 199
'post-work' world 165
poverty:
    Blackpool and 132, 137
    class and 4
    darkness and 96
    diet/weight and 137
    ease of slipping into 5
    Eastern Europe and 26
    monthly salary and 156
    as a moral failing 188–9
    press treatment of 66–7

time and 67
working poor living in 194
Preston, Lancashire 100, 105, 138–9
private school system 123
progressive thought 262
Public Accounts Committee (PAC) 107
Putin, Vladimir 71

Rand, Ayn 228–9, 235, 236; *The Fountainhead* 228, 229
recession (2008) 1, 45, 104, 121, 125, 156
'regeneration' 55, 60–1, 146
rent-to-own 157–8
retirement, working in 58–9
Reve, Gerard: *The Evenings* 160
Robin (Cwm) 196, 197
Rochelle (home care worker) 117–19
Romania, migrant workers from 11, 12, 13, 15, 20, 21, 22–7, 32, 44, 46, 51, 53, 61, 65, 71–5, 203, 206, 258
Ron (former miner) 170, 195
Royal London 59
Royal London pub, Wolverhampton 71
Royal Mail 151
Rugeley, Staffordshire 28–35
    Amazon distribution centre in 11–76, 79, 86, 119, 127, 128, 159, 258
    decline of coal mining industry in 31–2, 54–6, 57, 169
    disappearance of manufacturing jobs from 54–63
    high street 28–35
    immigration and 30–4, 193–4
    Tesco and 58–9, 62–3

Scargill, Arthur 175
scientific management theories 17
Scotland Yard 90
self-employment:
    'gig' economy and 214–15, 222, 229–30, 234, 243–4, 245, 246, 249, 250–1
increase in numbers of workers 2, 209
'independent contractors' and 209, 248, 251–2
Selwyn (former miner) 175, 178, 179, 263–4
Senghenydd, Glamorgan pit explosion (1913) 169–70
Shelter 104
Shirebrook Colliery, Derbyshire 55
Shu, William 250
Silicon Valley, California 210, 232
Sillitoe, Alan: *Saturday Night and Sunday Morning* 2, 3, 94
Sky Sports News 126
social democracy 3, 263
social housing 62, 206
socialism 7, 56, 131, 144, 148, 149, 173
social mobility 58, 199, 261
South Wales Miners' Museum, Afan Argoed 166, 196
South Wales Valleys 141–200
    accommodation in 150, 197
    Amazon in 145–6
    beauty of 148
    call centre jobs in 153–64, 180–6
    coal industry and 143–4, 147–9, 165–79, 180, 188, 189, 190–1, 193, 195, 196
    immigration and 197–9
    JB's family history and 143–4
    legacy of de-industrialisation in 187–200
    nostalgia and 147
    radical history of 149–50
    see also under individual place name
'spice' 95
Sports Direct 55
squatting 96, 99
steel industry 176, 180, 188, 189, 190, 196–7
Steven (housemate of JB) 124, 126, 127–31

Stoke-on-Trent 58–9
suicide 99–100
Sunday Times 175
  'Best Companies to Work For' 154
  Rich List 125
Swansea, Wales 145–6, 150–2, 154–64,
  176, 178, 197, 205

Tata Steel 190
tax 65, 69, 70, 118, 146, 158, 159, 163,
  164, 212, 229, 244, 246, 248, 251,
  255
Taylor, Frederick W.: *The Principles of
  Scientific Management* 17
Tesco 35, 57, 58–9, 62–3
Thatcher, Margaret 122, 123, 146, 174–5,
  193, 207, 263–4
Thorn Automation 57
Thorn EMI 59
trade unions:
  Amazon and 36
  B&M and 130, 131
  call centres and 160, 181, 184–5, 186
  care sector and 88
  coal industry decline and 55–6, 173,
    174, 263–4
  decline of 2, 3, 35
  'gig' economy and 230, 257, 261
  objectivism and 228
  oil crisis (1973) and 122
  Thatcher and 123, 174, 193, 263–4
  Wales and 144, 149
  see also under individual union name
Trades Union Congress (TUC) 173
transgender people 40–1
Transline Group 19, 20, 37, 38, 39, 40,
  41, 43, 65–6, 86
Transport for London (TFL) 211, 212–13,
  214, 233, 254, 256
Tredegar Workmen's Medical Aid Society
  247
Trefil, Wales 149

Trump, Donald 7

Uber 207, 211–57
  'account status' 221
  clocking in at 218
  corporation tax and 229
  customers 221, 222, 226–7, 237–41,
    244, 257
  driver costs/expenses 214, 217, 233,
    241, 246, 253–5
  driver employment classification/
    contract 214–15, 222, 229–35, 243,
    245,   250–2, 257
  driver hours 221, 226, 230, 232, 233,
    236, 246, 253, 255
  driver numbers 211–13, 233–5
  driver wages/pay 212, 218, 221,
    229–30, 235, 236, 237, 240, 241,
    244, 246, 252–5
  employment tribunal against (2016)
    229–34
  flexibility of working for 213–14, 218,
    230–3, 248, 250–1
  James Farrar and *see* Farrar, James
  migrant labour and 213, 236
  'Onboarding' class 224–5, 238, 241,
    256
  opposition to 215–17
  philosophy of 228–9, 235, 236
  psychological inducements for drivers
    222–3
  rating system 225–7, 232, 238, 239,
    243, 253
  rejecting/accepting jobs 221–2, 224–5
  ride process 219–21
  surge pricing 237, 238, 253
  TFL and 211, 212–13, 214, 233, 254,
    256
  Travis Kalanick and *see* Kalanick, Travis
UberEATS 256
UberPOOL 225, 240–2, 253, 255–6
UberX 212, 225, 240, 241, 255

VAT and 229
vehicle requirements 214
unemployment 2, 32, 36, 62, 121–3,
    132, 138, 148, 157, 172, 178, 179,
    189–95, 199, 218
Unison 88, 108
Unite 55, 160
United Private Hire Drivers 230, 257
university education 3, 6, 61, 62, 123,
    150–1, 152, 153–4
USDAW 130–1

Vettesse, Tony 138
Vicky (care sector supervisor) 86, 87

Wade, Alan 121, 123–4
wages:
    Amazon 18, 19, 37–9, 42–3, 65–6, 68,
        69, 70, 159
    call centre 155–6, 158–60, 164, 180
    care sector 107–8, 117, 118–19, 159
    living wage 1, 85, 160, 246
    minimum wage 1, 7, 55, 62, 84, 107,
        108, 118, 135, 155, 159, 173,
        189–90, 209, 212, 235, 236, 245,
        250, 262
    Uber 212, 218, 221, 229–30, 235, 236,
        237, 240, 241, 244, 246, 252–5
    wage stagnation 2
    see also under individual employer, job
        and sector name
Wealth and Assets Survey 207–8
wealth inequality 18, 73, 123, 125,
    207–8, 238

Wells, H. G.: The Time Machine 75, 264
Wilson, Harold 171, 174
Winter, Jeff 57–9, 61
Wolverhampton 45, 57, 71–4
Wonga 39
Woolworths 125–6
working-class 3, 4, 8, 145
    authors 5–6
    contribution to Britain's economic
        progress undervalued 145
    English seaside and 92–3
    erosion of class solidarity and 193–4
    football and 58
    immigration and 260
    interiors 56
    middle-class acceptance of toil of
        working class life 72–3
    politics of left and 262–3
    relationships and 33
    scientific management theories and 17
    Thatcher assault on 146, 175, 193,
        263–4
    time efficiency and 67–8
    university and see university education
    see also under individual job title and area
        of working class life
working men's clubs 55–6, 74, 144
working tax credits 159, 194

zero-hours contracts 3
    Amazon and 19, 58
    Blackpool and 122
    care sector and 87–8, 107, 116
    South Wales Valleys and 190, 191, 195